Date Due

CONTRIBUTIONS IN AMERICAN STUDIES
Series Editor: Robert H. Walker

The Modern Corporate State

Private Governments and the American Constitution

Arthur Selwyn Miller

Contributions in American Studies, Number 23

GREENWOOD PRESS
WESTPORT, CONNECTICUT ● LONDON, ENGLAND

Library of Congress Cataloging in Publication Data

Miller, Arthur Selwyn, 1917-
   The modern corporate state.

   (Contributions in American studies ; no. 23)
   Includes bibliographical references and index.
   1. Industry and state—United States—History.
2. Corporation law—United States—History. 3. Big business—
United States—History. I. Title.
HD3616.U46M55   322'.3'0973   75-35350
ISBN 0-8371-8589-0

Library of Congress Catalog Card Number: 75-35350
ISBN: 0-8371-8589-0

First published in 1976

Greenwood Press, a division of Williamhouse-Regency Inc.
51 Riverside Avenue, Westport, Connecticut 06880

Printed in the United States of America

. . . for Dagmar
con amor . . .

Contents

Preface

The time has come to rethink the nature of our constitutional order.

As the United States enters the third century of its history, Americans are beset as never before by doubts and uncertainties. Verities once considered to be immutable are being challenged. Distrust and cynicism about government and social institutions are widespread. To many, this nation was "the last best hope of man"; that belief has now turned to doubt, questioning, and confusion. We do not know where we are.

Much of this is healthy. There is little merit in hiding reality, historical or contemporaneous, however harsh it may be. "We the people" will never build a better social order unless we first understand what we have been, what we are, and what we can become. This volume tackles those questions from the perspective of constitutional theory. In the main, it is a descriptive analysis; no attempt is made to prescribe what should be. It seeks to raise questions rather than to proffer answers, to provide a way of thinking about the nature of the modern political economy—the constitutional order.

The subject matter is complex; of necessity, the exposition presupposes a minimum level of understanding about American history and American politics. It is, furthermore, an essay—a preliminary excursus into an immensely complicated area. No one (to my knowledge) has previously set forth the elements of a legal theory of the "corporate state, American style." Lawyers and those who write about law are apt to wax prolix, to draw every inference and pursue every side issue, to make every qualifying statement, and to attempt to insure (an unattainable) completeness. Such efforts may have some value for the legal specialist but surely not for the person who views the Constitution of the United States from outside the precincts of the priesthood of the law.

There is no simple, yet adequate explanation of any social phenomenon.[1] So it is here. I have tried to steer a middle course between the
rocks of oversimplification and the whirlpool of too much detail. I
made no effort to load the text with mountains of factual data; those
who wish that information will find it in many of the works mentioned
in the notes at the end of the book. Those works include not only
material from the literature of the law but also relevant texts in history, sociology, political science, and economics. This book, thus, may
be considered to be an effort to conduct an interdisciplinary investiga-
tion.

A point of view is presented, an argument if you will, but one that is
not intended as a polemic. My purpose is to call attention to the most
important constitutional development in American history. The book
is intended for the layman as well as the lawyer and the political theorist. I do not pretend that it is the final word on the subject. If it does
no more than to provide a way of thinking about the new American
political economy and constitutional order and to suggest some questions that are badly in need of study in depth, it will have amply served
its purpose.

It has had a long gestation period. My interest in the subject matter
began in the early 1950s when, while on active duty during the Korean
conflict, I had the opportunity to see at first hand a few of the details
of the way in which the Pentagon's procurement process works. My
first article in a legal periodical (in 1955) dealt with the government's
use of the instrument of contract as a means of social control, a clear
example of a close intermesh between government and business.
Other articles followed, traces of which can be found throughout this
volume. One of them, published in 1959 in condensed form by the
Center for the Study of Democratic Institutions under the title "Private Governments and the Constitution," is the springboard from
which the present study was launched. The wide readership that
paper received—it was reprinted in a number of anthologies—clearly
indicated a deep interest in the constitutional questions relating to
government and business.

Other articles of mine have appeared in several legal periodicals,
and I have used portions of some of them here. In a very real sense,
even so, this book is a preliminary statement of a complex, indeed

controversial, subject. By no means are the views expressed here in any way final. Constitutional theory can never be definitively stated, for the law that reflects that theory is always in a state of becoming.

My debts, intellectual and financial, are many. For the former, the many writers in law and economics, in political science and sociology, in history and philosophy, from whose efforts I have benefited are, I trust, sufficiently set forth in the notes at the end of the text. These notes both identify the sources for the references and also indicate some of the other literature on specific points. The listing is not exhaustive. No useful purpose would be served to publish an extended bibliography. Accordingly, choices had to be made; at times a book or article with a viewpoint that sharply diverges from the accepted wisdom of the day was followed over the more popular or orthodox treatment. I make no apology for this and mention it only to indicate that I am aware of the selective nature of the notes. Nonetheless, it must be emphasized that at no time was any contrary evidence ignored simply because it might not fit whatever theories are set forth in the text. I know that the greatest intellectual tragedy is the inconvenient fact that explodes the neat theory; I believe that I have considered all of the facts possible within the frame of reference chosen.

Financially, I have benefited from several sources over the years. A fellowship in 1957-1958 from the John Simon Guggenheim Memorial Foundation gave me the time to make my first inquiry into the nature of the modern constitutional order. Association as a consultant for the Center for the Study of Democratic Institutions enabled me to continue those studies. In 1960-1961, a Law Faculty Fellowship from the Ford Foundation again permitted me time to pursue my goal. I have also received fellowship aid from the Program of Studies on the Modern Corporation at the Graduate School of Business, Columbia University, and grants from the George Washington University.

ARTHUR SELWYN MILLER

Washington, D.C.
May 1975

Introduction

The key question is not whether Arthur Selwyn Miller is right—of course he is—but whether anything can be done about it. Has the United States gone so far down the path toward the corporate state that there is no remedy?

Miller sketches a chilling future. The giant corporation—that authoritarian, bureaucratic, and hierarchical private government—grows and spreads its influence. Political power moves to the national government, and within Washington to the executive branch and the national security managers. These growing concentrations of power need and increasingly support each other. An elite of top management and old wealth dominates the decision-making process, with the aid of the universities and the acquiescence of labor leadership. Big government, big business, big labor, and big universities come together in a symbiotic relationship that allows a small elite to run the whole system. This is the monolith whose legal and constitutional foundations are so ably analyzed in this book.

How does this American version of the corporate state differ from the classic patterns of fascism? In the first place, the corporate state in America does not normally use repression as a political instrument, although in the Nixon years we came close. Loyalty to the existing order is sustained by a variety of means. In normal times, economic growth provides rising living standards to most Americans, and the managerial elite is largely open rather than closed. Upward mobility, both economic and social, is the proffered carrot, and if one doesn't make it the ideology tells him it's his own fault, for opportunity was there within the system. There are psychic appeals, too: nationalism and racism for the chauvinist; anticommunism for the fearful; messianic democracy for the liberal reformer. A combination of these appeals allows the average American to revel in his affluence without bothering to ask who is running things, to what ends, and for whose benefit. As long as prosperity and economic growth is maintained, the continuing development of the corporate state goes unquestioned.

Second, there is no avowed ideology of corporativism, such as those developed in militarist Japan, Mussolini's Italy, or Hitler's Germany. Instead of an ideology stressing the subservience of the individual to the state and the subordination of individual to group goals, we still profess an ideology of individualism, competitive free enterprise, and pluralist democracy. The American corporate state retains the old ideology in the face of a new reality. We have not yet had the man on the white horse who preaches solidarity of the whole in order to preserve the existing order.

Third, traditional fascist authoritarianism is largely absent. Social choices are made by compromises and accommodations among the managerial elites. It is a pluralism of elites, so to speak, with much jockeying for position and power among corporate interests, union interests, military interests, bureaucratic interests, and what have you. In this respect we have much in common with the fascist regimes of Germany, Italy and Japan, where authoritarian governments were continually compromising the varied interests of differing power groups. But the President is, in many respects, a power broker mediating among rivals—and Nixon's effort to change that to presidential superiority led to his downfall.

Yet underneath the facade of the corporate state is a strong undercurrent of dissent and resentment. A large portion of America's young people realize that wealth and power, as ends in themselves, are empty goals. Many of them recognize that their parents acquiesced in the malign use of national power in exchange for relative affluence. Racial minorities see that they have been largely excluded from affluence, condemned to unsatisfying lives in menial, dead-end jobs. Internationally, the thrust to world power turned out to be very costly, and, faced with challenges from the less developed countries, perhaps even costlier in the future than in the past. It was just such a challenge from Vietnam that brought the American corporate state to its recent crisis.

These are only the outward signs of an even deeper economic malaise that is leading to what can be called a "master-servant" society. Automation and technical change limit the need for workers in the high wage manufacturing sectors of the economy. In addition, firms export capital to underdeveloped countries, where low wage workers produce goods for export back to the advanced countries, thereby limiting the need for workers in the high wage sectors still more. Meanwhile, modernization in the Third World itself stimulates further population growth and preserves the low wage structure there. This leaves the growing populations in the advanced countries with little new employment, except in the relatively low wage service sector of the economy, unless governments step in with government employment, military spending, or remedial and welfare programs. In practice, we have had all three. The expanding administrative operations of giant corporations, government bureaucracies, and the military, allied with the high wage sector of the work force, build a class of "masters," while the low wage service sector, the unemployed and welfare recipients are the "servants." We are just now beginning to understand the dimensions of this continuing transformation of the economy.

These changes put increased stresses on government. Large welfare, military, and government employment programs must be financed. Yet rising taxes bring resentment and political turnovers. Government then turns to borrowing, which generates inflation and more resentment and political turnover. There is a subtle three-way tradeoff between escalating unemployment together with other unresolved social problems, rising taxes, and inflation. In practice, the corporate state has brought all three.

Economic, social, and political conflict is endemic within the corporate state. And there lies the ultimate threat. For these conflicts can be expected to erupt from time to time in a series of crises that demand action.

One outcome may well be full-blown fascism, with the executive branch of government moving to full dominance under the banner of national solidarity in a time of crisis and conflict, using political repression to restore order and stifle dissent. Our recent history suggests that this outcome is quite possible. A second outcome may be a replay of New Deal reformism that makes adjustments around the edges of our basic institutions without fundamentally changing the structure of wealth and power. But such pragmatic reform may not be possible in a divided society distrustful of government and disillusioned about democracy. The third possibility is a true social revolution that redistributes wealth, breaks up or nationalizes giant corporations, takes the guns away from the generals, and decentralizes the powers of government. Many would consider such a program the most desirable but least likely. One alternative is no longer available, however—the traditional pattern of individualism, competitive private enterprise, and representative democracy.

These, then, are the options: a slide into fascist authoritarianism; continuation of the corporate state with some reforms to make it a little less malign; or democratic socialism. Before you choose, however, read Arthur Selwyn Miller's trenchant and perceptive analysis.

DANIEL R. FUSFELD

Professor of Economics
University of Michigan

part I
The argument stated

This is an essay in American constitutional law and politics. It develops the proposition that the American people are moving without constitutional amendment and with little fanfare into a new social order. The label for this is "the corporate state." The emerging native form of corporativism differs from its historical European antecedents. Exemplifying what Henry George once called an axiom of statesmanship, "that great changes can be brought about under old forms," the words of the Constitution of 1787 remain the same (save for a few amendments, the most important of which are rather ancient), but their content changes. As Woodrow Wilson said, written constitutions must be Darwinian, not mechanistic; they must follow the laws of life and not of mechanics. The coming of the corporate state, American style, illustrates that the Constitution of the United States truly is a living instrument of governance.

1

THE CORPORATE
SOCIETY

This is an age of collective action.

—JOHN R. COMMONS[1]

When in 1787 fifty-five men sat in Philadelphia to revise the Articles of Confederation, and instead produced the Constitution, they conceived a nation the development of which could not have been predicted by the most prescient of its founders. A straggling little group of allegedly sovereign states, perched precariously on the shoulder of North America and existing at the sufferance of the major European powers, in less than two centuries has become the most powerful and wealthiest nation in history—straddling a continent and having interests that literally transcend the planet. Small wonder, then, that those men are clouded in an aura of mystery and awe and are considered to have had superhuman qualities. The principal saints in the hagiology of a polity that acknowledges few heroes, they occupy front rank in the American mythology: they are the Founding Fathers.

Theirs is an undeserved reverence. The Constitution written in 1787, save in highest level abstraction, is not the fundamental law today. (Nor will today's be that of tomorrow.) Even with its few amendments (twenty-six), it is merely a skeleton—or, perhaps more aptly, an embryo, an inchoate mass whose lasting merit is less attributable to its internal provisions than to a set of unique external circumstances. Under those externalities, the United States has waxed both large and strong. Although the Constitution has a gloss, a patina of almost two centuries of experience, the original words are holy writ to Americans and the Founding Fathers occupy a very special position. Gladstone, in the late nineteenth century, with excessive praise termed the Constitution "the most wonderful work ever struck off at a given time by the brain and purpose of man."[2] That is fantasy—a classic example of the power of the human mind to endow people long dead with extraordinary characteristics. Every generation has its golden age; for Americans it is the late eighteenth century when men considered to be larger than life and wiser than those of today strode the earth and conversed—presumably—in language similar to Plato's philosopher-kings. The purported wisdom of the ancients thus enables Americans to engage in what Franz Neumann once called "constitutional fetishism," by which he meant the attribution of political consequences (such as individualism and personal liberty) and economic well-being "to isolated constitutional arrangements which have meaning only in a total cultural, and particularly social, setting."[3] Americans also worship, in a peculiar form of secular polytheism, a sheaf of old parchment, now enshrined in the National Archives, and the thirty-nine men who signed it. (Fifty-five out of a total of eighty-four named delegates attended the Convention of 1787, but sixteen left early.) There is a close congruence between the Constitution and avowedly religious literature, such as the Bible.

The purpose of this essay is more descriptive than prescriptive. Its principal theme is the coming of the "corporate state, American style" and how that development can be substantiated in constitutional (that is legal and politico-economic) theory. It is now fashionable to use the term "the corporate state." Writers employ it as if it had some accepted core of meaning, which, emphatically, it does not. Examples are easily found. John Kenneth Galbraith in *The New Industrial State* set forth an economist's version of American corporativism but with no reference to law or legal theory and very little mention of politics.[4] So, too, did Professor Charles Reich of the Yale Law School, whose best-seller *The Greening of America* seems to suggest that wearing beads and bell-bottomed trousers will liberate mankind and usher in some sort of terrestrial nirvana.[5] Reich calls the United States a corporate state but without reference to legal theory *or* politics (and little economics). A political scientist at the University of Wisconsin, H. L. Nieburg, suffers from the same malady: he too does not offer either a workable definition or a theoretical framework for thinking about the corporate state.[6] These, and others, merely say that it exists in the United States.[7] (To be fair, however, Galbraith is much more systematic and comprehensive than others—even though he is in essence an apologist for bigness in business.)

There is a need, then, for determining how under the fixed Constitution of 1787 the corporate state could have developed without formal amendment of the basic law. Before setting out the contours of an essentially new constitutional order, some discussion of the nature of constitutional change, followed by an outline of "corporate America," is desirable.

CONSTITUTIONAL ALTERATION

If one were to believe the constitutional fundamentalists, the only way to alter the document of 1787 is through amendment as set forth in Article V. There is, in this respect, more than a superficial resemblance between the Constitution and the Bible. Both are theological documents, one secular to be sure but nonetheless treated as sacred. Some Americans believe that the Constitution was divinely inspired, a notion that surely would have amused H. L. Mencken as well as Thomas Jefferson. And both are ancient, the Bible of course much more so; but the Constitution is swallowed up in that unimaginable past which historians try to plumb. The consequence is that the "intentions" of those who wrote or inspired these documents—God, in the case of the Bible, and a few dozen men for the Constitution—are thought to have a special, controlling relevance for the resolution of modern problems. That ain't necessarily so, as *Sporting Life* would have said.

Constitutions, including the American (the oldest written instrument extant), are always in a state of becoming. They are not static or frozen in time. Rather, they are open-ended, continuously being updated to meet the exigencies of succeeding generations. The origins of the Constitution of the United States, in other words, may be fixed in time—1787 for drafting it, 1789 for bringing the new government into being—but those dates are merely points of departure in the progression of what Woodrow Wilson once called the "vehicle of the nation's life."[8] Each term of the Supreme Court, each calendar year for other governmental bodies, brings new "origins" to the fundamental law. American constitutional law is common law—a body of precedent

produced through time. That law, paradoxically, must be certain but
it can never stand still. Just as each generation of intellectuals writes
its own history, so each generation rewrites the Constitution—not
wholesale, of course, for law is not made that way, but incrementally,
bit by bit, more like the slow building of a coral reef than a volcanic
explosion.

There is nothing novel in that idea. It could scarcely be otherwise.
The Constitution—all law—is Darwinian rather than Newtonian in
concept. It follows the laws of life rather than the mechanics of a fixed,
rigid, internally consistent system. It is a living instrument of governance, not a mere lawyers' document, such as a contract or a will or a
conveyance. Justice William O. Douglas asserted in 1962 that constitutional questions are "always open,"[9] and so they are. Any decision
that requires a Supreme Court decision on the merits must, by its very
nature, be law creating, a notion made explicit in 1966 by Justice
Byron White in *Miranda* v. *Arizona*. He said it was obvious that the
Court was making "new law and new public policy in much the same
way that it has in the course of interpreting other great clauses of the
Constitution."[10] (This nation is not alone in having a "living" constitution. Even the Soviet Union has a doctrine of "living Marxism,"
under which the "sacred" literature of Marx and Engels and Lenin is
updated from year to year.)[11]

The necessary implication is that the intentions of the Founding
Fathers cannot control the resolution in modern problems. At best,
those intentions are but one of the criteria of constitutional judgment—even if they are ascertainable, which in most (perhaps all)
present-day instances they are not. The Constitution's purported
immutable principles of law and justice are cast in such high-level abstraction that each generation of judges (and scholars) can pour what
it will into them. The words of the ancient charter remain the same
but their content changes through time. (A person has a good legal
mind if he understands how words and their application can at once
remain the same and change as social conditions are altered.) Not one
of the great generalities of the Constitution has ever had a fixed meaning: not due process of law nor equal protection of the laws, not interstate commerce nor taxing and spending, not freedom of speech nor
unreasonable searches and seizures, to name but a few. Not that they
are entirely unlimited in their application; rather, a rigid or fixed de-

finition cannot be given, else the Constitution would be ossified and ultimately ignored.

That is so precisely because social structures are always in flux, and law, including constitutional law, is a reflection of those arrangements as much as—perhaps more than—their determinant. Change is the law of life—and of constitutions—and we live in the midst of a period of the most rapid social change in history. Americans have witnessed more change since, say, the Civil War than did people in the previous centuries of human history—change, that is, in the environment in which the nation exists.

There is no need to restate the massive alterations in the United States since the men of 1787 wrote the Constitution. These are obvious. One factor, however, may be emphasized: the process of change has not stopped and indeed it may be accelerating (despite recent calls for an "end to growth"). Mankind, now living in a global village or on spaceship earth, is in the midst of the most profound social revolution since the agricultural revolution eons ago—the impact of science and technology upon historical habits and behavior patterns and upon social institutions. "No one—not even the most brilliant scientist alive today—really knows where science is taking us. We are aboard a train which is gathering speed, racing down a track on which there are an unknown number of switches leading to unknown destinations. No single scientist is in the engine cab and there may be demons at the switch. Most of society is in the caboose looking backward."[12] So said physicist Ralph Lapp in 1965, a sentiment echoed shortly thereafter by Professor John Platt: "There is only one crisis in the world. It is the crisis of transformation."[13]

The implications for law and the legal system, particularly for updating the Constitution, are readily apparent. Many constitutional commentators, not excluding Supreme Court Justices, ride in Lapp's caboose looking backward at the Founding Fathers for inspiration to decide present-day problems. Theirs is a touching faith, a view that history indeed can definitively prove the rights and wrongs of a given constitutional question today. Emphatically, that is not accurate. The dead hand of the past cannot guide the course of contemporary decisions. As Chief Justice Earl Warren said in *Brown* v. *Board of Education*, the 1954 school desegregation case, history is "inconclusive."[14] So it is with any other important question of the day. To invoke the shades of the Founding Fathers is merely to restate the question to be decided, not to answer it. Justice Oliver Wendell Holmes said it well in 1920: "When we are dealing with words that also are a constituent act, like the Constitution of the United States, we must realize that they have called into life a being the development of which could not have been foreseen completely by the most gifted of its begetters. It was enough for them to realize or to hope that they had created an organism; it has taken a century and much sweat and blood to prove that they created a nation. The case before us must be considered in the light of our whole experience and not merely in that of what was said a hundred years ago."[15] In like manner, Chief Justice Charles Evans Hughes said in 1934: "If by the statement that what the Constitution meant at the time of its adoption it means today, it is intended today that the great clauses of the Constitution must be confined to the interpretation of the Framers, with the conditions and outlook of their time, would have placed upon them, the statement carries its own refutation."[16]

One would have to probe deeply into the psyche, individual and collective, of the American people, or at least of lawyers and other constitutional commentators, to get an adequate analysis and resolution of why American's ancients are so revered. Some partial insight possibly may be derived from Dostoevski's Grand Inquisitor, who said that man requires three things: miracle, mystery, and authority.[17] To some marked extent the Founding Fathers fulfill those desires: they are thought to have wrought a miracle and so little is known about them that they are clothed in mystery. Small wonder, then, that they are invested with a spurious authority by people anxious to have some higher degree of certainty in a highly uncertain world. Possibly it would be wrong to attribute too much to the Grand Inquisitor's trilogy of human wants, but they have relevance to some themes that are the subject of later chapters; we will return, however, briefly, to the same thought later. It is sufficient now to maintain that the Founding Fathers have been buried; they should not—they cannot—rule us from their graves. Or, as Michael Kammen said in *People of Paradox*: There is "an awkward anomaly in American thought. Although the founders were themselves engaged in a continuous quest for modes of legitimacy appropriate to their times and needs, subsequent Americans have sought to validate their own aspirations by invoking the innovations and standards of our hallowed pantheon as unchanging verities. This nostalgic vision of the Golden Age actually conjures up an era when values were unclearly defined, when instability often seemed beyond control, when public rancor and private vituperation were rampant, and institutions frail and unformed."[18]

How, then, does the Constitution change through time? Whenever an authoritative text exists through time, the language of which remains substantially intact, there is a need for exegesis through a continuing process of interpretation to update the basic document to new conditions. Necessarily that exegesis has to be articulated in terms of a "living" text or document if the original version, often considered to be sacred, is to be preserved while simultaneously permitting its application to new conditions and new situations.

It is not only in law and in constitutions that this phenomenon is found. Within law, many statutes acquire over time a gloss far different from the original conception. The ready illustration is the Sherman Antitrust Act, which since 1890 has been interpreted and reinterpreted much like the Constitution. Outside of law, one need look no further than to such sacerdotal texts as the Ten Commandments and much of the fundamental theological literature. The Christian religion, for example, has been able to assimilate the teachings of Copernicus, Darwin, Freud, and Einstein without alteration of the ancient biblical language—but with considerable change in its application.

The four methods of constitutional change—formal amendment, judicial decision, a few highly significant legislative and executive actions, and some informal practices—are overlapping and interacting. Each could be given extended discussion, but that is not now needed. The essential point is that a difference exists between the "formal" and the "living" Constitution, between "formal authority" to make decisions and "effective control" over those decisions. By concentrating on the decisions of societal importance—a concept not easily defined—it is not difficult to locate those vested with the formal trappings of authority. Much more difficult is the task of identifying those who in fact control decisions. Even more difficult is a listing of those decisions that are constitutional in nature. But if we heed Aristotle's admonition to look for precision only in those subjects that lend them-

selves to exact delineation, then it may be said that constitutional decisions, each lawmaking in character, include the following: those
amendatory of the basic charter; those interpretative (by the Supreme
Court) of specific clauses of the charter; those that, although legislative or executive in origin, in effect alter the balances of power within
American society; those "political" practices that in cumulative effect
subtly but substantially change the governmental structure; and
those that, because of long-continued practice, bring new centers of
power into the decisional structure, such centers often being ostensibly "private" in nature.

One who reads only the Constitution might be led to believe with
some of the more fundamentalist interpreters that the only method of
changing the Constitution is through the process set out in Article V.
Nothing could be more erroneous, even though Justice Hugo L. Black
for years flatly asserted such a position.[19] He knew better, as does any
thoughtful observer of the Court and Constitution. Under Article V,
amendments may be proposed to the Constitution either by Congress
or through petition of three-fourths of the state legislatures. The
former has been the only one used, and then but twenty-six times. Of
those, eleven came before 1800. Since then, important amendments
have been few in number; other than those that came out of the Civil
War—the Thirteenth, Fourteenth, and Fifteenth—one is hard put to
find any of really basic significance.

If one asks how the 1787 document could last to the present for a
nation vastly different from that of the latter part of the eighteenth
century, the net conclusion must be that the Article V method of
change is by and large irrelevant. Were it the only means of alteration,
the 1787 charter would long ago have been supplanted. Justice Black
was clearly wrong when he said in *Griswold* v. *Connecticut*: "I realize
that many good and able men have eloquently spoken and written,
sometimes in rhapsodical strains, about the duty of this Court to keep
the Constitution in tune with the times. The idea is that the Constitution must be changed from time to time and that this Court is charged
with a duty to make those changes. For myself, I must with all deference reject that philosophy. The Constitution makers knew the need
for change and provided it. Amendments suggested by the people's
elected representatives can be submitted to the people or their selected agents for ratification. That method of change was good for our

Fathers, and being somewhat old-fashioned I must add it is good enough for me."[20] Cumbersome, seldom used, Article V has little meaning in the progressive adaptation of the fundamental law to new conditions and to the exigencies of new eras in the American experience. The very difficulty of mustering the necessary votes in Congress and in the state legislatures makes it obvious that amendment can be employed only in the most extreme circumstances. Even when used, amendments tend to deal with the relatively inconsequential.

That is not so, emphatically, with the second method—that of the Supreme Court's making decisions on constitutional questions. This is one of the main (but not the only) means by which the 1787 charter is kept viable almost two centuries later in a far different social milieu. Ironically not mentioned in the document itself, it was only by a bold and aggressive assertion of power in 1803 by Chief Justice Marshall that the Court has, since that time, made ultimate determinations on the meaning given in some specific circumstances of constitutional phraseology.[21] The Court operates in what may be called a quasi-religious manner. Because the Constitution is an object of awe and even of worship by Americans, the Justices act as a priesthood administering to the faithful. They have the task of official exposition of the sacred text. Not surprisingly, therefore, attacks on the Court by some critics bear a marked similarity to the attacks by the faithful on heresies and heretics. "Economics," Thurman Arnold was fond of saying, "is theology";[22] so too with Court and Constitution.

The point, however, is that the government acts—the nation survives—not *because* of the Supreme Court and the Constitution but *in spite* of them. Fundamentally, the Constitution organizes governmental power and is a set of limitations on the exercises of that power. Once having been brought into being, the new government (as of 1789) did not then, and does not now, need the Supreme Court to keep it viable. Too much power is accorded law and judges to assert that a group of decisions upholding national power over the states was a controlling factor in the growth of the Union.[23]

Further evidence of the theological nature of the supreme tribunal and the Constitution may be seen in the fact that both bear, similarly to the Supreme Being, capitalized word symbols; the Supreme Court is the only court that lawyers and other commentators habitually give the dignity of a capital "C." The Constitution receives the same reverential treatment. Perhaps, therefore, it is not surprising to note the existence of a school of fundamentalist interpreters of the document, not unlike those who adhere to a fundamentalist interpretation of the Bible. To cite but one example: Reed Benson, a prominent Morman layman and member of the John Birch Society, was quoted in 1965 as saying: "It's a part of my religious training that the Constitution is an inspired document, that the time will come when it will hang by a thread and it will be our task to save it. . . . We believe that the Lord helped raise up the Founding Fathers to establish the Constitution so there could be the opportunity for religious freedom."[24] His sentiment might well astonish the shades of those who wrote the Constitution, for they were, if anything, realists and hard-bitten men, who had come through a revolution and who had to struggle against both the wilderness and the superpowers of Europe. Dean Don K. Price, in *The Scientific Estate*, has discussed the nature of such attitudes as those of Mr. Benson:

Science, by helping technology to increase prosperity, has weakened the kind of radicalism that comes from a lack of economic security. But science has helped to produce other kinds of insecurity: the fear of the new kind of war that science has made possible, the fear of rapid social and economic change, and the fear that we no longer have a fixed and stable constitutional system by which to cope with our political problems. And these fears are breeding a new type of radicalism.

The new radicalism is ostensibly conservative. It springs in part from the resentment men feel when their basic view of life is unsettled—as medieval man must have felt when he was asked to think of a universe that did not revolve around the earth, or as some physicists felt a generation or two ago when their colleagues began to talk about relativity and indeterminancy. The new conservative radicalism has a fundamentalist faith in the written Constitution, and the high priests of that faith seem to have desecrated it. The Supreme Court has applied relative policy standards in place of fixed rules of precedent; but worse still it has admitted into its system of thinking not only the moral law as revealed in tradition, but arguments from the sciences, even the behavioral sciences.[25]

There are some who believe that the Court acts as a set of "Platonic Guardians" making decisions on the wisdom of governmental decisions. [26] The belief is only partially true. To the extent that the Court does make constitutional decisions, it also makes law, and in so doing, it does in fact rule on the wisdom of official action. Despite numerous protestations to the contrary by individual Justices, in final analysis they are driven back to their ideas of what is right and proper. The Constitution does not interpret itself. Neither does any decision follow inexorably as a matter of logic from the delphic terms of the fundamental law.

Whatever its methodology—a topic of great importance but beyond the scope of the present discussion—the Supreme Court has three primary functions: (1) it *validates* much of the change that takes place under and in the Constitution; (2) it acts at times as a *national conscience* for the American people; and (3) of growing importance, it is a supreme court of *statutory interpretation*.

The Supreme Court has had the main chore of updating the Constitution through time. This was its great historical function—that of legitimating constitutional change, accomplished by putting new content into the unchanging words of the document. The litigable, interpretable parts of the Constitution, deliberately written in cryptic language, enabled the Court in succeeding generations to alter the content of the terms.

How that is (and was) done is itself controversial. Theories explaining what men of action, including judges, have done are the province of academics rather than those who make the decisions. The task of updating the Constitution was not preceded by a carefully thought out ideology, nor need it be in the future. As Professor Paul Freund has said:

> Writing of the law of torts in England at the end of the nineteenth century, when the notion of absolute liability was making inroads on the unifying concept of blameworthiness, and when the academic jurists were disturbed at the resulting impurity and imprecision of doctrine, Professor Fifoot of Oxford has recently said: "Faced with the fragments of life, the current law of any place and time can but approximate to a principle or indicate a tendency. Looking back upon the individual torts as they

emerged at the end of the nineteenth century, it requires an act of faith to postulate that principle or to indicate the goal to which they were tending."[27]

So it is with constitutional law. The point is important, for future constitutional developments of American corporativism can be handled in the time-honored style of the Court. Put another way, the great and continuing function of the Court has been to act as a continuing constitutional convention, to update the fundamental law, to make it relevant in different times and for different peoples. Because it so acted for nearly two centuries, the oldest constitution in the world has survived. It has lasted only because it has been so flexible as to permit adequate resolution of the problems faced by succeeding generations. Those who wrote it were sufficiently wise to insert ambiguity in the fundamental law. (Perhaps, because of political exigencies, they had no choice.)[28] By updating the basic document through time, the Court helped to preserve the document while permitting the urgent tasks of government to be accomplished. As Woodrow Wilson said, "Whether by force of circumstance or by deliberate design, we have married legislation with adjudication and look for statesmanship in our courts."[29] That statesmanship, though performed with some deviation, preserved the Constitution. Had the Court not acted as a continuing constitutional convention, the document written in the far-off eighteenth century could scarcely do duty in the twentieth century.

The Supreme Court acts also as a "norm-setter"; or, in the words of Lord Bryce, as a "national conscience" for the American people.[30] When Bryce wrote, he spoke of the Court as a check on "impatient majorities" of legislatures. In recent years, however—not much before the end of World War II—that type of judicial decision making took a subtle but definite shift. No longer do the Justices strike down economic legislation, whether by Congress or the state legislatures, the product of "impatient majorities." Rather, the Court's attention is focused on civil rights and civil liberties, in short, the position of the individual in an age of collective action. Many of the important and controversial opinions of the Court since 1945 can be so analyzed, whether they are in ethnic relations (the position of the Negro in American society), church-and-state questions (as in the school prayer decisions), or in legislative reapportionment (the right of urban residents to vote equally with rural residents).

When acting as a national conscience, the Court erects what in effect is an affirmative standard toward which the American people may aspire. The flow of decisions is not so much toward negative limitations—what government *cannot* do, which was the historical content of constitutional adjudication—but toward what government *must* do if a democratic polity is to survive. Put another way, the tendency is toward finding affirmative duties of government, duties to act. The shift is subtle, and there are obvious semantic difficulties in differentiating between a negative prohibition and an affirmative command, particularly since the judiciary has long acted in specific cases only and its decrees bind only the litigants before the bench. But even if subtle, it is nonetheless pronounced.

The other principal task of the modern Supreme Court requires only brief mention. It is the resultant of an abdication of power by the Court, beginning in 1937, to the political branches of government in the area of economic policy making. Prior to 1937, the Court operated, in the words of John R. Commons, as the "first authoritative faculty of political economy in the world's history." [31] That abruptly changed in 1937, however, so much so that, other than in state taxation or regulation of interstate commerce, thereafter only one minor state statute (and no federal statutes) dealing with economic matters has been invalidated by the high bench. The withdrawal from that field, leaving it to Congress and the executive in cooperation with the states and the corporations, was accompanied by a vastly increased number of decisions concerning review of administrative actions. What happened is quite simple and of direct relevance to this essay: Congress, faced with staggering new responsibilities of government, transferred the day-to-day power of government to the public administration, thus creating the "administrative state."

The third function—judicial review—is, however, statutory, not constitutional, interpretation. It attains constitutional dimensions only with respect to some decisions involving the antitrust laws. There the Court, while construing those statutes, still attempts to guide the course and structure of the American economy (futilely, it should be

added). Judicial review also attained constitutional dimensions when
the Court upheld assertions of power by Congress to regulate (as in the
creation of the National Labor Relations Board).

No thoughtful person dissents from the idea that the Court acts as
an agent of constitutional change, however much some may deplore
specific examples of that process and however much some assert that
the Court is the cause (rather than the instrument) of change. Less
accepted is the third method of alteration in the fundamental law—
through certain legislative and executive acts of a fundamental nature. Some commentators maintain that only the Supreme Court can
make constitutional law (other than in the little used amendatory
process). Careful analysis of some of the actions of Congress and the
President, however, shows the contrary—not in all such actions, to be
sure, but in a few of their more fundamental activities.

Three statutes are particularly important: the Sherman Antitrust
Act, the Employment Act of 1946, and the Civil Rights Act of 1964.[32]
The Sherman Act of 1890 was written in the delphic language of constitutions: "Every contract, combination in the form of trust or otherwise, or conspiracy in restraint of trade . . . is . . . illegal." Soon the
question arose, Did "every" mean "all"? The answer the Supreme
Court gave ultimately was no; the statute, the Court said, applied only
to "unreasonable" restraints of trade. The point here is not what the
Justices did to emasculate the plain language of Congress, but that
Congress, by enacting the statute, in effect made a constitutional pronouncement. The antitrust laws relate to the nature of the American
political economy and to the extent to which government will seek to
control the size and activities of business. As clearly, then, as though it
were written in the form of an amendment, the Sherman Antitrust Act
is equal in stature to any part of the Constitution—and is far more important than most of the actual amendments.

The same conclusion is valid for the Employment Act of 1946, the
statute that may be considered the "charter" for a basically different
type of government in the United States. It epitomizes the concept
that government has a continuing responsibility to take action to
enhance the economic well-being of all Americans. As such, the
statute culminated the New Deal period in American history and in
effect ushered in what will be called the Positive State.

So, too, with the Civil Rights Act of 1964, a sweeping pronouncement by Congress in which it sought by means of legislation to redress some of the indecencies heaped on disadvantaged Americans because of their race, color, or national origin (and sex, too, for a part of the statute forbids discrimination in employment because of sex). The Civil Rights Act, still too new to have made its full impact, nevertheless is effecting fundamental changes in the nation. That impact will make it ultimately a change of constitutional significance.

Taken together, these three enactments—and there are others—clearly indicate that Congress has actual, if not theoretical, power to change the Constitution without benefit of amendment. It is true that the Sherman Act and the Civil Rights Act were approved by the Supreme Court, and thus were "constitutionalized," but the Employment Act has never been litigated and indeed is not likely to be. It is also true that Congress in each instance acted under express grants of power in the Constitution. But the point is that the size of the changes wrought by such statutes makes them of a different order of magnitude from the usual legislative enactment.

Much the same can be said for the President, whose grant of power for various reasons is nebulous and almost nonexistent, but who, in the words of social critic Amaury de Riencourt, is "the most powerful single human being in the world today." The President, Riencourt says, "wears ten hats—as Head of State, Chief Executive, Minister of Foreign Affairs, Chief Legislator, Head of the Party, Tribune of the People, Ultimate Arbitrator of Social Justice, Guardian of Economic Prosperity, and World Leader of Western Civilization."[33] The aggrandizement of power in the presidency can be applauded or deplored, but it cannot be ignored.

Ultimately, the question of constitutional change is one posed by Walton Hamilton in 1938 when he asked, What is a constitution?[34] A possible answer to that question, that the American fundamental law is a living instrument of governance, and that it is dynamic and organic and not static, is only the beginning of insight. Much more must be shown.

Some overlap is discernible between how the Supreme Court changes the Constitution and how it is altered through operation of the fourth method: certain long-continued practices. The point may be best seen, perhaps, through reference to the concept of the "living law" enunciated many years ago by the Austrian Eugen Ehrlich in a

seminal book, *The Fundamental Principles of the Sociology of Law.*
Ehrlich considered the living law to be "in contrast to that which is in
force merely in the Courts and with the officials. The living law is that
law which is not imprisoned in rules of law, but which dominates life
itself. The sources of its knowledge are above all the modern documents, and also immediate study of life itself, of commerce, of customs and usage, and of all sorts of organizations, including those
recognized by the law, and, indeed, those disapproved by the law."[35]

The usefulness of Ehrlichian jurisprudence in this connection is at
least twofold. First, it is possible to analyze and explicate the living
law of American constitutionalism. To do so entails scrutiny and
development of the total flow of decisions of a constitutional nature,
wherever made, not merely those made by the Supreme Court. Attention must also be accorded important legislative and executive decisions. Furthermore, there must be careful inquiry into certain decisions privately made that have constitutional consequences. Two
examples will illustrate what is meant here. Nothing is said in the
Constitution about political parties (or indeed about any other "private," "voluntary" association, such as the large business corporation
or the trade union). It is obvious, however, that the growth of the
political party has effected a substantial constitutional change. The
"two-party" system is now basic to American constitutionalism.[36]
The decisions parties make affect everyone in the nation and wherever
American influence is felt.

So, too, with the large business corporation: its growth and
acceptance during the twentieth century has wrought a change in the
Constitution as profound as anything expressly written in it, for those
huge enterprises set the tone for and dominate the American political
economy. As will be shown, much of American public policy results
from the interactions among these entities and their relationships
with government and with such other groups as the trade union. The
constitutional consequences of the rise of ostensibly private and
allegedly voluntary associations have been immense. These associations have developed a "living law of American constitutionalism"
that makes mockery out of the formal law of the Constitution. That
"living law" is concerned with the fundamental societal decisions
made by "nongovernmental" institutions—corporations, trade
unions, foundations, and the like.[37]

CORPORATE AMERICA

Americans have, then, a Constitution that is still viable after almost two centuries of national life and after enormous changes in the nation itself and in its commitments. That is one of the more remarkable achievements in the annals of government. Small wonder that the Constitution is worshiped. A symbol of certainty in a rapidly changing world, it is for many what the American Bar Association called it decades ago—"the Ark of the Covenant of our Fathers."[38]

If change is indeed the law of life—and of constitutions—and if law, including constitutional law (however made), is a reflection of the society of the time, brief mention of a fundamental social change in the United States in the past two centuries is in order. In the late eighteenth century, in colonial America and the beginning years of the republic, only two entities existed: the natural person and the state. The Constitution was drafted on that premise. Corporations of any type, profit or nonprofit, are not mentioned; indeed they scarcely existed. The United States was a nation of small towns and small shops, with a sturdy yeomanry in the small farmer. Fewer than 300 corporations, of any type, existed in 1800. By 1850 that situation had abruptly shifted; and in the decade before the Civil War more corporations were chartered than in all previous years under the Constitution.[39]

Thus there early began, slowly to be sure but with an accelerating pace, a tendency toward group action in economics and commerce. And thus there began a basic change in the nature of the American society. Another entity was created, somewhere between the natural person and the state: corporate or associational behavior. The net result today is that the most important social unit, despite the original theory of the Constitution, has become the pluralistic social group. The individual—the natural person—ever more is important only as a member of a group (or groups). The United States is *the* corporate society par excellence. William T. Gossett, former general counsel of the Ford Motor Company and past president of the American Bar Association, noted the tendency some years ago: "The modern stock corporation is a social and economic institution that touches every aspect of our lives; in many ways, it is an institutionalized expression

of our way of life. During the past 50 years, industry in corporate form
has moved from the periphery to the very center of our social and economic existence. Indeed, it is not inaccurate to say that we live in a
corporate society."[40]

The corporate form, then, has become the characteristic institution
of American society—corporate in the sense of group or organizational behavior, not necessarily devoted entirely to economic profit
making. The giant business corporation, however, is by far the most
important of the decentralized social groups that dominate the
nation.

What, then, is a corporation? There is no easy or quick answer to
that question. Under the corporate form may be found, in addition to
the business corporation, such a congeries of institutions as the
church, the university, the "think tank," the union, cities (municipal
corporations), the foundation, modern guilds (for example, the American Bar Association and American Medical Association), political
parties, cartels—the list is long. Its unifying thread is group behavior,
usually hierarchically organized to meet designated ends. (As Robert
Michels noted, and as will be expanded below, most groups tend to be
controlled by oligarchies.)[41] In 1816 Chief Justice John Marshall gave
a classic statement to the notion of a corporation (those that receive a
charter or permission from the state to exist) as a fictional "legal
person":

> A corporation is an artificial being invisible, intangible, and
> existing only in contemplation of the law. Being the mere crea-
> ture of the law, it possesses only those properties which the
> charter of its creation confers on it, either expressly, or as inci-
> dental to its very existence. Those are such as are supposed best
> calculated to effect the object for which it was created. Among
> the most important are immortality, and, if the expression be al-
> lowed, individuality; properties by which a perpetual succession
> of many persons are considered the same, and may act as a single
> individual. They enable a corporation to manage its own affairs,
> and to hold property without the perplexing intricacies, the haz-
> ardous and endless necessity, perpetual conveyances for the pur-
> pose of transmitting it from hand to hand. It is chiefly for the
> purpose of clothing bodies of men, in succession, with these

qualities and these capacities, that corporations were invented and are in use.[42]

The corporation is one of the great social inventions of mankind, a device that permits associational activity in perpetuity. Once termed by Thomas Hobbes "worms in the entrayles of the body politic,"[43] corporations are at once an economic entity, a political order, a sociological community, and a legal person. The corporation has a reality as much as the natural person, even though it has "no anatomical parts to be kicked or consigned to the calaboose, no soul for whose salvation the parson may struggle; no body to be roasted in hell or purged for celestial enjoyment."[44] No one can lay bodily hands upon United States Steel or AT&T or incarcerate the Ford Motor Company or the Chase Manhattan Bank. But they exist in contemplation of the law and they pose critical questions for American constitutionalism, particularly as the giant corporations interlock with government. Those questions are problems of theory. Before setting out the elements of American corporativism in the next chapter, we should consider the role that theory plays in human affairs.

Man is a systematic being; he lives by systems of thought, conscious or not, that guides his actions. Without some sort of system, people could not live their lives effectively; the world is much too complex to be grasped in its entirety. One of the most important tools in reducing the confusion of reality to manageable proportions is theory, or, as Professor Robert Axelrod has suggested, a "schema."[45] A schema is "a pre-existing assumption about the way the world is organized." The assumption (or hypothesis or schema) of this volume is the fusion of economic and political power into the corporate state, American style.

That formulation, of course, is only an approximation. It is manifestly impossible to take account of all the facts relevant to the politico-economic order. Nevertheless, there is utility in the theory, if it is sufficiently accurate—or at least more accurate than other theories of power in the modern state. Since social reality is constantly changing, the schema set forth here is one that needs continual reexamination to determine its validity.

With that cautionary note in mind, we now turn to an outline of American corporativism.

2

TOWARD A DEFINITION OF THE CORPORATE STATE

The United States has moved well down the path toward a corporate state.

—DANIEL FUSFELD[1]

There is no indigenous American corporatist theory, but the corporate state does exist in fact.

That paradox is explainable: there is little American philosophy, political or otherwise, that is worth mention—other than that poor substitute for not having a philosophy, pragmatism. American thought is largely derivative. It gnaws over the products of European writers much like medieval scholastics pored over Aristotle. Exegesis on themes struck early by Mill or Kant, by Hume or Locke, by Aquinas or Marx, among others, makes up the bulk of the American philosophical tradition. A nation of immigrants has looked to the homelands for intellectual inspiration—save for pragmatism. Conceived by Charles Peirce and nurtured into fruition by William James, the pragmatic "philosophy" substitutes action for thought. It eschews ends or purposes. Official action in the federal government provides apt illustration; there, as Charles Lindblom once put it, the science of "muddling through" prevails.[2] A policy issue is identified with a search for empirical data, and consensus is the test for validity. If it—a policy—works in the sense of being accepted by the common denominator of policymakers, it then is "good policy." Pragmatism thus is more concerned with method than with judgment.

In the early 1960s the pragmatic temper regnant was the ne plus ultra of governmental policymakers. To be a "hard-headed pragmatist" was equated with wisdom, with harsh realism rather than mushy idealism. The "best and the brightest" considered that the "facts" of policy were all that mattered—a dismal illusion that is based on the fallacious notion that "facts speak for themselves." That they do not should be obvious, but it is not. Facts do not exist, as Whitehead once said, "in nonentity."[3] There are no facts apart from a theory. The hard-headed pragmatists are intellectual prisoners of defunct academicians and of inarticulated major premises.

Hans Morgenthau (a European immigrant) pointed out in 1962 how pragmatism and empiricism are terms employed with pride in Washington (they still are): "They are used as though to be pragmatic and empirical when faced with a political problem were to be rational almost by definition."[4] Deep-seated thought habits permit officials to approach fundamental social problems with a series of piecemeal, empirical attacks, without the accompaniment of any thought-out plan. Problems are looked upon as headaches and handled accordingly—with the quick "fix," the aspirin tablet, the temporary expedient that will enable the problem to be "solved" and allow attention to be devoted to the next one.

That mind set is pathetic at best, dangerous at worst. It is entirely inadequate to the needs of the modern age, if not the past, as is evident from even a casual survey of the many problems or crises facing the United States (and, indeed, the entire planet). The net effect, as crisis piles on crisis, each one potentially more terrible or lethal than its predecessor or concomitant, is that the institutional capacity of the nation (the nation-state, as a generic group) has now come under its most severe test since its inception about 300 years ago.

It has long been obvious that the American dream has ended, although many still believe in its tenets. The process began with the closing of the frontier and the immersion, first begun in the Spanish-American War and accelerated in World War I, of the United States deeply and irreversibly into planetary affairs. Before 1900 it was possible to believe in the idea of progress and of a world in which things got better and better. Protected by the oceans and the British navy, the country prospered by exploiting the untold and seemingly endless resources of the empty continent. Much of that had been wrest away through imperialistic adventures, to be sure, but still the dream persisted that, in some way and somehow, Americans were special—a little better than people elsewhere. The bubble burst in the cynicism that followed World War I and collapsed entirely in the Great Depression.

The point, however, is not to retrace that well-known path but to suggest that adherence to pragmatism made little lasting difference when the problems were the relatively simple ones of filling and developing a virgin continent. Mistakes made could easily be corrected; the margin for error was great. We can no longer so indulge ourselves. The intellectual gap, unfilled by the pragmatic temper, must now be filled. Americans will need to know where they are, as well as where they have been, if ever they are to be able to attain a decent future. That future will not come by happenstance or by accident or by muddling through in a series of ad hoc decisions taken just before (or just when) a problem erupts into a crisis.

Americans are uneasy today simply because, for the first time in almost 200 years, they cannot contemplate the future with confidence. Although they continue to be short-term hedonists, perpetually searching for the quick return, the easy dollar, the immediate reward, and in so doing destroying their priceless and irreplaceable patrimony, some faint stirrings portending intellectual change are becoming evident. Still largely a nation of Micawbers, with a touching faith that something will turn up to rescue them from their present follies and pleasures, many Americans have substituted science for God and believe, deep down, there will always be a technological "fix" to extricate them from the quicksand of escalating problems. A few—far too few as yet—have a larger vision. The publication in 1970 of *A Theory of Justice* by philosopher John Rawls may well mark an intellectual watershed.[5]

The purpose of this essay, however, is not to chronicle the emergence of new strands of thinking that go far beyond pragmatism. Rather, it is the much more limited, yet still essential, aim of accurately describing the nature of the American political economy as seen from the perspective of constitutional theory; and then from that description extrapolating some of the present-day trends in order to call attention to certain dangers to the values inherent in constitutionalism. In other words, the corporate state, American style, will be described, as to both its contours and development. It is a product of pragmatism, which will explain how it can exist without any indigenous corporatist theory. It was not planned; it just grew—much like the Vietnam conflict grew without design by a series of small steps. Over the decades since 1787 a series of seemingly unconnected steps have little by little produced a new constitutional order—sans amendment and sans fanfare.

In this chapter the outlines of American corporativism will be set forth in skeletal form. Fuller details will come later. First, however, brief reference to European corporatist theory is desirable.

Forty years ago Mihail Lanoilescu maintained that the twentieth century was destined to become the "century of corporatism," a statement that, in 1934, was not a prediction but a description.[6] Many countries in western Europe were corporatist: Italy under Mussolini, Spain under Rivera, Portugal under Salazar, Austria under Dollfuss, and Germany under Hitler. In this hemisphere, Brazil under Vargas was corporatist. (In practice, however, many of the corporatist plans "either remained vague projects to be realized in some distant future or became passive instruments for carrying out the policies dictated from above by an absolute central authority,"[7] as in Italy.) Even the United States, in the National Industrial Recovery Act of 1933, experimented with a version of the corporate state. Although the NIRA was outlawed by the Supreme Court in 1935, the economic and cultural forces that brought it—as well as other examples of twentieth-century corporativism—into existence have not ceased to operate. And the government-business relations then formalized continued in another form. As the United States, as well as all other nations, fearfully enters in the 1970s into a period of an "end to growth" and sees massive realignments in historic Western-Third World relationships, there has come a resurgence of interest in ideas and concepts that have lain dormant since the 1930s. Further, informal accommodations have by now solidified into a corpus of customary law. But to speak glibly of the corporate state is not to define it or to determine how it could come into being under the fixed Constitution of 1787.

European corporatist theory is a view of society that sees a nation as made up of a number of diverse economic or functional groups rather than of atomistic individuals. It involves the rediscovery of society— more accurately, the group—as the basic unit and attempts to counteract what is considered to be excessive individualism. That, in briefest terms, is a call for a form of latter-day feudalism. (The United States today is appropriately labeled "neofeudalist.")

Historically, corporatist thought was mainly Roman Catholic. During the nineteenth century a reaction set in against a perceived undue emphasis on individualism brought about by the French Revolution. These Catholic (and other Christian) scholars proposed a reversion to the corporate character of medieval society. Two encyclicals, *Rerum Novarum* issued by Pope Leo XIII in 1891 and *Quadregesimo Anno* promulgated by Pius XI in 1931, are the intellectual landmarks of that stream of thought. The search was for "community" during a time when individualism was the sine qua non of Western life.

Corporativism also meant the discovery (or rediscovery) of a mystical entity called "society," itself a corporate organization, one with drives and purposes of its own that transcend the arithmetical sum of the private interests of the citizenry. The development in theory thus is cyclical. Using the French Revolution as a turning point toward the high point of discrete individualism, the trend today (during this century) is toward the decline of individualism and the rise of group behavior. Sir Henry Maine, writing in *Ancient Law* a century ago, opined that the development of "progressive societies" was from "status to contract"—in other words, from feudalism to individualism.8 At the precise time that he published those oft-cited remarks (1861), already society was turning back to a new form of feudalism. By 1939, two distinguished French economists characterized the developments as a "piecemeal emergence of corporatism [*corporatisation*]," noting a general tendency that "free contract has receded in the face of legal regulation. Markets . . . have been 'made sane' by the public authorities who, partly by legislation and partly by giving legal force to private professional agreements, have substituted statutory imperatives for the spontaneous adaptation of supply to demand."9

Corporativism as a formal theory all but collapsed with the fall of Nazi Germany and Fascist Italy. It remained in Franco's Spain and exists today in Sweden, Japan, and some other nations of the non-Soviet part of the world. There is much similarity between the United States and the Soviet Union. As Robin Marris has said: "The significant difference between managerial capitalism and managerial socialism lies less in the character of the rules of the game than in who sets them. In socialism, the rules are set by political government. In capitalism, they emerge indirectly from a body of law and custom, founded on the concepts of private property and slowly developed."10 But that does not mean that the U.S.S.R. is corporatist. The similarities go to the physical appearance of the two industrialized powers and to their bureaucracies. In Marris's words, who sets the "rules of the game" is of critical importance.

ELEMENTS OF AMERICAN CORPORATIVISM

Corporatist theory begins with the recognition of the group as the basic societal unit. The isolated individual does not exist as such. Hobbes could say that man in a state of nature had a life that was "solitary, poor, nasty, brutish, and short," a quintet of attributes that probably was at least 80 percent correct. It is only in the last 200 to 300 years that theories of atomistic individualism—the worth of the "natural" person qua human being—had any currency. Before that, and at the present, the individual merges, subtly or overtly, into some type of organizational activity.

Orthodox constitutional theory and doctrine recognize the existence of but two entities: government and the individual person. Nothing intermediate is envisaged. The Constitution limits government in favor of individuals, a notion based on the unstated assumption that individuals live and act as autonomous units. Not even the political party is mentioned in the fundamental law, and it is only through a dubious, sometimes disputed, but nonetheless impregnable construction that artificial persons (mainly corporations) are called constitutional persons.11 If anything, the Constitution, as drafted and surely as interpreted during the nineteenth and early twentieth centuries, is based on the Protestant Ethic. A basic tenet of this concept is individualism, both political and economic, an individualism that found expression in Adam Smith, Ricardo, Locke, Mill, Sumner, and Spencer, among others. These and other commentators extolled the sacredness of property, decried the spiritually debilitating effects of security, and asserted the supreme virtues of hard work, thrift, and independence—notions that received official approbation by British statesmen while the Irish starved during the

Great Hunger, by Herbert Hoover during the Great Depression, and by Richard Nixon in the depression of 1974.

The allegedly autonomous, isolated individual really spends his life as a member of groups; further, he is significant only as a member of a group or groups. As an individual he has neither political nor economic power. But when associated with others he gains the strength to prevail or to refute or at least to influence. The Protestant Ethic, accordingly, has been replaced by the Social Ethic: "That contemporary body of thought that makes morally legitimate the pressures of society against the individual. Its major propositions are three: a belief in the group as the source of creativity; a belief in 'belongingness' as the ultimate need of the individual; and a belief in the application of science to achieve belongingness."[12]

For the individual, the group provides a means for the escape from anomie by persons who are beset, as seems to be the general rule, with feelings of isolation, of nothingness, of rootlessness and purposelessness. It also enables, if one accepts Thomas Hill Green's views, individuals to increase and strengthen their liberty and freedom.[13] That seeming paradox is explained by the theory that through union persons may accomplish objectives which they as individuals would be unable to achieve and may also oppose coercive tactics of other and stronger individuals or associations. For society, on the other hand, voluntary groups and associations are a means by which some of the urgent business of society is performed. They are agencies of social control, operating as arms of the state in the performance of some of the preferred activities of society. They may be considered to be the recipients of delegated power from the state.

This is not new in history; apparently it has always been so. Nor is it new to this decade to suggest the importance of groups. In 1944 Robert Merriam asserted: "The lone individual does not figure either in family relations, in neighborhood relations, in state relations, in social relations, or in the higher values of religion. Nowhere is he left without guiding social groups, personalities, and principles."[14] There can be little question that group interests, as Charles Beard said in 1945,[15] have always formed the very essence of politics both in theory and practice. Associational activity thus is the way in which the individual achieves his meaning. That notion by John Dewey was echoed in 1952 by Earl Latham when he said that "the chief social values cherished by individuals in modern society are realized through groups."[16] And it is the organization, not the individual, which is productive in an industrial society.

Law and legal theorists, however, have lagged behind. Only in very recent years has the Supreme Court read a right of association into the Constitution.[17] Group theories of law have yet to replace the individualistic theories that have prevailed since the inception of the republic. The theory of the corporate state, American style, in final analysis is a statement of group legal theory, with particular emphasis on the business corporations. In the corporate state the social and legal role of the individual qua individual is supplanted by the individual qua member of group(s).

FUSION OF ECONOMIC AND POLITICAL POWER

The group as the dominant societal entity has one unavoidable consequence: sovereignty, Bodin and Austin to the contrary notwithstanding, is splintered. It is shared by public government and the private governments of the corporations.

To speak of sovereignty is to speak of power, the ultimate concept of politics and of constitutions—which organize the exercise of power and in the United States limit governmental power in favor of individuals and groups. For the moment, power may be defined succinctly as the capacity to make or influence decisions that affect the values of others. That, to be sure, is too abstract and says neither who in a given polity exercises power nor how it is exercised nor who is affected and how. Those questions will be developed later; it is sufficient now to emphasize one of the major segments of a definition of corporativism—the fusion of political and economic power.

The merger occurs in at least two ways. First is the influence that economic power centers can and do bring in fact upon public governmental structures. And second, there is the exercise of political power within the amorphous confines of the corporate community itself, the corporation being a political order as well as an economic entity (and a sociological community).

The close intertwining of public and private power is no new development. Depending on how one reads American economic and legal history, it can be seen far back into the nineteenth and even the eighteenth centuries. The line between public and private is blurred, and always has been blurred, in American law, the myth to the contrary notwithstanding. But what was relatively minor in the nineteenth century has in recent decades become central to the politico-economic order.

THE LEGAL NEXUS

To be corporatist, however, there must be a legal connection between public government and private groups—corporations and unions, in the main. Corporatist theory requires it and the European models all display that overt connection, by statute or fiat. But how, outside of perhaps the armaments industry where there is a contractual relationship between the major arms producers and the government, can it be demonstrated that necessary nexus exists?

To answer that question requires analysis of the nature of law itself, how it is created and promulgated and how it is enforced. If, as Professor Andrew Hacker has said, "neither our constitutional law nor our political theory is able to account for the corporate presence in the arena of social power,"[18] and if corporate managers do rule, at least in part, then it is clear that they have no direct, express delegation of power from the state. Corporativism in Europe has such a delegation. American views of law, however, are in the main based on Austinian notions of sovereignty, under which law is the command of the sovereign—that is, the government.

That conception is too limited; it does not take other power centers into account. Nor does it make a distinction between those who have formal authority to make power decisions and those who wield effective control over them. What is needed, accordingly, is a "living law" analysis, which requires primary focus upon the important societal decision and asks the question, *Who* makes those decisions, *how*, and with what *effects*? The living law is principally associated with Eugen Ehrlich, an Austrian jurisprudent who set out his theories in *The Fundamental Principles of the Sociology of Law* in 1912. Ehrlich maintained that the living law is to be seen in contrast to that which is in force merely in the courts and with the officials. It is law not imprisoned in rules of law but which nevertheless dominates life itself. It is to be found in "the modern documents, and also by immediate study of life itself, of commerce, of customs and usage, and of all sorts of organizations, including those recognized by the law, and, indeed, those disapproved by the law."[19]

In other words, the living law is the flow of decisions important to Americans. Some are made by private officers, others by public officials. It is what important decision makers actually do, a flow of decisions, a process rather than a static system. The myriad routine transactions between the two characteristic institutions of the day—big government and big business—make up a body of the living law. At times put into statute, administrative ruling, or court decision, it also exists as an inchoate set of "working rules" by which the corporate state gets its business done. A series of laws (in Ehrlich's sense) rather than a logical whole, the living law is the grease that keeps the wheels of government going. The living law, often not codified, is the legal nexus between political and economic power.

THE CORPORATE STATE AS GROUP-PERSON

The corporate state is the hypostatization of the public interest, and the public interest is greater than the arithmetical sum of the private interests of the nation. Government has a momentum of its own, separate from and greater than individual interests. At a 1962 press conference, President Kennedy was asked about a statement of Secretary of Labor Arthur Goldberg about the need for a third person—the public—at the bargaining table when collective bargaining agreements were negotiated. Said the President in reply: "These companies are free and the unions are free. All we [the executive] can try to do is to indicate to them the public interest which is there. After all, the public interest is the sum of the private interests, or perhaps it's even sometimes a little more. *In fact, it is a little more.*"[20] With that statement, Kennedy (perhaps unwittingly) articulated a view of government at odds with the historic Constitution. He revealed his belief in a transcendent public interest. (The phrase "perhaps unwittingly" is used deliberately, for by no means is it clear that the President did not know what he said. After all, it was in his inaugural address that he uttered the statement, often repeated, about citizens asking not what their country could do for them but what they could do for their country—a sentiment perilously close to the *Todo Por La*

Patria slogan seen on public buildings throughout Franco Spain. And Spain is a corporate state.)

A considerable body of constitutional law illustrates the dominance of society as a corporate body over the individual. Government, the voice and instrument of society, has drives and interests of its own to further. Thus, as Justice Holmes once said, a man can be marched up to the front with a bayonet at his back, there to die for his country, and the Constitution will not prevent it. And as Justice Hugo Black said in 1943, in a case involving the exclusion of Japanese-Americans from areas on the West Coast, citizenship has its duties as well as its rights; and therefore the Japanese-Americans should not (and could not, constitutionally) complain about being deprived of their homes and, at times, penned up in concentration camps.[21] The sordid history of treatment of the Indians by government, with systematic violations of solemn treaties upheld by the Supreme Court, is another example of the triumph of the societal corporate entity over the individual.

At no time, in fact, when the interests of government or society are really at issue does the individual prevail. As President Kennedy said, the public interest is a little more than the sum of the private interests of the nation. That, in brief, is another way of saying that the state in the modern era has become an anthropomorphic superperson whose reality is as real as that of human beings. American constitutional law, as well as other law, recognizes this; even when the Supreme Court issues decisions that appear to further individual rights, the Court has in fact been talking about individuals as members of groups. And even group rights have to give way to the rights of "society."

The net result is that the state is some sort of group-person. Not only are groups, such as corporations, real persons in the eyes of the law, but so too is the national state. The constitutional problems posed by that are discussed in Chapter 7.

OTHER CHARACTERISTICS

Two other attributes of American corporativism require only brief present mention. First is the idea of citizenship as attaching as much to the corporation as it does to the nation-state. It is becoming more and more obvious that the identifications and loyalties, the reciprocal rights and duties, of natural persons run to and from the corporate entity to a degree that times equals and even surpasses those to the nation. Government (society) seeks to counteract such tendencies, to be sure, by making nationalism a secular religion and by creating a congeries of symbols and myths about the nation and its heritage. But the steady growth of the corporation and its place both as a unit of "functional" federalism and of a "new" separation of powers means that, much as sovereignty is being eroded, so too is the ancient concept of citizenship as attaching only to the nation-state. The development has reached its apex in the managers of the multinational corporations.

Second, there may be seen definite and significant changes in the individualist categories of law—contract and tort and property, the bedrock of a laissez-faire theory of government and of society. Each is being fundamentally altered—away from a basis in individual volition (contract) or individual responsibility (tort) or even individual ownership (property) to "contracts of adhesion," liability without fault, and a new form of property in the promises made by corporate enterprises (including government). Adolf A. Berle put the matter well some time ago: "We are seeing the gradual transition (in historical time not gradual at all) of our vast country from a system of individual possessory property (the norm a century ago) to a system of non-individual, non-statist, non-possessory economic and social power (a system of corporations, corporate insurance companies, and pension trusts, of labor unions, professional guilds, and voluntary associations) which has concentrated economic power to a degree unknown in recorded history." [22] Berle chronicled the alteration in property; implicit in his analysis are concomitant changes in contract and tort. Most contracts are at best only partially volitional. And most civil wrongs (torts)—those that revolve around the automobile—have now produced a movement toward no-fault insurance.

That adumbration of the elements of American corporativism will serve to provide a basis for thinking about what is said below. In Part II, the argument is further elaborated. The corporate state has arrived, unsung and unheralded, and is now an essential aspect of American constitutionalism.

part II
The argument defined

Corporate America has arrived, as part of a condition of constant social and constitutional change. The American economy is dominated by the supercorporation, which finds a ready ally in the rise of "positive" government. The two overmighty entities of the day—corporation and government—interact in a synthesis that is leading to the formation of a type of corporativism. In this process the intellectuals, far from being a separate power center, are "servants of power"; they service the bureaucracies of the supercorporations and of the state. In Part II, these strands of thought are developed; the argument of the book is set out in detail.

3

THE CORPORATION
AND THE STATE IN
AMERICAN HISTORY

*A corporation . . . may be defined in the light of history as a
body created by law for the purpose of attaining public
ends through an appeal to private interests.*

—HENRY CARTER ADAMS[1]

Something like the modern corporation is "the inevitable product
of an industrializing society," Dean Edward S. Mason observed in
1960—a statement that anticipated Galbraith's assertion in 1967 that
"technological imperatives" demanded the modern giant business
corporation.[2] Mason and Galbraith *may* be correct—although, as
will be shown in Chapter 4, at least Galbraith, and perhaps Mason,
can be faulted. But whether they are accurate on the score of inevita-
bility and technological determinism, surely they are in saying that industrializing societies—whether essentially capitalist or socialist in
makeup—tend to produce similar economic institutions. Those in-
sights do not, however, define the nature of a corporation; nor do they
reveal how they have developed side by side with the nation-state as
twin instruments of public-private governance.

The modern nation-state is a relative latecomer as a political order.
It arose out of a disintegrating feudal system, and thus is not much
older than 300 years. (It was not until late in the nineteenth century
that Italy and Germany became nations rather than collections of
feudalities.) Its growth antedated and created the need for corporations, private organizations created by law, as Henry Carter Adams

said, "for the purpose of attaining public ends." Until very recent years that public side of the private corporation has been lost in the historical development of those economic and financial institutions, even though the Supreme Court said in 1905 that "the corporation is a creature of the State. It is presumed to be incorporated for the benefit of the public."[3]

So seen, the corporation is one of the great social inventions of all time. In law it is an artificial person, "invisible, intangible, and existing only in contemplation of the law," as Chief Justice John Marshall put it in 1819.[4] Corporations are "juristic" persons, as distinguished from "natural" persons. They have most of the legal rights and almost all of the legal duties of natural persons. But they are more: they can be immortal, or come as near to immortality as a secular society can provide and they have no corpus and thus cannot be imprisoned. The corporation, as Professor Christopher Stone recently said, "is a 'legal fiction' with 'no pants to kick or soul to damn.' What is meant is that while we can point to the corporation's steel and glass factory, or to its tangible chairman of the board, or to its offices on Rockefeller Plaza, there is no physical entity *the corporation* that we can point to—or that can, of itself, adulterate foods or pollute rivers. The corporation *itself* 'does no act, speaks no word, thinks no thoughts'."[5] On the other hand, corporations are less than natural persons in having no inherent capability of acting; they can operate only through agents in the form of natural persons.

The modern corporation, thus, is a relatively new phenomenon, just as the nation-state is relatively recent. Both are not only new, they also—until very recent years— were characteristic of only one part of the world. Today, nation-states as the characteristic form of political order number more than three times those in existence when the United Nations was created in 1945. Corporations, as juristic persons formed for specific purposes by their members, have become the characteristic form of economic order—if not in numbers, then surely in importance and influence. They have, as Professor James S. Coleman recently said, "created societies with different structural foundations than those which existed in the past."[6] It is those different structural foundations that create the need for reexamination of the nature of American constitutionalism.

Since 1886 the corporation has been considered a constitutional "person."[7] That, too, is a major social invention, of crucial importance during a time when corporations were waxing larger and stronger; they were able to invoke judicial protection against legislative regulation. It was only when the giant corporation had become an established fact of American life that the legal tide turned so that regulation became valid. (Some exceptions may be noted, as in public utilities, which were always subject to regulation; but the statement is accurate for most businesses.)

There was no need for such judicial protection prior to the last part of the nineteenth century. Neither the states nor the federal government were interested in regulating business. The national government was quiescent, and the states were far more interested in creating new corporations and maintaining a close connection with them. There was an immense population growth in juristic persons during the first half of the nineteenth century, one that far exceeded in terms of percentage the population explosion of real persons. Witness a statement by an Illinois judge in 1857: "It is probably true that more corporations were created by the legislature of Illinois at its last session than existed in the whole civilized world at the commencement of the present century."[8]

The point, in short, is that government encouraged the growth of corporations, both in numbers and in size. It is to that continuing symbiotic relationship that we now turn.

THE HISTORICAL SYMBIOSIS

Two factors coalesced to produce the large numbers of corporations that were created in the United States in the seventy-five years before the Civil War: economic need and legal permissiveness. Capital was required beyond the capacity of individual persons. That capital could be pooled in a corporation by permitting several persons (stockholders) to form a corporation; and when the law established the principle of limited liability, then there was even greater impetus to incorporate. Added to that was the peculiarity of the American Constitution that left to the states the right to charter corporate bodies, whether "municipal corporations" (cities) or business corporations. (Congress' right to incorporate was read into the Constitution by Chief Justice John Marshall in 1819, but it has been seldom exercised even to the present day.)[9]

Each state, having the power to incorporate, could and did compete for business—by offering such attractions as tax benefits, land grants, and lax to nonexistent supervision of the business corporations by state governments. The result was a large increase in the numbers of corporations. Consider, for example, the experience in Michigan; in 1894 an observer chronicled the change there:

> Before 1850, we had about forty-five mining corporations, seven or more railroad corporations, a few banking corporations, several plank-road corporations, and a few of a miscellaneous character; all, of course, under special charters [with the exception of religious corporations].
>
> General laws to the number of one hundred and fifty-six have been passed from time to time since 1850 for incorporating almost every kind of lawful business and association, and the result has been that we now have [in Michigan] about eight thousand corporations which are organized under those general laws. . . .
>
> To this great number of domestic corporations must be added one hundred national banking corporations, and a large and not ascertainable number of foreign corporations . . . which do business in this state by express permission.[10]

But then, as in England, the corporation was not simply an organization for the convenient prosecution of business. It was considered to be a public agency, to which had been delegated the regulation of trade.

Even so, an apparent movement of the corporation from a public agency to an institution for purely private gain began soon after the Civil War. It was the business corporation, as Professor Merrick Dodd said,[11] that although practically nonexistent in 1780, "supplied the medium" by which a nation of fewer than 3 million engaged in agriculture, fishing, and small shops was transformed by 1860 into a nation with ten times that population and that was already deep into the process of industrialization. With greater numbers came greater size—and with both came greater economic power for the corporations. Economic power then, as now, meant social and political power. This may be seen in the manner in which the Supreme Court adapted constitutional law to the growing demands of the business interests.

The tale, though thrice told, merits repeating for two reasons: first, because it reveals the way in which law follows power (both constitutional law and, as will be seen, the "private" law of contract and tort and property); and second, because it is a classic historical example of litigation being a pressure group device.

LAW AND POWER

Law, in this country as well as elsewhere, follows economics. That is no statement of crude Marxian economic determinism. It has always been that way.

Economics—that is, wealth either in the traditional form of property (real and personal) or the modern form of promises—means power, power that however exercised finds its ultimate statement in the positive law of the state. The central concept of constitutional law and politics, power may be defined as the ability or capacity to make or influence decisions of societal importance. It is the ability to coerce, either subtly or directly. "Those who own economic goods exercise a kind of governmental power," Professor Edmond Cahn once said. "Being entitled to retain their property or part with it as they choose, the owners like petty sovereigns can dictate terms and conditions their neighbors must perform in order to have access to the property. In this sense every lawful economic power becomes a type of political power, and every economic inequality poses a question of political equality. Property so viewed is 'private government'."[12] In short, property means the power to state binding norms, formal (as in law) or informal.

The law, then, has never been passive or colorless. It has been employed, overtly or covertly, as the means to compel adherence to the values of those who hold economic wealth. This may be seen in both constitutional law and in the private law of contracts, torts, property, and crimes.

CONSTITUTIONAL LAW

The myth to the contrary notwithstanding, the state has never been hostile to business interests (to economic wealth) in the United States. The Constitution itself provides ready illustration in the clause prohibiting states from making laws impairing the obligation of contracts—a provision designed to protect creditors and to proscribe legislatures from interfering with private agreements. During the early decades of the republic, the Supreme Court used the precept to strike down adverse legislation concerning corporations. Two cases show the pattern, *Fletcher* v. *Peck* and the *Dartmouth College Case*.[13] Beginning in 1809 and running through 1861, the Supreme Court in thirty-seven decisions declared state acts unconstitutional. Of them almost half—eighteen—were based on the obligation-of-contracts clause. (During that same period, only two acts of Congress were invalidated, neither of which was on economic grounds.)

Fletcher v. *Peck* dealt with the so-called Yazoo land frauds. It is an early, classic example of the interplay between economic power and influence on the one hand and political subservience on the other. The facts that led to the *Fletcher* decision are these. Four influential land development corporations bribed the Georgia legislature to sell a huge part of the western part of the state (35 million acres) for a penny and a half an acre. (This territory made up much of what is now Alabama and Mississippi.) The leading promoters of the scheme, it might be noted, included two United States Senators, two Congressmen, and three prominent judges, including an Associate Justice of the Supreme Court. The land, or much of it, was eventually sold to another group of prominent politicians. When a successor Georgia legislature tried to void the original sale, suit was brought that the new statute violated the obligation-of-contracts clause. Relying on an opinion of Alexander Hamilton, which was probably written in 1796 (soon after the frauds), the Court upheld the claim, saying that public grants were contracts within the meaning of the Constitution.

Language from Hamilton's opinion, which was undoubtedly known to the Court when it decided *Fletcher* in 1810, merits quotation. The repeal, he said, contravened "the first principles of natural justice and social policy," particularly so far as it was made "to the prejudice . . . of third persons . . . innocent of the alleged fraud or corruption.''[14] Therefore, the repeal was void under the Constitution—the first time a state statute had been declared invalid by the high court. Language by the Court, speaking through Chief Justice Marshall, is apposite because it points the way toward subsequent judicial actions. The state of Georgia, Marshall. said, "was restrained" from passing the rescission "either by general principles which are common to our free institutions, or by particular provisions of the Constitution of the United States." In sum, the Supreme Court announced its freedom and capacity to ascertain "general principles . . . common to our free institutions," thereby rewriting the Constitution—a process that continues to the present day. A concurring opinion by Associate Justice William Johnson is even more explicit than Marshall on this point. In the only statement ever made by a member of the Court that even God could be bound by a judicial decree, Johnson said: "I do not hesitate to declare, that a state does not possess the power of revoking its own grants. But I do it, on a general principle, on the reason and nature of things; a principle which will impose laws even on the Deity."

Thus the Court accepted the argument of the attorney for the land companies, Alexander Hamilton, and thereby began a series of legal victories that continues to date. And thus was born, together with other decisions, what the late Edward S. Corwin called "the basic doctrine of American constitutional law"—vested rights.[15] "The doctrine of vested rights," said Corwin, "represents the first great achievement of the courts after the establishment of judicial review. In fact, in not a few instances, judicial review and the doctrine of vested rights appeared synchronously and the former was subordinate, in the sense of being auxiliary, to the latter."

The decision in the *Dartmouth College Case*, also written by John Marshall, provides ready illustration of Corwin's thesis. Marshall accepted almost without change the argument of Dartmouth's lawyer, Daniel Webster, and held that a charter granted by the British crown to the college could not be altered by the state legislature of New Hampshire. Making law wholesale, New Hampshire was thus bound by the terms of the British charter, even though the American Revolution had severed legal connection with Great Britain. Dartmouth had a "vested right" that could not be impaired by the state.

These decisions are fundamental; they set the intellectual pattern for subsequent judicial action. The development took two forms: first, the uncritical acceptance of arguments made by corporation lawyers was clearly evident in the post-Civil War period; and second, the Justices felt free to find new rights buried within the cryptic clauses of the Constitution. The further point is that the Supreme Court was the object of pressure group tactics designed to advance property rights; it was, that is, the target of litigation. That it succumbed quite easily to the blandishments of lawyers for business interests should not be considered astonishing. Judges, historically and contemporaneously, have been drawn from the "ruling class" in the United States, and it would be odd indeed if they did not generally reflect the values of that group.[16]

The population growth in business corporations that took place in the mid-nineteenth century created islands of economic power that pressed upon the political and legal orders. Corporate lawyers, soon after the Civil War, drew on the early Marshall opinions and added to them, creating a protective constitutional umbrella under which corporations could wax even larger and more powerful. Professor Wallace Mendelson put the matter strongly when he said in 1960: "Conservative tradition insists that by putting the sanctity of 'contracts' above other considerations of ethics and public welfare, Marshall and his associates promoted economic stability. Would it not be more accurate to suggest rather that they encouraged the flagrant corruption of state politics and reckless waste of natural resources that marked the nineteenth century? Surely judicial protection of fraud in the Yazoo land scandal paved the way for the Robber Barons and their Great Barbecue at the expense of the American people."[17] Politics were manipulated to gain favors from legislators and other politicians, for despite the myth to the contrary, government intervention in economic affairs has always been the norm in American history—but to help, not to regulate, business enterprise. Peter d'Alroy Jones summarized the point in *The Consumer Society:* "Despite the prevailing orthodoxy, government intervention in economic life was supported by leading political figures and public policy took the form of local, state, and federal subsidization of the transportation revolution, federal creation of two national banks, and manipulation of the economy through Treasury fiscal operations, the deliberate use of tariffs to divert the allocation of resources into desired lines of development, and government subsidies to certain industries (fishing, small arms, and, at a state level, agricultural bounties on grain and silk production)."[18]

When the Fourteenth Amendment was added to the Constitution after the Civil War, business interests made an immediate attempt to have it interpreted to protect them. The first efforts failed: the Court simply could not accept the notion that a corporation was a "person" within the meaning of the amendment's due process clause (reading in part "no person shall be deprived of life, liberty, or property without due process of law"). Due process had always meant "due procedure," and that was what the Court held in the *Slaughterhouse Cases* (1873) and *Munn* v. *Illinois* (1877).[19] And a "person" meant only the freed slaves and other human beings.

But the setback was merely temporary. By 1886 the Court was ready to accept without argument the proposition that a corporation was a person within the meaning of the Fourteenth Amendment. Thus began the formal reign of "substantive due process," the most important judicial invention in American constitutional history, which lasted in economic questions until 1937 and which exists today in other issues. The "liberty" protected by due process of law became the freedom to contract—something not mentioned in the Constitution. The freed slaves were forgotten; replacing them in the eyes of the Court were the business corporations. Thus it was that the Justices announced that "liberty of contract . . . cannot be unreasonably interfered with"; and they equated the right of an employee to quit his job with "the right of the employer, for whatever reason, to dispense with the services of the employee." Legislation that disturbed "that equality is an arbitrary interference with the liberty of contract which no government can justify in a free land."[20]

One would have to be naive indeed if he supposed that the Justices did not know what they were doing. Of course they did. They freely struck down statutes designed to ameliorate working conditions as violative of due process (liberty of contract) in as high-handed an example of judicial fiat as has ever been seen. Of course they knew that "necessitous men are not free men" and of course they had doubtless read the *Federalist Papers* in which Hamilton had observed that "the power over a man's subsistence amounts to a power over his will.''[21] The point is that they did not care. Building on Chief Justice Marshall's validation of fraud in *Fletcher*, they created a constitutional framework under which laborers, many of whom were immigrants, had to pay the dreadful costs of an industrializing society. The Supreme Court encouraged business to organize collectively but created obstacles out of the whole cloth to prevent labor from doing so. (There is a sobering lesson here for those who today look upon the courts as ultimate protectors of the weak and disadvantaged.)[22] The willful blindness of the judges to the dismal facts of life among the working classes in industrialized cities has not been sufficiently emphasized in recent years. Judges are drawn from that stratum of society that identifies with the wealthy and the powerful. An off-bench statement by Justice Samuel F. Miller succinctly sums up the point: "It is vain to contend with judges who have been at the bar the advocates for forty years of railroad companies, and all the forms of associated capital, when they are called upon to decide cases where such interests are in contest. All their training, all their feelings are from the start in favor of those who need no such influence."[23]

Small wonder, then, that the courts were the target of business interests, which importuned them to protect business. The Supreme Court, the federal courts generally, and indeed the Constitution itself were viewed as roadblocks toward any attempts to interfere with the rights of property. In the vanguard was the American Bar Association, a group of corporation lawyers who banded together in 1868 and who since then have been preeminent in the defense of property ("vested rights"). "The bar," Benjamin Twiss said in 1942, "actually looked upon itself as a priesthood, serving and protecting the Constitution and its interpreters from any sort of profane attack. Probably as good a statement as any of this position was made by John Randolph Tucker in 1892 [to the American Bar Association] when he said, 'Can I be mistaken in claiming that Constitutional Law is the most important branch of American jurisprudence; and that the American Bar is and should be in a large degree that priestly tribe to whose hands are confined the support and defense of this Ark of the Covenant of our fathers, the security of which against the profane touch of open and covert foes is the noblest function and the most patriotic purpose of our great profession?' "[24] One can snicker, as one should, at such sanctimonious balderdash. The pitiful, the pathetic thing is that the lawyers actually believed it. And when those leaders of the bar found themselves on the bench, as they often did, they simply could not help ruling in favor of the group from whence they came. It is worth more than passing mention that since 1937 when hydraulic social pressures finally broke that barrier to social welfare legislation, the bar—including the American Bar Association—no longer views the Supreme Court or the Constitution as did Tucker in 1892. The effort now, usually successful as will be shown, is to manipulate the political branches of government rather than to rely on the judiciary.

PRIVATE LAW

As with constitutional law, so with the private law of contracts, of property, and of torts. Judge-made rules in those fundamental categories had the result of transferring the social costs of private enterprise from the enterprise itself to the workingman or to society at large. Tort law provides apt illustration. Under its doctrines, a person who willfully or negligently harms another's person or property must answer by paying money damages. The analogue of contract, which is a consensual obligation, a tort is a nonconsensual legal obligation. Who, then, bore the costs, in accidents and in deaths, of the new industrialism? Not the businessman. Not the corporation. The worker himself. (Often those workers were children.) And who bore the costs of pollution and other social costs? Society at large.

How did this come about? In tort law judges created doctrines of "contributory negligence," "assumption of risk," and the "fellow servant rule," all of which served to insulate the enterprise from liability. By "freely" taking a job, said the judges, the workers "assumed the risk" of any accident that might occur. That they did occur (and still do, for that matter, at a terrifying rate) is all too evident. And when legislators enacted "workmen's compensation" laws, under which accidents would be paid for by the corporations, the first such laws were invalidated as unconstitutional.

So law indeed followed power, economic power, whether that law was the fundamental law of the Constitution or private law. Judges articulated it. They maintained for decades that *their* law prevailed over that of the legislature, drawing on those "first principles of nat-

ural justice and social policy" that Marshall had discovered in
Fletcher v. *Peck*. That law still follows economic power, but in other
ways, is also true (as will be shown).

Litigation, thus, was a pressure-group device, employed by the
dominant economic interests to further their goals. The courts are not
usually so viewed. The myth has it that judges are impartial arbiters
between parties and that they discover the law in some preexisting res-
ervoir of legal principles rather than create the law. Long under attack, the myth no longer has any credible intellectual adherents.
Judges make law routinely, as Justice Byron White acknowledged in
Miranda v. *Arizona*: "The Court has not discovered or found the law
in making today's decision, nor has it derived it from some irrefutable
sources; what it has done is to make new law and new public policy in
much the same way that it has in the course of interpreting other great
clauses of the Constitution. This is what the Court historically has
done. Indeed, it is what we must do and will continue to do until and
unless there is some fundamental change in the constitutional distribution of governmental powers." [25]

Sophisticated lawyers have long known this; they have realized that
judges have far more discretion in making decisions than is accorded
them by the traditional model of "justice blindfolded." Accordingly the Supreme Court historically was the governmental policymaker
that corporation lawyers sought to influence—as, indeed, they did
with other judges, state and federal. Litigation was a specialized form
of interest-group lobbying insofar as it dealt with ultimate constitutional questions. With its self-assumed power to invalidate actions of
other governmental agencies, the Supreme Court long reigned as "the
first faculty of political economy in the world's history," [26] making
economic policy for the nation, but to the benefit of the limited
groups—the "ruling class" and their legal votaries—who could sway
it to those undefined principles of natural justice that Chief Justice
Marshall found in *Fletcher* v. *Peck*.

Small wonder, thus, that the Court and Constitution were viewed in
sacerdotal terms by those who benefited from them. And there should
be little cause to wonder why, since economic policy has been "constitutionalized" since 1937—that is, become a matter of political choice
rather than constitutional requirement—the businessman is no
longer among those who extol either the high bench or the fundamen-

tal law. Congress, in the first instance, and the bureaucracy, more generally, are now the targets of business. Litigation as a pressure-group device has become the technique of the disadvantaged—the black, the American Indian, the consumer, the unrepresented multitude—in short, all of those who do not themselves have much political muscle.

It should not be thought that the pattern outlined above was clear-cut. The tapestry of history is far too complex. So, while the courts were used to protect business interests, so too were the legislatures. And judges on occasion did rule against business interests, as in *Muller* v. *Oregon* in 1908 when a state law setting maximum hours for working women was upheld.[27] By no means, however, was it a mere coincidence that the Supreme Court discovered substantive due process and liberty of contract at precisely the time that an expanded franchise and the rise of new farmer and labor groups to some positions of power enabled them to get legislation ameliorating working conditions enacted. In law, as in life, those "coincidences" are usually the result of design, not of happenstance.

4

THE RISE OF THE SUPERCORPORATIONS

The industrial capital of western democracies is no longer
divided into two classes, "public" and "private," but
rather into three, "public," "private," and "corporate."
The corporate sector likes to be described as "private,"
but this may represent no more than a desire to conceal.

—ROBIN MARRIS[1]

Corporations, small and sparse in 1800, had by 1900 become many and large. In the period immediately after the Civil War, the "supercorporation" was born. Spawned by the rising tide of industrialism, the supercorporations are a genus apart from the small, localized, family-owned companies that characterized the early years of the republic. They are sui generis; nothing quite like them has been known in human history. Early attempts were made to regulate and, indeed, to control them. The Interstate Commerce Commission was established in 1887 in an effort to keep the railroads—then the most predatory of the "trusts"—under some minimal control. That the ICC did not succeed needs no restatement. But when the ICC was followed in 1890 with the Sherman Antitrust Act, the movement toward federal intervention into business affairs became solidified.

Whatever else may be said about them, the antitrust laws have not stayed the trend toward bigness in business. Corporate enterprise today has become the largest ever known, far greater in size and resources than were the trusts that concerned Senator Sherman. As America grew in size geographically, its business units paralleled that growth. Today a few hundred corporations so dominate the economy that they set its tone and present serious problems of governance to the American people. These firms—the supercorporations—number not more than 500. They are the giants that straddle the continent and that spill over into other countries, that make the United States a common market in fact, and that have a definite and important impact on politics and law. Their names are familiar—General Motors and General Electric, U.S. Steel and AT&T, to name but a few—and sometimes unfamiliar—for example, the Cargill grain company. However many there may be—the precise number is of little significance—they exemplify the transition, as Adolf Berle said,[2] from a system of individual possessory property to a system of nonindividual, nonstatist, nonpossessory property; the result is a concentration of economic power to a degree unknown in history and a sharing of sovereignty with the state. In this chapter, the rise of one of the groups (the supercorporations) having that characteristic is discussed. In economic terms, the supercorporations culminate the industrial revolution and create the greatest social change since the agricultural revolution eons ago. In political (hence, in legal) terms, they present critical problems of governance in all industrial nations, both those said to be democratic (such as the United States) and those considered authoritarian (such as the U.S.S.R.).

THE NEED FOR THEORY

The existence of the supercorporations needs neither documentation nor extended discourse. No one disputes the fact, however much opinions may differ over what to do about it. But what *is* the corporation?[3] How may it be defined? The question is not easily or quickly answered, save on a superficial level. There is no such thing as a single descriptive model that will fit all of the enterprises incorporated in the United States. In legal parlance a juridical person, it is in fact a collective entity, a confederation of disparate interests, "more nearly a method than a thing" (as a New York court put it several decades ago).[4]

The need is for an adequate descriptive model of the firm. None exists. Professor Fritz Machlup of Princeton University noted this in 1966. He identified ten concepts of the firm while indicating that at least eleven more existed in the literature of business and economics. Some of his concluding language merits quotation:

This exercise should have succeeded in showing how ludicrous the efforts of some writers are to attempt *one* definition of *the* firm as used in economic analysis, or to make statements supposedly true of "the" firm or of "its" behavior, or what not. Scholars ought to be aware of equivocations and should not be snared by them.

I hope there will be no argument about which concept of the firm is the most important or the most useful. Since they serve different purposes, such an argument would be pointless. It would degenerate into childish claims about one area of study being more useful than another.

I also hope the specialist who uses one concept of the firm will desist from trying to persuade others to accept his own tried and trusted concept for entirely different purposes. The concept of the firm in organization theory, for example, need not at all be suitable for accounting theory or legal theory; and I know it is not suitable for either competitive price theory or for oligopoly theory.

Most of the controversies about "the" firm have been due to misunderstandings about what the other specialist was doing. Many people cannot understand that others may be talking about altogether different things when they use the same words . . .

I conclude that the choice of the theory has to depend on the problem we have to solve.[5]

(Machlup's final statement is only a half-truth; the converse may also be valid: the choice of problems scholars undertake to solve may depend on the theory—the ideology—they bring to the subject matter.)

The basic problem, however, remains: how to define the supercorporation so as to transcend the simplistic formulations of lawyers or the narrowly focused conceptions of economists. We may begin with the proposition that the firm is a collective organization, a collectivity, and that it is only by a transparent legal fiction that it is called a person. That fiction may be useful, but it is still manifestly untrue—known to be such, but with the untruth being (at times) used for beneficial ends. Going beyond the legal make-believe that the corporation is a person is necessary. Required is a conception of the firm as a sociological entity. Neither the economist nor the lawyer, the political scientist nor the sociologist, has evolved a viable theory of conscious cooperation.

Nevertheless, a growing literature exists that attempts to define a corporation functionally, as an institution, in contemporary American life. Drawing on that literature and adding to it, one may conceptualize the corporation as a collection of cooperating interests. Far more than the property interest of the stockholders, although legal theory still looks upon it that way, it is a sociological organization and a political instrument, an economic force and a juridical person—in short, something new in the manner in which humans order their affairs. So considered, one can pierce inadequate definitions and present the supercorporation for what it is. The mythology of "free enterprise" speaks of the firm as if it were to be equated with a natural person. That simply is not accurate.

For purposes of constitutional analysis, what, then, is an adequate descriptive model of the corporation? The first attribute is that it is a creation of the state. As Justice Louis D. Brandeis said in 1933, "Whether the corporate privilege shall be granted or withheld is always a matter of state policy. If granted, the privilege is conferred in order to achieve an end which the State deems desirable."[6] But when granted, the corporate charter—the legal instrument that creates the entity—becomes for the most part insignificant and irrelevant. Once a firm has grown to the size of a supercorporation, whether a charter exists is a matter of the smallest moment. No one could seriously argue that by rescinding the charter of (say) General Motors that firm would cease to exist. It is no more dependent on the act of conception than is a natural person; the firm takes on a character of its own. As such, it far transcends the description of Chief Justice John Marshall in 1819, in which he said that a corporation was "an artificial being, invisible, intangible, and existing only in contemplation of law."[7]

A useful model of the corporation must take into consideration those who have claims of some sort against the firm, those who have some type of legal relationship with it, and those who merely because they are a part of the same polity cannot help being affected by the actions of the firm. These diverse groups make up a federation of interests—not conflicting interests, although superficially the contrary might seem true, but those that exist at least in a state of antagonistic cooperation. That federation may be broken down into two groups—the internal order of the corporation and the external order, all existing together in a sociological community. So viewed, the various interests include the following:

The security holders. The usual legal conception of the corporation recognizes only one interest—the property of the stockholders and others who supply capital. Long seen as too simplistic, nonetheless that view identifies the group that constitutes a major segment of the corporate community. What they own in most supercorporations, however, is not the corporation, but a piece of paper, usually transferable, which is a claim on profits if and when those who control the firm decide to distribute them. This does not mean that some large stockholders, particularly institutional investors, do not have a high degree of control; but the usual or small investor in the publicly owned corporation exercises no control at all. The Berle-Means thesis[8] of the divorce of ownership and control may well be valid only for the small investor, not those with substantial holdings. In actual fact, then, no one really owns the corporation; it exists as though it has a life of its own. In much the same manner as no one really owns nonprofit corporations such as universities, the supercorporation, once brought into being and into full maturity, transcends any of the groups in its federation of interests. If it did not exist, like Voltaire's God it would have to be invented, for what it does is essential to the type of society the United States has become.

The corporate managers. These are those who control, even though often they may not necessarily own. Included is the board of directors and the managerial hierarchy. They are the top stratum of the corporate bureaucracy, with interlocking links to large investors and financial institutions. (They intermesh also with government and the centers of knowledge.)

Rank-and-file employees. Often these are members of a union. They are to be distinguished from the managerial class and the white-collar worker who is not a member of the union.

The technostructure. John Kenneth Galbraith identifies this group as the locus of real power in the corporation: it includes "all who bring specialized knowledge, talent or experience to group decision-making."[9] Admittedly, this is a vague classification with considerable overlap with the other categories. Galbraith is far from specific as to its membership and his viewpoint has been sharply challenged.

The union managers or leaders. To an immeasurable yet marked extent, the officers of the union are a separate segment of the corporate community. Possibly they attempt to see themselves as part of the ruling class of that community. Accordingly, in their relations to the union members, they may be analogized to corporate management and its relationship to the stockholders.

That listing of the elements of the internal order of the supercorporation is not all inclusive, but it is sufficiently accurate to serve as a working model of a bureaucratically managed, hierarchically structured entity. Seen in this way, "the" corporation clearly is not a monolith; the "it" indubitably is a "they." Just as property can only be defined as "a bundle of interests," [10] so too the corporation is best seen as a federation of associational groupings. It is a method or a process, not a thing, an amorphous collectivity built around a principle of organization for production and operating in accordance with a general concept of cooperation. In many respects, it is the most meaningful unit of American local government. The general point has been made by Michael Young: "Every industrial society is governed by a series of managerial bureaucracies, and it is surely right to speak of them conforming to a common type. Managerial organizations are strikingly similar, in industry along with government, in education and research along with the armed services. Almost all institutions in almost all advanced societies are run by graded hierarchies of managers, officials, or officers, who do not 'own' but control; the posts filled by appointment nominally on grounds of merit instead of by election or inheritance; the officials salaried, permanent, and pensionable; the whole structure governed by written rules and regulations." [11]

If the principle of federalism can be fruitfully employed as an organizing concept in constructing a model of the internal order of the supercorporation, it can also be applied to the relations among large companies and to their posture to the state. Similarly (possibly because political thinkers see federalism or pluralism everywhere) the "external order" of the firm may be so structured. It too consists of a number of disparate elements, some with legal links to the supercorporation and one with no direct connection but with a pervasive interest in it. These external groups number at least four.

Direct satellites of the supercorporation include the *suppliers* and the *dealers*. The former, many corporations themselves, provide logistic support to the principal firm in the making of its final products. They also can supply services to the firm. They are tied to it by the legal link of contract, either on a continuing or on a one-time basis. Dealers are those who sell the products of the supercorporations. Some supercorporations, of course, have no dealers; for example, weapons producers have only one customer, the government. But others, notably the automobile industry, have a complex web of dealerships, again tied to the "mother" firm by contract.

These are direct claimants and contributors to the wealth and welfare of the organization. They are integral parts of the corporate constellation of interests, perhaps not as obviously as are those identified as elements in the internal order but nontheless so closely connected to the firm that they should be considered a part of it. Furthermore, they make up in large part "the second economy" of small business.[12]

Not so obvious, but nevertheless present, are the indirect claimants on the corporation—those who have a continuing, more than small interest in the decisions made by "the" firm. These include *consumers*, the individual members of the public who buy the product, and *the public generally*. Consumers have a fleeting legal tie through a sale, either from the mother firm or from a dealer, a tie, it should be noted, that is now recognized in law; the consumer in some instances can bring lawsuits directly against the supercorporation. For example, a person who is injured in an automobile may be able to sue the maker directly (as well as the dealer) even though he had no direct contractual link with the maker. This means that law is beginning to recognize the dealer as part of the greater corporate community. It is less so with respect to suppliers to the firm, although here too the mother company may be held liable for defects in the final product emanating from items originally produced by a satellite company.

Admittedly the group called consumers is nebulous. It is, in fact, no organization at all but a collection of individuals. Only very occasionally, as in boycotts of some companies, do consumers take on the characteristics of organizations. Nevertheless, they are part of the corporate community in that they have some sort of claim, albeit tenuous, against the firm. The same may be said for the public generally, although in a different way. The most uncertain of all, this concept involves the public interest or the interest of society in the activities of the firm. Articulated through government, it is the embodiment of societal concern with and the dependence of the people of the nation on it. The public interest in the supercorporation is a matter of surpassing importance, for those firms pose clearly and continuously the problem of faction that James Madison discussed: factions are groups made up of citizens "actuated by some common impulse of passion, or of interest, adverse to the right of other citizens, or to the permanent and aggregate interests of the community." He went on to say that regulation of "these various interfering interests forms the principal task" of legislation—that is, of the state. [13]

The model of the firm sketched here is obviously rough; equally obviously, it does not fit all of them. Some have only one customer; some have no suppliers; others have no dealers. But the general idea is valid. It sets forth a conception of the company that enables one to view it as a group, not as a fictitious person.

REASONS FOR THE SUPERCORPORATIONS

This is the age of the supercorporation. The American economy may well be, as Michael Harrington and others assert, [14] really two—that of the large firms and that of the small businessman—but there is little dispute about which is in control. America is dominated by huge collective organizations, which are "private" in that they are not actually owned by government but which in fact are instruments of governance and should be considered "public."

The phenomenon is not worldwide; it is largely confined to the nations of the North Atlantic littoral plus the U.S.S.R. and Japan. For that matter, it is not typical of all the nations of what often is propagandistically called the free world; the supercorporation exists in Europe (Volkswagen, Philips of Eindhoven, etc.) but as the exception rather than the rule. No doubt the peak of the development is in the United States; there is nothing elsewhere to compare with the sheer size of some United States corporations. Even the Zaibatsu of Japan, Volkswagen and Krupp of Germany, Philips of the Netherlands, or Unilever of Great Britain do not have the magnitude of General Motors or AT&T or the other giants of the American economy. (Nor, for that matter, do most of the nation-states of the world.)

The others are large, of course, and even when smaller, they can be thought of as being of a similar basic nature. As Michael Young has

said, industrial societies tend to be governed by a similar set of institutions. Young's statement, which appears in his foreword to the 1961
edition of James Burnham's well-known *The Managerial Revolution*,[15] indicates both the prevalence of the supercorporations (in
both open and authoritarian nations), whatever their actual label may
be, and the fact that industrialized nations are systems of overlapping and interacting bureaucracies.

We concentrate now on one of those bureaucracies—the giant corporation—and seek to determine the reasons for its development. To
sharpen the discussion, the point of departure and principal target of
criticism will be Professor John Kenneth Galbraith's confident (un-
documented) assertion in *The New Industrial State* that "imperatives of technology and organization, not the images of ideology, . . .
determine the shape of economic society." The question, in short, is
how to explain gigantism in American business. The development includes introductory matter to show the nature of the corporate economy in the United States and an examination of alternative hypotheses.

At one time economic determinism was at least a fad and perhaps
even fashionable. Marxists, neo-Marxists, and crypto-Marxists all
espoused it in one form or another. Even those who must strenuously opposed Marxism nevertheless were economic determinists. "Economic man" was said to control not only the market but the means of
production, the flow of goods, the very technology on which
production depended. A generation ago, however, Peter F. Drucker
chronicled "the end of economic man" and the coming of "industrial man."[16] He was correct, but the ancient ideology and shibboleths have lived on: the form has remained but the substance has
changed.

Today we are told that the position has been neatly reversed: not the
market, not economics, but technology determined the shape of
things that are as well as those to come. Economic determinism has
been replaced by technological determinism. Witness, for example,
the statement of Dean Don K. Price of the John F. Kennedy School of
Government at Harvard University: "The main lines of our [public]
policy, over the long run, are likely to be determined by scientific
developments that we cannot foresee, rather than by political doctrines that we can now state."[17] Such assertions, to use William
James' classification, appear to be based on a "strict" or "hard" de-

terminism—a unilinear cause-and-effect relationship between scientific-technological discoveries and the institutions created and maintained within any nation or society.

So it is with Galbraith, who perceives technological and organizational necessities as the main determinants of the supercorporations. And so, too, with Dean Edward S. Mason: "Something very like the modern corporation is *the inevitable product* of an industrializing society, whether that society follows a capitalist or a socialist trend of development. Lawyers love to describe the corporation as a creature of the law, but law in a major manifestation is simply a device for facilitating and registering the obvious and the inevitable. Given the *technologically determined* need for a large stock of capital, the managerial requirements set by the problem of administering the efforts of many men, and the area of discretion demanded for the effective conduct of an entrepreneurial function, the corporation, or a reasonable facsimile thereof, is the *only* answer."[18] Mason, however, did not define "the" corporation, although he seems to be talking about the corporate giant.

The Galbraith-Mason position is at best too simplistic, at worst erroneous. It illustrates, perhaps unwittingly, that "craving for an interpretation of history" that Edward Hallett Carr tells us "is so deep-rooted that, unless we have a constructive outlook over the past, we are drawn either to mysticism or to cynicism."[19] Technological determinism, in the Galbraith-Mason mold, tends toward mysticism. They attribute the fact of the supercorporation to one or at most two factors. If one, then, is to avoid cynicism—saying that history, in the immortal words of Henry Ford, "is bunk"—something more is required. That something is a careful analysis of social causation, built around the theme of the rise of the supercorporations. The net conclusion of what follows is that new scientific discoveries and new technologies permit changes in social institutions and even values because they create new possibilities for human action and thus alter the range of options available to men. The operative word in that sentence is "permit"; our conclusion is not that new technologies require—determine—certain social organizations but that they make them possible. Whether such organizations or institutions will result seems to be dependent on a number of other factors: "A new device," says Lynn White, "merely opens a door; it does not compel one to enter."

To pose the question of how to explain the rise of the supercorporation is, then, to venture upon the unruly sea of social causation. That sea is not uncharted, but there is a wide variance among those who have sought answers to the basic as well as the specific questions. In attempting to sort out the most plausible or the most valid explanation(s) of the creation of the large business firm, we should heed the admonition of economist William Letwin. [20] He maintains—rightly—that the road that American economic policy follows in its historical development is winding and murky. Tracing all of its permutations is an enormously difficult task. When faced with such a problem, historians (economic and otherwise) refer, as perhaps they must, to simplifying notions. The problem becomes one not only of following the path of policy or institutional development, but of not oversimplifying. Ready-made patterns may be used instead of mapping all the twisting and turning of the real path; rough though those patterns may be (and are), they make up the professional tool kit of economic (and other) scholars. That tool kit contains a few such models; they bear such names as laissez-faire, socialism, communism, mercantilism, and welfare state. Letwin did not mention science and technology, but he could, perhaps should, have.

Analysis of the supercorporation in the United States should be seen against a backdrop of what economist Kenneth Boulding has aptly termed "the organizational revolution." [21] The United States is the organizational society par excellence; it has carried the principle of organization into "private," "voluntary" groups to its apex in history.

The term "business gigantism" is itself susceptible of varying definitions. For example, it is possible to focus on the degree of concentration within certain industries. Market power exists when one firm or a small group of firms in a given industry can or does exercise significant discretion over production, distribution, pricing, and related decisions. Measures of market concentration, which means that a small group of firms control a substantial share of the economic activity in an industry, are the best available index of the degree of market power in an industry. Furthermore, one may speak of "aggregate concentration," which means the overall position that the supercorporations occupy, because they are conglomerate firms or because they are interlocked with actual or potential competitors, in total activity within, say, manufacturing.

For present purposes, however, attention will be on the total assets (the property and income) of the largest corporations. No distinction will be drawn between firms in manufacturing or in distribution, in transportation or in communications. What counts is sheer size—the amount of the total economic pie that the few hundred largest (super) corporations own or control. A ready guide is the annual listing by *Fortune* magazine.

SEVERAL ALTERNATIVE EXPLANATIONS

One would be rash indeed to venture upon the turbulent sea of social or historical causation. In this section, accordingly, "explanations" of business gigantism postulated by others are merely outlined, followed by possible alternative "explanations." No attempt is made to suggest a single, all-important explanation.

1. GALBRAITH'S TECHNOLOGICAL IMPERATIVES

In Chapter 2 of *The New Industrial State* Professor Galbraith sets forth his explanation of the rise of the supercorporations. He begins by mentioning the development of the Mustang automobile by the Ford Motor Company, showing the time and cost involved, and compares it to the beginnings of the company (and the Model T) in 1903. In Galbraith's view, nearly "all of the effects of increased use of technology are revealed by these comparisons." Technology, he says, forces the division and subdivision of the application of scientific or other organized knowledge into its component parts. Just why this is so he does not say. His basic conclusion is stated flatly (and without documentation): "Nearly all of the consequences of technology, and much of the shape of modern industry, derive from this need to divide and subdivide tasks and from the further need to bring knowledge to bear on these fractions and from the final need to combine the finished elements of the task into the finished product as a whole." He then lists six consequences as being of considerable significance: (1) the time separating the beginning from the completion of any task tends to increase; (2) an accompanying increase in the amount of capital devoted to production may be discerned; (3) time and money tend, in large industries, to be committed more and more inflexibly to the performance of a specific task; (4) specialized manpower is required,

those with special skills within specific technical areas; (5) specialization inevitably means that "organization" must come, for the
specialists must be coordinated; and (6) advance planning becomes a
necessity, both for the enterprise and also for the economy (which is
dominated by the huge firms).

There are several shortcomings in Galbraith's position. His thesis is
a monumental non sequitur, at best an example of post hoc reasoning
(with all of the fallacies of that type of thought). It also has aspects of
anthropomorphism: technology is said to have a "need," which by
implication is a human characteristic. Whatever technology may be
and however it is defined, it cannot in and of itself—that is, without
reference to human actors—have the characteristics of living beings.
That needs neither documentation nor expansion. It is obvious. Technology as applied knowledge, which is Galbraith's definition, furthermore suggests the requirement that someone must apply it, which in
turn is grounded on the (psychological) desire to apply it. But Galbraith never confronts that important matter.

Although the difficulties with Galbraith's position are multiple,
they may be divided into two main questions: (1) does technology require business gigantism, and (2) given the existence of the supercorporation, does it have characteristics that are comparatively beneficial? The latter question is not within the scope of our present inquiry;
however, some attention will be paid to it, for it bears on the conclusions one makes about the desirability or usefulness of continuing the
corporate giant in its present form. Our principal question is the relationship between technology and size of business units. Some of the
shortcomings of Galbraith's position follow.

a. Certainly there is no logical relationship between the existence
of technological knowledge, in and of itself, and business gigantism.
It is not enough to point to the U.S.S.R., as does Galbraith, and to
postulate a "principle of convergence" of industrial nations and their
institutions. His "sample" is too small. Not all nations, even with the
technology available as a store of knowledge, create such entities.

This is not to say, of course, that some nations—Great Britain,
Germany, France, Italy, Japan—do not have relatively large enterprises and that the U.S.S.R. does have large decentralized economic
units constructed in accordance with "the plan." And, furthermore,
there may well be a tendency or trend of development toward larger
business units. Whether there is would require considerable empirical

study throughout the world. But, again, this is only to point out the fact of the existence of those enterprises; their causes are not proved by asserting that since technology makes them possible, therefore they are inevitable. The logic of that relationship simply does not exist. Galbraith's model is the United States, but whether American enterprise is relevant to other nations is at best dubious.

b. Galbraith also fails to take into account the fact—at least, it seems to be a fact—that social or historical events are matters of multiple causation. To single out one factor from the totality of past events and say that it is the single cause is far too simplistic. (Possibly it would be preferable if human affairs were that simple; if they were, then "rational" solutions would be much easier to come by.) Social scientists delude themselves when they give simple cause-and-effect "explanations" to complex, aggregative occurrences. As Professor David S. Landes has said; "Economic development . . . is a process that, particularly when it takes the form of industrialization affects all aspects of social life and is affected in turn by them." And further; "One is not justified in speaking of uniform causal ties or influences." [22]

c. There is no economic or technological necessity for, say, General Motors to be as big as it is. Chevrolets can be built without the larger organization. General Motors is large not because of "technological imperatives" but because of other reasons, reasons that might be summed up in the statement that it has proved advantageous economically and commercially to be gigantic.

d. There is no hard evidence that proves that the huge industrial unit is technologically more innovative than is small business. The evidence, in fact, tends to prove the contrary.

e. Galbraith's six consequences of technology tend, on the whole, to be descriptions of large business units. The connection between their size and technology are at best post hoc rationalizations. This is not to say that no connection exists—for obviously it does—but that more than his flat statement is needed to "prove" the conclusion.

f. Professor Galbraith thus finds himself in the company of those who overtly or by implication counsel acceptance of the giant business enterprise, using it for public policy purposes rather than trying to break it up—men like A. A. Berle, David Lilienthal, and John K. Jessup. [23] What these social commentators failed to foresee is the newest of the large business units, the "conglomerate" firm. By definition the conglomerate is not a "technological unit." Accordingly, it is again obvious and needs no documentation that the imperatives of technology cannot have led to its existence. Yet conglomerate firms are now among the very largest of American enterprises. History—in a very few years—has refuted Galbraith and the others. That ought to be a sobering lesson, although probably it will not be, for those who are dogmatic about historical causation of aggregative events.

The coming of the conglomerates suggests that there are other reasons for the rise of business gigantism. It is to some other possible hypotheses that we now turn.

2. LAW AND THE LEGAL SYSTEM

With invincible parochialism, lawyers tend to view law and the legal system—and particularly the Supreme Court—as being far more important than possibly they were and are. Witness, for example, the statement of Professor Felix Frankfurter, written before he became a member of the Supreme Court, a statement that illustrates the unilinear thinking often employed by practitioners of any discipline:

> The raw material of modern government is business. Taxation, utility regulation, agricultural control, labor relations, housing, banking and finance, control of the security market—all our major domestic issues—are phases of a single central problem: namely, the interplay of economic enterprise and government. . . . In law . . . men make a difference. It would deny all meaning to history to believe that the course of events would have been the same if Thomas Jefferson had had the naming of Spencer Roane to the place to which John Adams called John Marshall, or if Roscoe Conkling rather than Morrison R. Waite had headed the Court before which came the Granger legislation. The revolution of finance capital in the United States, and therefore of American history after the Reconstruction period, would hardly have been the same if the views of men like Mr. Justice Miller and Mr. Justice Harlan had dominated the decisions of the Court from the Civil War to Theodore Roosevelt's administration. There is no inevitability in history except as men make it. [24]

Frankfurter's foray into an individualistic interpretation of history does not wash. His statement assumes the answer he is looking for; he begs the real questions. He could scarcely take a different position: it would not be easy for one who had spent his life studying the Supreme Court to question its power. He speaks as does Galbraith: the flat assertion, not the empirical study and not even (as did Max Weber) [25] the tentative hypothesis. But the learned Professor Frankfurter does raise, however incompletely, the role that law plays in the construction of a given economic order.

As was shown in the previous chapter, law was used to help create a favorable social environment that permitted the growth of corporate enterprise; however, it did not have an independent "force" of its own. In creating that milieu, the Supreme Court did help and thus, in a very limited way, can be said to evidence what Felix Frankfurter said about it. Legislation was also helpful. "If one includes all the activities of government [state and federal], and takes into reckoning all the costs, one must conclude," says William Letwin, "that an economic policy, aimed particularly at encouraging the internal growth of the nation's economy, was pursued with great energy and at considerable expense." [26] That is statutory law, legislation designed to encourage and aid the growth of corporate enterprise, legislation that seldom got judicial cognizance and never received Supreme Court disapproval. What that Court did was summarized in 1949 by Justice Robert H. Jackson: "Our system, fostered by the Commerce Clause, is that every farmer and every craftsman shall be encouraged to produce by the certainty that he will have free access to every market in the nation, that no home embargoes will withhold his exports, and no . . . state will by customs, duties, or regulations exclude them. Likewise, every consumer may look to the free competition from every producing area in the nation to protect him from exploitation by any. Such was the visions of the Founders." [27] Jackson's history is dubious, but his general point is valid.

An examination of Supreme Court decisions in an effort to determine whether law—the legal system—had any direct causal connection with corporate growth must result in a negative conclusion (or, in Scottish terms, "not proven" at best). That law and the legal system were favorable to the growth of the corporation is clear. Law could not, in and of itself, produce the giant enterprise. If today one of

the new nations of the world, for example Chad or Tanzania, were to
legislate the formation of large corporations, they would not spring
instantly into being. More than law or judicial decision is behind the
growth of the supercorporations. Not that law was unimportant, but it
is derivative rather than prescriptive. Law formalizes conditions and
social structures already in existence rather than prescribes what they
should be.

At the very least, then, the Supreme Court has acted in ways that
favor the growth of giant business—not only in constitutional law, as
we have seen, but also in interpretation of the antitrust laws. Those
laws merit brief mention. In 1890 the Sherman Antitrust Law was
passed, in which Congress said that "every contract, combination in
the form of trust or otherwise, or conspiracy in restraint of trade . . . is
. . . illegal." The question soon became one of interpretation: did the
word "every" mean "all"? In 1904 the answer was yes, but by a bare
five to four majority.[28] In 1911 the Court had so changed that by a
vote of eight to one it enunciated the famous "rule of reason," which
meant that only "unreasonable" actions were proscribed by the
law.[29] What this meant is that the Court was to have the final word as
to which contracts or combinations or conspiracies were prohibited,
for reasonableness was to be determined judicially. Later on, an
equally important ruling held that bigness in and of itself was no
violation of the antitrust laws (*United States* v. *Swift & Co., 1932*), the
Court thus insuring that no legal barrier—constitutional or statutory—existed for the growth of supercorporations. And while the
Court was interpreting the Sherman law so as to permit giant enterprises to grow, the government continued to take parallel action that
affirmatively aided such growth, as Walter Adams and Horace Gray
have shown.[30] Furthermore, as Thurman Arnold argued in 1937 in
The Folklore of Capitalism, those laws in many respects are a facade.[31] They permit the public to believe that something is being
done about giant enterprise, while simultaneously allowing corporate
managers to expand and operate almost at will. Thus the famous advice of Richard Olney, Attorney General under President Cleveland,
is true not only for the Interstate Commerce Commission (about
which he wrote) but also for the antitrust statutes. Said Olney, when
queried by a president of a railroad as to whether it would be advis-
able to try to get the Supreme Court to declare the ICC invalid: "My

impression would be that looking at the matter from a railroad point of view exclusively it would not be a wise thing.... The attempt would not be likely to succeed; if it did not succeed, and were made on the ground of the inefficiency and usefulness of the Commission, the result would very probably be giving it the power it now lacks. The Commission, as its functions have now been limited by the courts, is, or can be made, of great use to the railroads. It satisfies the popular clamor for a government supervision of railroads, at the same time that supervision is almost entirely nominal. Further, the older such a commission gets to be, the more inclined it will be found to take the business and railroad view of things. It thus becomes a sort of barrier between the railroad corporations and the people and a sort of protection against hasty and crude legislation hostile to railroad interests.... The part of wisdom is not to destroy the Commission, but to utilize it."[32] A sager or more prescient analysis of the independent regulatory commission would be difficult to find, and much the same can be said for the tortuous history of the administration and interpretation of the antitrust laws.

Paralleling the judicial development was direct governmental aid to business. The growth of the supercorporation is, in no small part, attributable to affirmative aid from government. Not only a favorable legal system helped, but direct subsidies were the norm—and still are, for that matter (this will be the core of a separate hypothesis).

That something other than "technological imperatives" operated to help create the supercorporations should, thus, be obvious. No doubt it is valid to say that technology is one of the principal underlying causes, but it is not the sole cause. Multiple factors coalesced—a virgin continent, huge natural resources, no foreign wars, cheap labor, large amounts of capital (often foreign), the urge to monopolize, a favorable legal system—with science and technology at a particular time in history. The unique nature of the American experience may be seen when it is cast against what other nations did. Certainly Canada and Australia, France and Germany, to say nothing of the remainder of the world, had available the mysteries of technology—"technological imperatives"—yet few giant industries were created. The persistent question is: Why? Why even today are many of the other industrialized nations of the world noted for the *absence* of supercorporations?

Galbraith neither poses nor answers this question. But he must answer it if he is to demonstrate an empirical base for technology as the key to growth of the huge firm. It will not do, in such an effort, to point to Unilever and Volkswagen, to Philips and Renault, for these under any criterion are the exception in England and Germany, Holland and France. We are thus left with an unanswered, possibly unanswerable, question. The fact of the supercorporation is obvious, the reason for it obscure. Other hypotheses, however, may be advanced.

3. GOVERNMENTAL PROMOTION OF CORPORATE GIGANTISM

We have seen that science and technology cannot alone explain the rise of the supercorporations and have inquired into the role of law and the legal system to conclude that, as Emerson said, at the very least, "The law is only a memorandum."[33] But it could well have been more, in that it was employed to further the interests of the business class. We turn now to a third hypothesis, one with obvious overlaps with the first and particularly the second: business gigantism is a consequence of affirmative governmental promotion of monopoly. The word "monopoly" is used as do Adams and Gray in their well-known *Monopoly in America* and as do Paul Baran and Paul Sweezy in *Monopoly Capital.*[34] As the former pair say, monopoly "denotes an industry situation where a single firm or a small group of firms—by virtue of horizontal, vertical, or conglomerate integration—possess substantial economic power." Baran and Sweezy, in like manner, use "monopoly" synonymously with "oligopoly." Because such firms, in whatever industry, tend to be large, the term "monopoly" can be used to characterize giant business or business gigantism.

Americans have had an ambivalent attitude toward concentration of economic power. On the one hand, the antitrust laws seem to be a commitment to competition and small business units. But the way that they are administered seems at least to permit bigness, a sentiment that the Supreme Court has approved. A. D. H. Kaplan has said in his *Big Business in a Competitive System* that there is a schizophrenia in American public opinion, the people wanting the results of both competition and monopoly.[35] Adolf Berle goes so far as to say that "few of the major segments in the community really want a regime of unlimited competition."[36]

Whatever the merits of that, the thesis that size of business units can be traced to affirmative governmental programs (which are formalized in public-law pronouncements) gets a trenchant presentation by Adams and Gray. They say: "Our thesis is that the currently popular deterministic explanations of economic concentration are inaccurate and misleading, that concentration is largely an artificial, institutional phenomenon which originates in, or derives sustenance from, the actions and policies of the federal government. Our study [*Monopoly in America*] indicates that some of these policies, whether or not so intended, have had a profound effect on the structure of the economy, that they have served to promote concentration and to restrict and weaken competition; in short, that the federal government—although by tradition, popular regard, and legal mandate the defender of competition—has by a process of functional perversion become one of the principal bulwarks of concentration and monopoly." [37] Adams and Gray do not propound a doctrinaire Marxist interpretation. On the other hand, Baran and Sweezy do put forth a Marxist viewpoint—and in so doing, parallel the Adams-Gray conclusions about the causes of business gigantism.

Evidence produced for the thesis includes the following: public utility regulation; tax and expenditure policies; defense procurement; disposal of surplus property; and such specialized areas as the atomic energy industry. All combine to make the antitrust laws no barrier at all to business size—and only a slight impediment to what a businessman might want to do. A few years ago Robert Heilbroner said that there was no substantial intellectual (or other) opposition to giant business, a situation not much changed today.[38] Those firms acquire a patina of intellectual respectability when such writers as Berle and Kaplan, Lilienthal and Galbraith, either counsel their acceptance as preferable or consider them to be inevitable. Adams and Gray put it rather more harshly. After noting that competition at one time was "a way of life, a social philosophy, a plan or social organization calculated to attain maximum freedom and individual well-being for all men," they go on to say that during the twentieth century values have changed. Individual freedom no longer is preeminent: "Many are prepared to sacrifice freedom for some collective goal that is assumed to be superior, such as order, stability, security, efficiency, productive power, or abundance." Or, as Professor William Withers has observed, when Americans have had to choose between freedom and material well-being, they have chosen the latter every time.[39]

That, in briefest terms, is the thesis. It makes a powerful case. But, again, ultimate questions are not answered—or even asked. Perhaps the basic question is this: Just how were these public policies tending to promote gigantism promulgated? Who influenced them? The question looks to the nature of the American constitutional democracy and in large part shades off into the fourth of our hypotheses.

4. THE "GOVERNING CLASS" HYPOTHESIS

If governmental policy did actively promote—or at least encourage—the growth of large business units, our immediate question is: How and by whom is governmental policy set? This is beyond the scope of the present exposition. We posit now a fourth hypothesis: that business gigantism is a resultant of a drive for economic position and power by the American "governing class," with the corporation as a source of wealth. Intangible promises, in the form of shareholdings, rather than property are the base of both wealth and power. The members of the "ruling class" also "co-opt" the intellectual talent necessary to provide it with a base of capable employees: in present-day terms, the "knowledge revolution" is a device employed to service the giant enterprise (and universities and other centers of knowledge serve as talent pools). This hypothesis, admittedly controversial, draws on some of the literature of social protest—from William Domhoff and Wright Mills, from James Weinstein and Michael Harrington, plus others.[40] It is predicated also on the "principle of cumulative causation," which Gunnar Myrdal proposed.[41] Latter-day Marxists tend to espouse it.[42]

The giant firm is a creature of the latter half of the nineteenth century, a period Louis Kelso and Mortimer Adler describe as one of "primitive capitalism."[43] The "tycoon"—the individual entrepreneur—organized the early corporate giants. Typically, he was a person who used the corporate device for individual gain, which he promoted at times by building up a company and at other times by dissolving it. His modern-day counterpart is the "corporate raider" rather than the usual corporate officer, who is an "organization man" par excellence. In 1904 Thorstein Veblen described this type of person: "With a fuller development of the modern close-knit and comprehensive industrial system, the point of chief attention for the businessman has shifted from the old-fashioned surveillance and regulation of a given industrial process, with which his livelihood is bound up, to an alert redistribution of investments from less to more gainful ventures, and to a strategic control of the conjunctures of business through shrewd investments and coalitions with other businessmen."[44] A recent fictional description of this type of person may be found in Cameron Hawley's novel *Cash McCall*.

The corporation in primitive capitalism, in short, tended to be a one-man affair, with the entrepreneur—the tycoon, the robber baron, the mogul—dominating business firms for his own ends. Today the picture has shifted, not in the sense that business executives do not try to maximize profits but in the sense that the end sought is the welfare of the company. Company welfare, in turn, means enhancement of the economic status of those whose wealth now is largely in the form of "promises."[45] Individualism has been replaced by a notion of the "company" or the "organization" man. The present-day exemplification of the tycoon is Harold Geneen of ITT. (Conglomerates, in some respects, represent a reversion to primitive capitalism, which may help to explain the reaction they are getting from centers of old economic power and from the government.)

The company man illustrates how the principle of cumulative social causation operates. He is dedicated to the advancement of the firm as such, pursuing the goals of enterprise viability, growth, and—ultimately—size. Profits are the means by which these goals are attained. James Earley of the University of Wisconsin put it this way: "The major goals of modern large-scale business are high managerial incomes, good profits, a strong competitive position, and growth . . . . High and rising profits are . . . an instrument as well as a direct goal of great importance."[46] Once, then, that an enterprise is started, the effort is to effect growth. The corporate manager is, under this conception, as much homo economicus as were the tycoons and other predecessors; the difference is that the firm molds the man rather than the man using the firm for his own ends. Not that all corporations succeed or wax large and strong. Far from it. Most no doubt fall by the wayside or never achieve the dizzy pinnacle of the supercorporation. But once those that do become supercorporations begin on their way, the Myrdal principle of cumulative causation may be seen in operation. Success begets success; "them as has, gits" in the old frontier slogan; "the way to achieve and retain greatness is always to be striving for something more"; [47] through a process of upward causation, once having made a breakthrough certain firms become giants. Equilibrium is seldom, perhaps never, achieved. Firms become huge under this view for several reasons, which can only be outlined here:

a. There is a marked attempt to reduce risk taking, accomplished in two principal ways: through what Joseph A. Schumpeter called "co-respective" behavior [48] toward other corporate giants and through influencing public policy (tariffs, resale price maintenance legislation, etc.). Galbraith has said that the modern corporation can be understood only as a systematic attempt at reducing risk. [49] So it may well be. Co-respective behavior means that the reigning principle is reciprocity rather than "cut-throat competition." Alliances, tacit or actual, are entered into with other firms in the same industry. Trade associations, which may be called a loose form of cartel, often set the rules of the game.

b. The tendency of corporate managers is not to go to the "money market" for financing unless absolutely necessary. Rather, profits are plowed back into the corporation to finance growth. Dividends are kept small or just large enough to satisfy the small investor. The large investor—individual or collective (as in a pension fund)—is quite willing to settle for a relatively small annual return provided that the basic value of the shares is steadily increased through corporate growth. He then can profit from capital gains.

c. Corporate managers, Herbert Simon and others to the contrary notwithstanding, tend to be profit maximizers rather than what Simon calls "satisficers." [50] Business propaganda, sedulously cultivated by public relations experts, is otherwise. The talk is of business "statesmanship," with the manager "balancing" the various interests of the corporate community; ostensibly, profitability is only one of those interests.

d. The persistent drive is for more and more. Size becomes an end in itself.

e. Success begets success; profits plowed back mean more profits—in a chain of upward causation.

An analysis such as this takes an astringent view of corporate enterprise. As with the other hypotheses that have been advanced, it may have some validity, but it surely does not fully explain corporate growth. In briefest terms, it postulates an urge to "monopolize" for the purpose of achieving and maintaining positions of great wealth, and consequent social status and political power, by the members of what Mills has called the "power elite" and what Domhoff terms the American "governing class." [51] In many respects, even so, the hypothesis seems to be better than the others advanced. It is more all-encompassing for it suggests that technology, law, and American public policy are all merely instruments of power and position. In other words, the "governing class" uses such means as are available to enhance its own position, co-opting intellectual talent it needs from other classes.

Having said that, one must hasten to add that it seems to be too "easy," too facile, too neat—in a word, too simplistic. The "governing class," assuming that it exists, may not have the cohesion that seems to be required for the "class" to operate as such. There can be little doubt that American society is much more stratified than the myth would have it, but this does not mean that those at the top are monolithic. Much more empirical data will have to be produced to show "a power elite"—or an economic elite that is able to use the corporate device as a means of controlling wealth.

Nevertheless, the hypothesis—as unsubstantiated as it is and as unaccepted by the bulk of scholars as it is—is the most appealing thus far examined. Without accepting it in toto, one may say that, taken as a whole, the burden of proof is on those who challenge it to show its lack of validity. A prima facie case can be made out for the thesis.

One challenge to it may come from those who point to the general affluence of the American people—even admitting the millions of disadvantaged poor—and conclude that wealth differentials have been reduced. Arnold Rose, in his well-received *The Power Structure*, so concludes. [52] But the available data indicate that concentration of wealth is as great now as it has ever been and that the economic pie has grown larger—thus enabling more people to improve their level of living. The net conclusion, to telescope a very

complicated process, is that "the rich and the super-rich," as Lundberg calls them, use corporations as the base of wealth (and power)
in much the same way their predecessors in feudal days used land
ownership. The corporate rich are the feudal lords of modern
America.

The myth is to the contrary, of course. It speaks in terms of an un-
stratified nation, of atomistic individuals with roughly co-equal social
and political power. The reality, as has been seen, is otherwise: the
basic social unit in the United States is the "voluntary" association, the pluralistic group of which the supercorporation is the most
important.

To summarize: under this hypothesis, the supercorporation is a
product of a drive for wealth and power, with technology used to
further that end. Essentially the theory is one of methodological individualism. The hypothesis appears to have more validity than any
examined thus far. Even so, it is not a complete—in Ernest Nagel's
term, a "meaningful" [53] —explanation, for it lacks sufficient empirical foundation and does not refer to the social milieu in which the
"governing class" operates.

5. THE TELEOLOGICAL HYPOTHESIS

Our fifth hypothesis is difficult to state, except in broad terms. Historically the supercorporation arose in the United States at about the
same time as what de Tocqueville called the trend toward equality had
produced the Granger and Populist movements and the rise of the
labor unions. In essence, these movements were aimed at attaining
greater material well-being, "a larger slice of economic pie" for members of the burgeoning groups. These groups became sufficiently
powerful politically as to be able to get legislation enacted for better
working conditions and other benefits. This hypothesis, then, suggests that the giant firm, to some extent however immeasurable, is a
resultant of the need for mass production and for a higher degree of
general economic welfare. It may be broadened in this way: a given
community—"society"—tends to produce the institutions necessary
to fulfill its assumed goals within—and this is a very important pro-
viso—the limits of its capabilities or means. The shorthand label for
this is the "teleological" hypothesis. (It will be noted that the thesis is

based on a fundamental assumption—that "society" is to be considered a collective organism with drives and purposes of its own.) Some support for the proposition may be found in historian David M. Potter's *People of Plenty*; in that book, Professor Potter argues that American institutional development—including social, economic, political, and cultural—has been shaped and formed by the search for and enjoyment of material abundance.[54]

With the coming of the Positive State (see Chapter 5) and the consequent express acceptance of responsibility by government to create and maintain conditions of economic well-being (and other goals), society and its mechanism (government) then produced the giant business firm as the instrument to fulfill the assumed goals. That economic unit can most effectively harness technology and produce the immense quantities of consumer goods desired. Had the supercorporation not existed, it would have had to be invented. Professor Howard Perlmutter, writing in the *Columbia Journal of World Business*, has expressed that notion, at least in part, in the context of a discussion of multinational corporations. He claims that the multinational corporations—he calls them "geocentric" or "world oriented" firms— are *indispensable* institutions.[55] Perlmutter argues that the geocentric firm performs for the world what no other institution can. Further—and this takes us back to Galbraith's thesis—it is a new form of social architecture, one that perceives in the planetary potential of modern technology an opportunity to be world oriented and to be an organization that maximizes its economic opportunities—and thus helps to fulfill the vast demand for material goods by the peoples of the world.

In brief, under this hypothesis the character of society determines its economic institutions, within the limits of its resources. Just as the corporation may mold the behavior of its functionaries, so the social milieu—with the demands and aspirations of the people—helps mold the corporation. To the extent that the thesis is valid, it will explain, at least in part, the revisionist theories of history that now view the robber barons as (perhaps unwitting) public benefactors.

But is it valid? The thesis can only be stated; it cannot be proved. But it may well have some basis in fact. Surely the social context had something to do with nineteenth- and twentieth-century economic institutions. Surely the facts of no foreign enemies, protection by two

oceans and the British navy, an empty continent waiting exploitation, a flow of capital and cheap labor from Europe all coalesced, with
the movement toward equality, into deep-seated demands for larger
economic pies to be cut up and the slices passed around. However, if
so, the ultimate questions are still not answered. Not explained, for
example, are the reasons for the drive toward equality. Nonetheless,
the giant firms and their satellites may now be indispensable for
reasonable realization of the goals of the Positive State.

Furthermore, the thesis does not include what is often assumed
without argument: first, that the giant firm is more "efficient," if
efficiency is taken to mean both profits and social costs; and second,
the business giant, the oft-stated belief to the contrary notwithstanding, may not be more "innovative." In fact innovation may come
more from small firms and even individuals than from the corporate
giant. Some observers go so far as to maintain that no significant technological development has come from the supercorporations in the
past few decades.[56]

But even so, without the supercorporations it is difficult, perhaps
impossible, to visualize the flow of consumer goods necessary to fulfill the demands now being made by people in the United States and
throughout the world (particularly in the so-called Third World). As a
productive unit, then, the firm is a requirement—and to that extent validates the hypothesis. Possibly some evidence to buttress that
conclusion may be found in the U.S.S.R. Galbraith views the industrial complex of the U.S.S.R. and uses it to buttress his "principle of
convergence" of industrial societies, which he traces to technological
imperatives. But cannot that same evidence be used—that Russian
economic enterprises tend to resemble those of the supercorporations (save for who controls)—to shore up the teleological hypothesis? The "plan"—within, of course, the limits of resources—determines the nature of the enterprise.

6. THE "WORLD FRONTIER" HYPOTHESIS

Quite obviously, there is an overlap between the fifth hypothesis
and the sixth: that the unique social conditions that existed in the
United States during the later part of the nineteenth and early part of
the twentieth centuries were a special mix that permitted the growth

of the supercorporation. In some respects, this builds on Walter Prescott Webb's "great frontier" hypothesis—the "four-hundred-year boom" precipitated by the great discoveries of the New World and opening up commerce to worldwide proportions. [57]

Webb suggests a direct relationship between colonial expansion and social development in the nations of the North Atlantic littoral. Perhaps, in examining this proposition, we should refer to historian David S. Landes's book, *The Unbound Prometheus: Technological Change and Industrial Development in Western Europe from 1750 to the Present*. [58] There Landes directs attention to two questions: Why did the Industrial Revolution occur first in western Europe? and Why within Europe itself, did economic change take place when and where it did? His book is mainly concerned with the latter, but he does devote some attention to the first. As to it, he says that "a definitive answer is impossible." Landes mentions two elements as being salient: "the scope and effectiveness of private enterprise; and the high value placed on the rational manipulation of the human and material environment." Says Landes:

> The role of private economic enterprise in the West is perhaps unique: more than any other factor, it made the modern world. It was primarily the rise of trade that dissolved the subsistence economy of the medieval manor and generated the cities and towns that became the political and cultural, as well as economic, nodes of the new society. And it was the new men of commerce, banking, and industry who provided the increment of resources that financed the ambitions of the rulers and statesmen who invented the policy of the nation-state . . . .
>
> . . . The role of private economic activity was far larger in western Europe than in other parts of the world and grew as the economy itself grew and opened new areas of enterprise untrammeled by rule and custom. The trend was self-reinforcing: those economies grew fastest that were freest . . . .

Why, then, did Europe leap ahead, soon to be followed by the United States, while the rest of the world failed to develop a business class of vitality and influence? There is no ready answer to that question; it is more a question of speculation than of proof. Rational manipulation of the environment provides another partial key, combined with the Faustian sense of mastery over nature (and man). In many respects, the application of rationality to business affairs may be seen in the Protestant Ethic—and it is here that Weber's analysis can be appreciated.[59]

The mastery over nature and things—the Faustian ethic—has reached its apotheosis in the modern day: many believe that there literally is no limit to what man can accomplish by science and technology. It had its origin centuries ago and has been accelerating since.

But it is obvious, and Landes would agree, that this is not a sufficient explanation of the Industrial Revolution. Certainly the ultimate questions are left unasked and unanswered. One other aspect of his exposition deserves mention, for it bears upon the Webb hypothesis: that colonial possessions contributed to the enrichment and thus to the development of some European countries. In other words, some say that had there been no overseas expansion, there would have been no Industrial Revolution. But, says Landes; "It is hard to prove or disprove this kind of contrafactual hypothesis."[60]

That observation is relevant to our examination of the "great frontier" hypothesis, stated by Webb in his book with the same title. The boom hypothesis, simply stated, means that the vast new body of wealth in the New World was the principal cause of an unprecedented and unique boom in business. The theory is Frederick Jackson Turner's American frontier hypothesis[61] writ large so as to encompass the entire Western world. The ratio of population to land and resources was radically altered; that ratio, said William Graham Sumner, determined "the possibilities of human development [and] the limits of what man can attain in civilization and comfort."[62] (Sumner wrote in 1913 and Webb in 1952. Neither took into account the new frontier, one that had little to do with land as such: science and technology.)

Webb expressly disavowed any effort to trace the processes of corporate growth in business, although he did describe corporate development and said that it was the outstanding example of a process of reintegration of society (after society had been splintered following the breakup of feudalism). But he does make the following relevant observations:

> [Corporate] growth extends first to national limits, and then reaches out through cartels to other nations. In its early stages, it

proceeds by competition operation in a laissez faire manner, and in its later stages it grows by elimination to near monopoly. *The view advanced in this study is that the frontier has been a prime contributing factor which made possible this dynamism.* The frontier increased many fold the room over which European people could move, and the body of wealth which they could acquire. The physical facts called for motion and volition. As long as there was room, more work than men, more material than machines, the process of expansion was socially and politically safe. In the very dynamics the people could have a maximum of freedom, political and economic, for the boom was such that all could live, many could prosper, and government could look on while men had their way. The result is that a whole civilization evolved in this atmosphere of expansion with institutions adapted to it.[63]

Supercorporations, in short, are the institutions appropriate to the "great frontier."

There may be at least a partial insight here. Certainly the giant firm is characteristic of only a small part of the world, one that—save for the U.S.S.R.—largely encompasses Webb's frontier. And even the Soviet Union is itself a large land mass, until recently underdeveloped, so that it cannot be said to disprove Webb. However, Webb concentrated too much on land as a source of wealth and institutional development and failed to see the potentialities of science and technology, which together have opened up vistas undreamed of before modern times.

Our net conclusion is easy to state and may seem to be an empty truism: the corporate giant is a complex entity that has resulted from multiple causes. Each of the hypotheses we have examined appears to lend some insight but alone is not a sufficient explanation. Taken together, they tend to overlap and to complement each other. Accordingly, it may be said that the supercorporation is a resultant of (1) technological imperatives, (2) law and political institutions, (3) affirmative governmental policy, (4) activities of the "governing class," (5) a quest for equality and for a larger share of material well-being, and (6) the social milieu in which the firms have waxed large and strong. None of these, taken along, is a sufficient explanation; all,

taken together, help us to understand the characteristic and
dominant institution of the day.

No discussion of the supercorporation would be complete without emphasizing what is easily the most significant post-World War II
develoment in American business: the trend toward multinationalism. Ten years ago the idea was novel; today it is a truism. Major
impetus to acknowledgment of the larger-than-national character of
American business came in 1968 with the publication of the English
translation of the J.-J. Servan-Schreiber's *The American Challenge*,[64] in which the French journalist maintained that in the near
future "it is quite possible that the world's third greatest industrial
power, just after the United States and Russia, will not be Europe, but
American industry in Europe." Whether Servan-Schreiber is
accurate is beside the point (probably his focus was too narrow, for
multinationalism characterizes corporations chartered by other
countries as well); what is important is the way in which the businessman is spilling across national boundaries.

Although the development is unique in history—nothing quite like
it ever existed before—corporations ("joint-stock companies") were
used in the past mainly as a means by which Europeans could exploit the wealth of the New World. So it was in America. "Colonial
culture," Peter d' Alroy Jones asserts, "reveals at the briefest glance
a highly complex fusion of religious faith, political conviction, economic interest, and social idealism." Jones goes on to say: "There may
be some truth in the often-made claim that the nation was 'founded as
a business enterprise' and that the early history of American society
can be explained in terms of the given relationships among the economist's 'factors of production' (physical resources, labor, and capital).
Thus it was that private business enterprise played a large part in set-
tling the original colonies in North America during the seventeenth
century. The British government had a much smaller role."[65] The
state of Virginia is an example: its colonization was conceived in business terms as a joint-stock company organized for profit. This is not to
say that economic motivation is a completely meaningful explanation of the early settlement of North and South America. But surely it
was one of the prime factors. Multinationalism in business, then, can
be traced at least as far back as the private companies that were
formed to exploit the wealth opened up after Columbus. In a seminal

article published in 1952 Sigmund Timberg stated the development in these terms:

> England, Holland, and the other great trading powers of the seventeenth and eighteenth centuries were delegating *political* power to their foreign merchants, when they permitted those merchants to engage—collectively and under the corporate aegis—in foreign trade. In Maitland's classic phrase, these were "the companies that became colonies, the companies that make war." The same proposition holds for the modern large corporation. The modern state undeniably delegates *political* power to large private corporations, as it does to large labor unions with which the corporate behemoths deal. [66]

The East India Company provides a particularly apt illustration. In it can be seen the fusion of economic and political power to which Timberg alludes (and which is becoming more and more evident in the modern era). Timberg puts it this way:

> In the seventeenth century, a new and more ambitious field was carved out for corporate action. The economic exploitation of the wealth to be found in the new hemisphere of the Americans and the old continent of Asia became the province of compact and aggressive groups of merchant adventurers collectively organized as an English (or Dutch or Portuguese) East India (or a Hudson Bay, or a Muscovy) Company. These companies, in addition to their monopoly privileges and (shall we say sovereign?) immunities from import and export laws and custom duties, had the power to tax their own members, decide their own disputes, and defend themselves against pirates and other external enemies. The English East India Company . . . ruled India with an iron grip until the middle of the nineteenth century. In fact, the maintenance of fortifications and consular agents and the governmental functions of these trading companies justified their existence even after their economic functions had terminated. . . .

But if business was multinational early on, nevertheless its main focus for centuries was domestic. Save for new areas (for example, petroleum and other extractive industries) certainly most American enterprise was ethnocentric—necessarily so, for there was a continent to be subdued and harnessed. Only when the frontier closed and only after the fabulous store of natural resources began to run low did American business turn outward. The trend in this century has been one from "going national" to "going multinational," as Michael G. Duerr of the Chase Manhattan Bank said in 1963:

> Many U.S. companies today are looking at European opera- tions not as an isolated arm of their domestic business, but as part of an integrated world-wide business. It is easy to exag- gerate this, but the president of a U.S. company with its head- quarters in Chicago is now more likely to look on his plant in Amsterdam and his plant in Atlanta as interrelated parts of the company's global operation than he might have a few years ago. I think this is a trend which will continue—as markets over- seas continue to grow and as American companies become bet- ter and better educated in the ways of serving them.
>
> I had a conversation two years ago with a New England manu- facturer that has stayed in my mind ever since. I had commented on his ambitious plans for overseas expansion, and he said:
>
> "About 40 years ago I remember the big topic of conversa- tion was whether to confine themselves to the territory they knew well—the Northeast—or to 'go national.'
>
> "Our company did decide to 'go national,' and—although we had some anxious moments—we did very well.
>
> "Now," he went on, "I look back to that period and, do you know? It's hard to remember the names of the firms that de- cided not to venture outside of New England. Most of them have disappeared.
>
> "Today," he went on, "I have the feeling I've lived through this before. Maybe I'm exaggerating a little," he concluded, "but if you ask me today you 'go international' or you're dead." [67]

The physiognomy of American business is changing dramatically. No longer is the continental United States the limit of the interest or thinking of the corporate executive. National boundaries are no longer important in business thinking. Like the several states, they are merely a nuisance to doing business on a larger-than-national scale.

For the supercorporation, going multinational has become by and large a necessity.

The development may be best seen as a trend that began, as has been said, deep in American history and that is just now accelerating. What its ultimate development will be is speculative at best. But it may be said with assurance that the trend will continue. "The world is entering a new age—the age of total industrialization. Some countries are far along the road; many more are just beginning the journey. But everywhere, at a faster or slower pace, the peoples of the world are on the march toward industrialism. They are launched on a long course that is certain to change their communities into new and vastly different societies whose forms cannot yet be clearly foreseen. The twentieth century is a century of enormous and profound and world-wide transformation."[68] So spoke four economists in 1964 in an important book, *Industrialism and Industrial Man.* Few today would disagree with that general diagnosis. What might be disputed is the shape of things to come. What specific form will industrialization take? What institutions will be created? What roles for the corporation and for government?

No systematic development of answers to those questions can be given here. It must suffice to postulate that the global corporation of the future will rival the nation-state, and *it may well become the most significant unit of government in the world arena.* Already observers like Adolf A. Berle and Peter F. Drucker [69] call the multinational corporation a more efficient tool of governance than the territorial state itself. So it may be. World commercial matters are more smoothly run and subject to fewer abrasive disputes than are political affairs (although, of course, there is an overlap between the two). According to Arthur Barber the "world corporation" (his term) is challenging governments for power; there are about 1,000 major corporations, 750 of them American, now engaged in foreign operations in a significant way. "They have international staffs, international funding, international communication networks, and—in the computer—even an international language," says Barber. [70]

In the next two or three decades, 400 to 500 global corporations will own about two-thirds of the fixed assets of the world, Barber maintains. Now being determined is how this international corporate structure will evolve; it is evolving even though few people as yet perceive it. Ultimately, if Barber is correct, the political officers of the nation-state and the corporate officials will come into conflict. Tensions will arise. Some accommodation will have to be worked out, for one or the other will be dominant. Barber holds that "the victory of the technocrats [the corporate managers] is assured," barring a nuclear war.

That may well be. Just as the businessman has been the major power holder within the United States, so he likely will be—may already be—in international affairs. But what this will mean is not the disappearance of political forms entirely. Much more likely is that there will be a merger of political and economic power into a series of corporate states. International institutions will increase in power, particularly in economic matters; the International Monetary Fund is a ready example. As power shifts from the nation-state to the corporations and to international organizations there may come a growing obsolescence of the nation-state as a form of social order. But it will remain, just as the fifty American states have stayed intact; its power will be shared, however. Corporativism then, as will be seen, will be worldwide.

The basic mistake that Servan-Schreiber made is in seeing the challenge as *Le Defi Americain*. Although the United States is far and away the most powerful and American companies the largest, others exist. The challenge is from business to government—from economics to politics. In this process, a few hundred supergiant corporations will control world economics and, in so doing, dominate the world unless adequate social controls are developed. The small firms will probably increasingly find themselves able to survive as the "second economy." The small "one-man" or "one-family" unit will continue mainly because the giants will not be interested in the "small-change" activities involved. Much less secure are the middle-sized firms. As Professor Howard V. Perlmutter of the Wharton School says: "The middle-sized firms find it hard to get the human and financial resources, the geographical and product scope to function as worldwide entities. They are targets for take-overs—with the large firm as a suiter promising world-wide markets for its products."[71] Perlmutter foresees about 300 firms of the supergiant character and agrees with Barber that they will vie with the nation-state for power.

The supercorporation has already come to the American domestic economy and is being born in the global economy.

Why has the global supercorporation grown? Not, surely, because of "technological imperatives"; we have already seen that that is not an adequate explanation of the phenomenon. Professor Perlmutter lists the following factors as important: (1) they will find it easier to get capital; (2) they are able to diversify, replace obsolescent products rapidly, and still maintain worldwide production and distribution of all their products in both developing and developed countries; (3) they can maintain a high level of research; (4) they have the resources to acquire middle-sized firms; (5) they can afford to hire the best specialists and managers to carry out their operations; and (6) there is "an absence of effective countervailing forces in the world community." As to the latter, consumers are not organized, the unions are on the decline, and the nation-state itself has weapons too puny to effect meaningful control. Business and government will tend to enter into a "partnership." Perlmutter ends by asking how the 300 supergiants he foresees can be held to a social responsibility. Although this anticipates a later discussion, it is desirable to set forth his conclusion at this time:

> There are no easy answers here, but I feel there is a need for rules and laws at the world level. By 1985, such laws will become more and more indispensable because the quality of life of the world's citizens, and their survival cannot be made to depend on the policies of international firms.
>
> The nation-state will not wither away. There is a positive role for the nation-state in the second half of the twentieth century. It should be worked out in partnership with national political and business leaders, not bilaterally but multilaterally, in an atmosphere of mutual confidence and trust. There is a key role for the United Nations in their endeavor.

Former Under-Secretary of State George Ball has stated a similar view of the need for some type of world law—an "international companies law"—administered by a supranational body as a means of effecting social control on the supergiants. Whether this will be done is, at best, speculative. What can be said is that the multinational firm of a truly gigantic size is already in being. It is the dominant economic institution of the age.

So, big business there is and big business there will be. But there is also big government, and it is to that phenomenon that we now turn.

5

THE COMING OF THE POSITIVE STATE

The first principle of the law for the control of the economy is that the government is responsible for the general level of employment. Twenty-five years ago even the idea was not taken seriously. . . . For better or for worse, the idea has disappeared that the state can be but a passive spectator while booms alternate unpredictably with busts. . . . American law, like the law of other capitalist democracies, has accepted the view that prolonged depressions and inflations threaten the fabric of society far too gravely to be tolerated.

—EUGENE V. ROSTOW[1]

One of the convenient, even pleasant, fictions with which Americans like to bemuse themselves is that they live under a written constitution. This supposedly makes the United States different from other nations—say, Great Britain, which is said to have an unwritten constitution. The idea does not accord with reality; it is at best a half-truth, probably a quarter-truth. Nowhere may the point be better seen than in the new form of government that has been established during the past forty years in the United States: affirmative or responsible government, or, in shorthand terms, the coming of the Positive State, which is beyond measure the most important *constitutional* change in American history. That it came without amendment makes it all the more remarkable.

In briefest terms, the Positive State is a label for express acceptance by the federal government—by government generally and thus by the people—of affirmative responsibility to further the economic well-being of all the people. It is a societal undertaking of a duty to

86

attempt to create and maintain minimal conditions within the economy—of economic growth, of employment opportunities, of the basic necessities of life. Not that the efforts are fully realized. Far from it. Millions of Americans today live below the poverty line; that is, they do not have income adequate to furnish them with a decent standard of living.

In constitutional terms, the development is toward the creation of a concept of "constitutional duty"—and that is something new. In politics and economics, it is the American version of the welfare state, although that term, because of invidious connotations placed on it (usually by those who have it but decry the desire of others for it), is not expressly used. And in terms of trend analysis the development is toward increased governmental intervention in economic affairs. The history of the United States could be written around that theme, a trend that is culminating in the progressive merger of the concepts of liberty and equality and in the increasing blurring of the line between what is thought to be private and what is said to be public.

The roots of the Positive State lie deep in the American experience, but the exponential jump from negative to positive government is relatively recent. No clear line of demarcation can be found, however, to denote the change in concept. Here, as elsewhere, hindsight enables one to discern regularities that in all probability were not even remotely in the contemplation of those who exercised power in the past. The year 1937 may, nonetheless, be used as a watershed between the two conceptions of government. In that year, soon after President Roosevelt's overwhelming victory in 1936, a series of Supreme Court decisions were rendered that exemplify the new conception in clearest terms.

Behind the change were hydraulic pressures built up within a rapidly changing nation. By the 1930s the impact of science and technology on the social structure, as well as on the political and economic order, had utterly and irreversibly changed the United States. The modern age was ushered in. The United States was no longer a small-shop, agricultural economy (which it had been in 1800 and even in 1850); federalism had changed; the frontier had disappeared; isolationism had in fact died with American entry into World War I (although it had a brief renascence in the 1930s); cities began to explode in size as farmers left the land; population began an enormous

leap even though immigration had been stifled; the demand for
equality, long before noted by de Tocqueville, became more insistent;
and the pent-up pressures in the populace were increasingly translated into legislative programs, both federal and state. All of this is
familiar history and needs no extensive restatement now. It is mentioned to underscore a truism: government, including the Positive
State, is neither the creation of an ideology nor the result of a conspiracy of "creeping socialism." It may be Machiavellian in the sense
that power and not law is the more pervasive influence—the notion of
a government of laws, not of men, is a mere shibboleth—but that is
merely another way of saying that those who have political clout or
muscle, to use current jargon, can achieve their objectives within the
confines of the American Constitution.

Professor William Anderson in 1943 effectively compared the
world of 1789 to the new social context in language still pertinent:

> Then a small area, with a small and sparse population, mainly
> agricultural and poor. Now one of the world's greatest nations
> in both area and population, largely urban and highly industrial,
> with tremendous national gain.
>
> Then largely a debtor people and an exporter of raw materials.
> Now a great creditor nation and large exporter of manufactured
> as well as agricultural goods.
>
> Then meager and slow transportation facilities, and even
> poorer provisions for communication. Now an equipment of rail-
> roads, steamship lines, highways, trucks and buses, air trans-
> port, and communication of all kinds unexcelled by any nation
> and undreamed of in the past.
>
> Then state citizenship, state and local loyalties, interstate sus-
> picions and tariffs, localized business, and considerable internal
> disunity. Now a nation, with national citizenship, primarily na-
> tional loyalties, a nationwide free market, and nationally orga-
> nized business, agriculture, labor, professions, press and
> political parties.
>
> Then an upstart and divided people, an international weak-
> ling, threatened from north and south, with very poor defense
> arrangements, and looking out over the Atlantic at an essentially
> hostile world. Now a great world power, an international leader,

with a powerful army and navy, and with strong friends and interests (as well as enemies) across both Atlantic and Pacific.

Then inactive, negative, laissez-faire government with very few functions, and with only business leaders favoring a national government, and they desiring only to give it enough vigor to protect commerce, provide a nationwide free home market, and a sound currency and banking system. Now active, positive, collectivist government, especially at the national level, rendering many services with the support of powerful labor and agricultural elements, while many business leaders have reversed their position.

Then local law enforcement with state protection of the liberties guaranteed in bills of rights. Now increasing national law enforcement and national protection of civil liberties even against state and local action.

Then practically no employees of the national government and very few state and local employees. Now a national civil service of normally over a million persons reaching into every county of the country, plus extensive state and local civil services.

Then small public budgets at all levels. Now public budgets and expenditures, especially for the national government, that reach astronomical figures.

Then (before 1789) no national taxes at all for decades after 1789, only customs and excise taxes on a very limited scale, with state and local governments, relying almost entirely on direct property taxes. Now tremendously increased and diversified taxes at both national and state levels, with a national government rising swiftly to a dominating position with respect to all taxes except those directly on property.

Then (before 1788) state grants to the Congress of the United States for defense and debt purposes. Now grants-in-aid by the national government to the states in increasing amounts and with steadily tightening national controls over state action. [2]

Hence, the context in which today's Constitution must operate bears little or no resemblance to that of 1787, of 1800, of 1900, or even of 1930. Massive societal changes during the past hundred years have so altered the milieu that the ancient words must do duty for a nation and a people that know no historical counterpart. There should be little wonder, then, that the most important parts of the Constitution are in fact unwritten. One has only to ponder the quaint ceremonies that celebrate the American Revolution each July Fourth to realize how the United States became by the 1970s a force against revolution and to discern the vast gap that exists between the late eighteenth and the latter part of the twentieth centuries. Less than two centuries in chronological time, the periods are really light years apart. A nation born in revolution is now engaged in fighting off change in other parts of the world—at precisely the time in history that social change has become a social constant. The United States today tries to maintain the status quo at the very time that science and technology make it an impossibility.

The context includes the future as well as the present and the past. Justice Holmes once said that adherence to the past is not a duty but merely a necessity. So it is. Knowledge of the present is both a necessity and a duty, and some idea of the future is also a necessity. Only by attempting to determine what the United States will become can current doctrines and practices be adequately evaluated (and extrapolated). But that depends on being able to anticipate what scientists and technologists will develop. This ultimately will force social scientists to know the methodology of the natural sciences and for natural scientists to realize that in the modern era all science tends to be social science.

Although it would be rash to try to predict the constitutional future in full detail, its main contours are already apparent. This chapter states the hypothesis of the Positive State and discusses four principal attributes of that form of government: (1) a change from a Constitution of limitations to one of powers; (2) the affirmative duties of government, both those accepted politically (by Congress) and those sought to be imposed judicially; (3) governmental promotion of associational activity, particularly in industrial relations; and (4) the intellectuals as servants of power. The basic trend discussed is: *toward increasing intervention of government into social and economic affairs*. Socioeconomic matters have been "politicized"; politics, not law, is the name of the game. Despite the myth to the contrary, our government is "emphatically a government of men, not of laws."[3]

CONSTITUTIONAL REVOLUTION

The "Positive State" is the label for a fundamentally new form of American government. Rooted deep in the American experience, it came with a rush in recent decades. The year 1937 is the dividing line between the "negative, nightwatchman state" and the Positive State, although the change really is one of degree and emphasis rather than of type. American government, never neutral to economics, became much less so and in different directions during the political period of the New Deal. Rooseveltian programs, many of which were invalidated by the Supreme Court prior to 1937, finally received judicial approval in a series of cases beginning in that year—by all odds the most important year constitutionally in American history, more important even than 1791, which saw the addition of the Bill of Rights to the Constitution, or the post-Civil War period in which the antislavery amendments were added. In 1937 there began a process of revision that has resulted in an entirely new Constitution, at least so far as economics are concerned. Since then, the Court has assisted Congress and the President in working out the details of the Positive State, but it has not made ultimate judgments of its validity. Rather, the Justices found a new role in the protection of individual rights and liberties, thereby adding a new dimension to the Positive State. (The relationship, if any, between abdication from making final economic policy judgments and rendering decisions in civil libertarian matters has never been demonstrated. Indeed the question has not been posed, save by those constitutional historians who note the change in issues since the late 1930s. Just why the Court has been so preoccupied with civil liberties in the past twenty years would be a fascinating question to research. Certainly that emphasis was entirely new for the high bench.)[4]

What, then, is the Positive State? What is so new and remarkable about it? Why is it considered to be such a marked change from what went before? These questions may be answered briefly, but not without some reference to history.

Writing several decades ago, the Fench legal philosopher Leon Duguit asserted: "Any system of public law can be vital so far as it is based on a given sanction to the following rules: First, the holders of power cannot do certain things; second, there are certain things they must do."[5] The "cannot do" of that statement is a shorthand expression for much, perhaps most, of historical American constitutional law—at least, insofar as that law was formulated by the Supreme Court. It should be recognized that many actions of government—indeed, most of them—never got or today get judicial cognizance; this means that in between the "cannot do" and the "must do" is a vast area of official action, some of it based on only the flimsiest of constitutional pegs. Historical constitutional law, then, was naysaying in large part when matters got to the Supreme Court. Quite often, however, public policy questions never got there, de Tocqueville's aphorism that in America the Court eventually decides such questions to the contrary notwithstanding.[6] Even when matters did get to the Court, furthermore, the Justices tended to *uphold* governmental action, particularly that of the federal government. Once validated, a particular activity or doctrine has a tendency to expand; it is employed to justify a wide range of other actions not before the Court.

The "must do" of modern government is just now coming into view, so far as constitutional doctrine is concerned,[7] although it has been a familiar political feature during the past three decades. In other words, American government is no longer merely limited government; it is also responsible government; in place of adherence to the notion that "that government is best that governs least," Americans have moved into a situation where the basic notion is, "that government is best that governs best." The Positive State has undermined the preconceptions of classical constitutional theory in much the same way that the modern corporation, according to Gardiner C. Means, "has undermined the preconceptions of classical economic theory—and similar to the manner that the "quantum undermined classical physics at the beginning of the twentieth century."[8]

The Positive State received its charter in 1946 when Congress enacted the Employment Act, surely one of the most significant legislative actions in American history. In form a statute and thus outwardly not of the dignity of a constitutional precept, it nevertheless overshadows most, if not all, of the true constitutional amendments.[9] Written in "constitutional" language of high-level abstraction, with little particularity or precision in prescription, the act makes constitutional law—but by Congress and not, as is the usual situation, by the Supreme Court. It symbolized a series of other statutes that brought about a radically different government-business symbiosis from that which existed prior to the 1930s.

Often mislabeled the "full employment act" (it does not call for "full" but rather for "maximum" employment), its purpose may be found in the preamble:

> The Congress declares that it is the continuing policy and responsibility of the federal government to use all practicable means consistent with its needs and obligations and other essential considerations of national policy, with the assistance and cooperation of industry, agriculture, labor, and state and local governments, to coordinate and utilize all its plans, functions, and resources for the purposes of creating and maintaining, in a manner calculated to foster and promote free competitive enterprise and the general welfare, conditions under which there will be afforded useful employment opportunities, including self-employment, for those able, willing, and seeking to work, and to promote maximum employment, production, and purchasing power. [10]

With that pronouncement, economic planning, which has always been a feature of American government, became overt and expanded. Prior to 1946, a series of governmental acts of a planning nature had been given the Supreme Court's imprimatur—or had been ignored by one of the several means that tribunal has of evading sticky questions.

The Positive State exemplifies in classic style a synthesis along Hegelian lines: thesis-antithesis-synthesis. The *thesis*: During the nineteenth century the state actively encouraged, through assistance programs and the legal system, the growth of business enterprise. The *antithesis*: A trend toward egalitarianism, particularly in the post-Civil War period, may be seen in the Granger and Populism movements. The liberty of the corporations, protected by law including the Supreme Court, came to loggerheads with the rising tide toward equality and the spread of mass suffrage. Something had to give; that "something" was the co-optation of welfare programs [11] by the business community—the "ruling class"—in a *synthesis* that at once kept the "masses" quiescent and enabled the rich to remain rich and even to wax richer. The Supreme Court, ultimate guardian of

corporate privilege, tried for a time to stave off that synthesis, but it
had to give way in the 1930s when the economic system broke down in
the Great Depression. That debacle produced the political programs
of the New Deal, programs that in essence saved the private enterprise
system at a minimum of cost. (One of the ironies of history is that
Roosevelt is hated by the very people his policies did most to help—in
his terms, the "economic royalists," who then as now sat atop the
politico-economic structure.)

CONTOURS OF THE POSITIVE STATE

The new constitutional order has not yet fully jelled; however,
enough is now known to be able to indicate some of its principal characteristics.

First, and perhaps most basic, is the change from a constitution of
limitations to one of powers. Although government has always been
interested in economics and has throughout history been as strong as
was considered necessary by the American elite structure, nevertheless the theory of a limited government was fundamentally altered in
the "constitutional revolution" of the 1930s. The turning point came
in three sets of decisions—those validating the Wagner labor relations
act as a permissible exercise of Congress's power to regulate
commerce, those upholding the Social Security legislation (both old
age annuities and unemployment compensation), and those
upholding state regulation of minimum wages and maximum hours
in certain industries.[12] Language from *West Coast Hotel Co.* v.
Parrish, dealing with the latter, classically sets forth the new
conception:

> The principle which must control our decision is not in doubt.
> The constitutional provision invoked is the due process clause of
> the Fourteenth Amendment governing the states, as the due pro-
> cess clause in the Adkins case governed Congress. In each case
> the violation alleged by those attacking minimum wage legisla-
> tion for women is deprivation of freedom of contract. What is
> this freedom? The Constitution does not speak of freedom of
> contract. It speaks of liberty and prohibits the deprivation of
> liberty without due process of law. In prohibiting that depriva-

tion, the Constitution does not recognize an absolute and uncontrollable liberty. Liberty in each of its phases has its history and connotation. But the liberty safeguarded is liberty in a social organization which *requires* the protection of law against the evils which menace the health, safety, morals, and welfare of the people. Liberty under the Constitution is thus necessarily subject to the restraints of due process, and regulation which is reasonable in relation to its subject and is adopted in the interests of the community is due process. [Emphasis added.][13]

That statement, implicitly if not expressly, changed the nature of liberty under the Constitution and ushered in the Positive State. Liberty became a social, as distinguished from an individual, right. The Supreme Court recognized that liberty could be infringed by forces other than public government (which was the historical concept) and that its protection at times would require affirmative intervention of government to counteract those other forces. In the context of the *Parrish* case, in which Chief Justice Hughes spoke, these forces could be only the corporations, which by 1937 had become giant in size and which had effective control over the terms and conditions under which most people worked. In other words, the Court saw that the giant firms were in fact private governments, governments of as much constitutional importance as the organs of official government, and gave the latter carte blanche to regulate them. Professor Edward S. Corwin put it succinctly: "From being a limitation on legislative power, the due process clause becomes an actual instigation to legislative action of a levelling nature."[14]. Without announcement and with little contemporary appreciation of the implications of the shift in judicial attitude, a quiet but massive constitutional revolution began.

Individuals—including those artificial persons, the corporations—could now be limited by due process, something that previously had been applicable only to federal and state governments. In economic terms, the power of the state to countervail the power of private collectivities became, for all practical purposes, unrestricted. Due process, after the *Parrish* case, was not only liberty against government; it could be used by government to restrain the liberty of some in the interests of the community. The "requirement" (per

Hughes) of the protection of law against the evils that menace the welfare of the people was truly revolutionary doctrine, the full implications of which are yet to be seen.

Hughes's hint lay dormant in the judiciary for a number of years.
World War II, plus the progressive enactment of social welfare programs uniformly upheld by a permissive Supreme Court as quick to
recognize the rigors of an urbanized and industrialized nation as were
the Congress and the President, made it unnecessary to use judicial
power to effect the Hughes suggestion. Leon Duguit's formulation
was being met. The "must do" part of public law grew apace, save in
the area of civil rights and civil liberties. There the Court found a new
role in the twentieth-century phenomenon of concern for human
rights and liberties. A means was provided for expansion of Hughes's
delphic language. Having relinquished its position as an authoritative
faculty of political economy (unique in world history), the Court in the
past thirty years has become an authoritative faculty of social ethics.
Tossing aside the idea that the Constitution enacted Herbert
Spencer's *Social Statics*, it found that the Constitution in effect enacted Thomas Hill Green's concept of positive freedom and of collective well-being. The idea of positive freedom, as enunciated by the
English philosopher, "reflected the rediscovery of the community as a
corporate body of which both institutions and individuals are a part,
so that the idea of collective well-being or the common good underlies
any claim to a private right."[15] Since necessitous men cannot be free
men, this idea is an assertion of the philosophical basis for positive
government and for social insurance programs that provide the
economic foundation for people to be free—if they so desire. The duty
of government, in this conception, is not so much to maximize individual liberty per se but rather to insure the conditions for minimal
well-being: a decent standard of living, of education, and of personal
security below which proper governmental policy requires that no
substantial part of the population shall be allowed to fall.

This is not to suggest that the Justices (or others) openly avowed the
almost forgotten Green, but it is to say that freedom became a social
right as well as something of value for the individual. Green tried to
reunite the individual with the social order of which he was a member
and without which his existence has no meaning. Instead of an absolute and doctrinaire individualism, based on a theory of natural

rights, he considered individual freedom to be a social phenomenon, one protected by the legal and other institutions that can be provided only by the community. "When we speak of freedom as something to be so highly prized," said Green, "we mean a positive capacity of doing or enjoying something worth doing or enjoying, and that, too, something that we do or enjoy in common with others. We mean by it a power which man exercises through the help or security given him by his fellow men, and which he in turn helps to secure for them." [16]

When the *Parrish* case was followed by decisions upholding the Wagner labor relations act and the Social Security legislation, the legal barriers to the Positive State crumbled. In the Wagner Act case, congressional encouragement of union activity was validated, apparently on the premise that "free collective bargaining" between management and labor would redound to the public good. The *Social Security Cases* upheld use of the taxing and spending powers to further the general welfare. [17] Those decisions opened the gates to other acts of Congress and of the executive, usually but not always in tandem, which brought overt welfarism to American government. The point should be refined: what happened is that government largesse, which had been confined to the business community, was now extended to other societal groups. No doubt government bounty in the nineteenth century benefited others than its main recipients, the business interests. Subsidies to the railroads in the form of land grants were of ultimate benefit to the nation at large. One observer (who, it should be noted, spoke as a representative of the railroads) went so far as to say that "whatever may have its shortcomings, the land grant policy touched off national and individual energies which in a few short years accomplished the greatest engineering, construction, and colonization project ever undertaken up to that time, a project which transformed the West from a wilderness to a civilized community and welded the nation into one." [18] Even tariffs tended to help other segments of the corporate community than the entrepreneurs (one reason for the anti-free trade policy of so many unions today). The point, in short, is that the federal government assumed responsibility for the guidance of economic affairs in the interests of all; the principle of equality, long present in the nation, received official cognizance—and was spelled out explicitly,—in the Employment Act of 1946. In constitutional doctrine, this has meant the desuetude of the concept of economic due process and the decline of the Supreme Court as an authoritative spokesman of political economy.

The basic point of the movement from a Constitution of limitations to one of powers should not be taken to mean that, even with the Employment Act of 1946, all Americans prosper equally (or at all) under the new form of government. What it does mean is that the potential is there, lacking only the will—and perhaps the constitutional structure—to make it a reality.

Second of the principal characteristics of the Positive State is government's express undertaking of that responsibility just mentioned. The development is both political (that is, congressional and presidential) and judicial (by the Supreme Court). Obviously this characteristic overlaps with the first.

At this juncture, we concentrate first on the judiciary, then on economic planning. A concept of constitutional duty, of obligation on the part of government to take action, is being evolved out of a series of decisions rendered in the past three decades—a time of turmoil and stress, actual and potential, paralled in American history only by the era of the Civil War. Included are cases on racial relations, legislative reapportionment, administration of the criminal law, and (less directly) administrative law. All are familiar. [19] What is stressed here is their implication rather than the specific doctrines enunciated. Taken together, they add up to at least a strong suggestion, if not a command, by the Supreme Court to the political branches of government on how they must behave in certain circumstances. Since those circumstances all involve individual human beings, the decisions may be seen as judicial efforts to enhance the quality of life in America. That those admonitions have not been empty words may be seen in a number of political programs promulgated after the Court had energized what Lord Bryce (in a different context) called the "conscience of the people." If the thesis is valid, it marks an exponential jump in the jurisprudence of the Supreme Court, though the development is far from complete. (It may point the way to greater judicial activity in effecting the nexus between bureaucracy, public and private, and the individual person.)

The change came unheralded. The Court did not announce a shift in emphasis—no doubt the Justices would be reluctant to do so—and in the great bulk of its work, it still operates in the traditional way. However, a growing number of decisions now exemplify how the nine Justices, as Alexander Pekelis advocated a quarter-century ago, have immersed themselves in "the travail of society" and are helping to build a jurisprudence of welfare to complement the political programs of the Positive State.[20] It illustrates Henry George's dictum "that great changes can be brought about under old forms." [21] Usually, of course, change is evolutionary, not revolutionary. But the concept of constitutional duty is of considerably greater magnitude than the routine development of constitutional law by the Supreme Court. As such, it presents novel problems to the high bench, a supreme tribunal in a government of affirmative responsibilities for the well-being of the people. Required as a consequence is a thorough re-examination of the very concept of judicial review, not so much to say what the Court should not do but to try to find out what it can do and to develop the institutional techniques to assist it. [22]

In analyzing the idea of constitutional duty, attention must be paid to the effects of judicial decisions as well as to the abstract statements of principle set out in the opinions. The need is for development of a jurisprudence of consequences to assess the societal impact of judicial decrees, particularly the extent to which the political branches of government follow the Court's particular norm with promulgation of a general norm. A "jurisprudence of consequences" or "impact analysis" requires also that the Court have an institutional means of forecasting the probable effects of consequences of given decisions.

The coming of the Positive State as a form of affirmative government with self-imposed duties has been "constitutionalized," as we have seen, to the extent that the programs of that state have received the imprimatur of the Supreme Court. The Court, thus, may be said to have cooperated in the promulgation of a set of obligations enunciated by the political branches of government. That exemplifies the other side of "separation of powers"—cooperation rather than conflict. The disputes between branches of government receive attention, but they should not be allowed to hide the more pervasive and more important cooperative activities. Cooperation among the various organs of government is a necessity and their warfare "fatal," as Woodrow Wilson averred. The genesis of the concept of constitutional duty, accordingly, can be traced to decisions finding no objection in the fundamental law for politically articulated duties.[23]

Third, the Positive State is characterized by the promotion of group activity. This tendency can be traced at least as far as 1886, when the Supreme Court in as casual a piece of lawmaking as it ever performed, unanimously said that the corporation was a person within the terms of the Fourteenth Amendment. [24] That remarkable example of the way in which the Court updates the Constitution was not lawmaking by inadvertence. Quite obviously, the Justices knew exactly what they were doing in bending the Fourteenth Amendment's purpose of protection of freed slaves, which only a few years before seemed to be its only purpose, to the needs of the corporations. And it was by no accident that the Justices—then and today—refuse to call the union a person. Rather it is an unincorporated association, a status less than that of business corporations. Just why this is so is puzzling, perhaps impossible to determine. Gus Tyler, in his volume *The Political Imperative: The Corporate Character of Unions*, contends that the union is a political entity: "the labor organization of twentieth-century America is, among other things, an instrumentality for the performance of governmental functions that the government itself is either unwilling, unable, or not yet ready to perform."[25] The legalistic form may not view unions as "persons" as are corporations, but as we have seen the union should in fact be considered part of the corporate community. It is one of the disparate groups in the federation of interests that make up the corporation. Even if thought to be a separate entity, it is, as Tyler argues, a corporate form of organization, one Hugo Krabbe describes in these terms: "The group itself has ends which it pursues with more or less consistency; it has a settled policy which no individual can modify at will. Its collective character is as fixed as the character of an individual. It can assert collective rights and assume collective obligations. In short it has the same type of energy and inertia which in the individual we call will or personality."[26]

Even though the union has not been accorded constitutional status by the Supreme Court, it has nevertheless been recognized—in fact, legitimized—by Congress. The basic charter for that process is to be found in the National Labor Relations Act (Wagner Act) of 1935, which stated that "employees shall have the right to self-organization, to form, join, or assist labor organizations, to bargain collectively through representatives of their own choosing, and to engage in other concerted activities for the purpose of collective bargaining or other mutual aid or protection." In essence, that was governmental encouragement of union—group or associational—activity. It was "constitutionalized" in fact, if not in theory, when the Supreme Court upheld the statute as a valid exercise of the power of Congress to regulate interstate commerce. This means that it has many of the benefits of being a constitutional person without some of the shortcomings.

Once a union has been certified as the bargaining agent in a company or industry, it then has authority under the Wagner Act to operate in behalf of its members; it thus has official standing in law—a status peculiar to its needs. The employer must by law bargain in good faith with the union, which speaks for all the workers in the bargaining unit. When the collective bargaining agreement is signed, it is something more than a mere contract; it is more like a constitution for the bargaining unit. Under it, the union represents the workers—all of them, whether or not they pay dues. As Tyler puts it: "In effect, the union that wins the election is 'chartered' by law to 'do the business' of representing a body of workers as certainly as if the government had issued a charter of incorporation."[27] Adolf Berle, in discussing the relationship of unions to the state, concluded:

> The National Labor Relations Act recognized the collective associations, known as labor unions, but did not undertake to settle how they should run. It legitimized them as bargaining agents for groups of workers and provided a method (election) by which workers could indicate that choice. It did not undertake to instruct either employers or labor unions as to bargains they could or could not make. It did insist that where workers organized, or were organized, and so chose, agreements as to wages, plans, and benefits must be negotiated with the group and not with each individual.[28]

In short, encouragement of union action was a program of the Positive State—based, be it noted, on the unstated assumption that the results of collective bargaining would redound ("by the invisible hand"?) to the public good. (That the assumption has serious shortcomings will be argued below.)

Unions and corporations (or the two together as constituent segments of the corporate community) are not the only associations furthered by government effort. A constitutional "right of association" has been recognized by the Supreme Court. The leading case is *NAACP* v. *Alabama* (1958), in which the Court said that Alabama could not require the NAACP to reveal its membership. [29] Taking the position that group association unquestionably furthers effective advocacy of both public and private viewpoints, the Court said: "It is beyond debate that freedom to engage in association for the advancement of beliefs and ideas as an inseparable aspect of the 'liberty' assured by the Due Process Clause of the Fourteenth Amendment." For the first time in history the Justice expressly recognized a constitutional "right of association." "Of course," Justice Harlan went on to say for the Court, "it is immaterial whether the beliefs sought to be advanced by association pertain to political, economic, religious or cultural matters, and state action which may have the effect of curtailing the freedom to associate is subject to the closest scrutiny." The decision was echoed in *Bates* v. *City of Little Rock*, [30] upholding a refusal of the NAACP to turn over membership lists to the city clerk because of fear of harassment, economic reprisals, bodily harm, and the violation of the Constitution. The right of peaceable assembly protected by the First Amendment, was said "to lie at the foundation of a government based upon the consent of an informed citizenry." Accordingly, "it is now beyond dispute that freedom of association for the purpose of advancing ideas and airing grievances is protected by the Due Process Clause of the Fourteenth Amendment from invasion by the States."

In effect, then, the Constitution protects the right of association and, further, the right to do so without disclosure of membership to government if such disclosure, as Justice Douglas said in 1961, "results in reprisals against and hostility to the members"; "regulatory measures," according to Douglas, "no matter how sophisticated, cannot be employed in purpose or in effect to stifle, penalize, or curb the exercise of First Amendment rights." [31] But the law is not that simple, for there are "good" associations and "bad" associations. Anti-Ku Klux Klan laws have been upheld, even those requiring disclosure of membership. [32] The distinction between good and bad is not at all clear; it will be left to future cases to spell out the details of the constitutional right of association. It is enough now merely to note its existence, as a part of the encouragement of group activity by the Positive State, and to set forth some pertinent observations of Professor David Fellman:

> The right of association is central to any serious conception of constitutional democracy. In the big states of modern times the individual cannot function politically with any measure of effectiveness unless he is free to associate with others without hindrance. In fact, most people find much of their identity, in either economic, social, political, professional or confessional terms, in some form of group activity. "If we are individualists now," Ernest Barker once observed, "we are corporate individualists. Our 'individuals' are becoming groups." It follows that *government has an obligation to protect the right of association* from invasion, and to refrain from making inroads into that right through its own activities. . . .
>
> As the courts devote more and more time to the emerging problems which touch upon the right of association, it is becoming increasingly evident that the basic problem of defining its scope is very much like the problem of spelling out the metes and bounds of any similar right. [33]

The right of association is not an absolute; choices and accommodations must be made in specific cases by the Justices. But it is high on the hierarchy of protected rights and as Professor Fellman asserts, there may even be an "obligation" (read "duty") on government to protect that right.

The final example of governmental encouragement of group activity is particularly apt, for it at once combines historical development, legislative programs, administrative action, and Supreme Court approbation: the farmer, or, more particularly, the American Farm Bureau Federation. The story is well told in Grant McConnell's *The Decline of Agrarian Democracy*: [34] Beginning not later than 1862 with the passage of the Morrill Act, systematic government subsidization of agriculture has been a cardinal tenet in almost every administration that has come to power. The Morrill Act married education and agriculture by establishing the land-grant colleges; public land, vast in quantity, was used to endow colleges "for the benefit of agriculture and the mechanic arts."

During the latter part of the nineteenth century, farmers organized into political movements to battle the rising power of the new capitalists of the Northeast. The Grangers and the Populists were essentially grass-roots efforts to stem primitive capitalism and to preserve a form of agrarianism. They failed, but in failing did something not contemplated by the Granger and Populist leaders. The farmers, rather than fighting power, embraced it—and thereby became one of the prime movers in the American political order. McConnell puts the matter in these terms:

> The structure of power whose rise has been the outstanding feature of agricultural politics in the first half of the twentieth century now extends from a base of social organization in a multitude of localities to a peak of direct influence over the exercise of government authority in the entire nation. To say that it is a pressure group, a grass-roots association of farmers, or an alliance of special interests is to ignore the whole of which these are but parts. Neither the size of the American Farm Bureau Federation, nor the position of the county agents, nor the character of the Department of Agriculture, nor the personnel of the committees of Congress explains the quality or the extent of this power. It is a vertical structure that rises through every level of political organization in America. [35]

Here, then, is an example of "corporativism" in agriculture. The farmer as an individual has diminished in importance. The group— the American Farm Bureau Federation—is all important. It has close ties with the Department of Agriculture. As McConnell concludes, the federation was an outgrowth of the county agent system that the Department of Agriculture and business interests had promoted. The point, for present purposes, is the fact of governmental promotion of agricultural associations (the federation); but more generally, the development is the analogue, perhaps the complement, of the American system of corporativism.

In net, government promotion of associational activity—whether in business or labor or agriculture—ties the major economic interests of the nation closely to the federal government. That is not all: lesser economic interests also have close ties with government, both state and federal. An example is the legal profession.[36] On the state level, the profession polices itself; it says who can practice law, disbars in a few of the more blatant instances of dereliction, and is used by the Department of Justice as a screening unit for nominees to the federal bench. Lawyers, accordingly, operate not only as "officers of the court" (their traditional role) but in a governmental capacity to administer certain policies relating to the profession. So, too, with many other professions and trades; they are self-governing, and as such, also perform a governing function for others.[37] People in many occupations in the United States today have to get a license or join a union or otherwise become a member of a group. The guild has indeed returned to the United States. A new form of feudalism has arisen, with public government using private, voluntary associations to perform some of the urgent tasks of government. Under the Positive State the development has been accelerated and broadened. The right of association is not only constitutionally protected, it is often an economic requirement for the individual if he wishes to survive. True, some examples of yeomanry and the individualism persist, but they are noteworthy for their paucity rather than for being the norm.

The scientific-technological revolution that has been the primary cause of so much social change—its early form made up the Industrial Revolution—has at once made the world smaller, by way of communication and transportation, than the original thirteen states and has permitted the growth of the private collectivities that we have called the supercorporations. These centers of economic power are closely allied to the organs of the Positive State. The two dominant institutions of the modern era—the supercorporation and government—together with their alliances with the centers of learning (the universities, the "thinktanks," etc.) are slowly but steadily growing closer together. The merger of political economic power involves intellectual power as well.

The politico-economic theory of American constitutionalism has been irretrievably shattered. It simply will not do any longer to think in terms of outworn theories and doctrines; the shibboleths of the past can no longer do duty for the technological age. The development may be applauded or deplored, depending on one's set of values, but it cannot be ignored.

We turn now to another part of the "argument" — the rise of the centers of knowledge to prominence and to enhanced power.

The fourth characteristic of the Positive State is the way in which the intellectuals have both grown in size and power and have become the servants of economic (and political) power. As D. N. Chorafas put it: "We are entering an era in which only the mass-oriented industries will be able to compete in world markets. This state of affairs can only harden in the Knowledge Revolution—and the Technological Age it defines. And the Knowledge Revolution promises to be as great an upheaval in its way as the Industrial Revolution was in its time." [38]

During recent decades, knowledge, says Peter F. Drucker, "has become the central capital, the cost center, and the crucial resource of the economy." [39] If that be so—and there are many who would agree with Drucker—then even more can be said about the knowledge revolution and the rise of the new men of power. A knowledge explosion is indeed taking place, but the holders of knowledge, far from being people of power for their own ends, are beholden to those who exercise real power—the corporate managers and others who in fact exercise significant influence over public policy decisions in the United States. The argument, advanced by such observers as Daniel Bell, [40] that power is shifting in America from the businessman to the intellectual does not wash, even though there can be little doubt that, as Chorafas says, "brain power is the key to the future." [41]

The thesis recognizes the coming of the new intellectuals—the "technocrats"—and their great importance in the nation. In *The New Industrial State*, Galbraith discusses the technostructure, made up of all those who bring specialized knowledge to group decision making, and asserts that this group is the repository of real power in the modern state. This may be doubted, but, if so, it is not to be denied that the economists and computer technologists, mathematicians and engineers, to say nothing of scientists generally, have in recent decades become considerably more significant. The essential problem or question, however, is who makes the ultimate decisions; or stated another way, for whom and for what goals do the technocrats toil? There is little or no evidence that those who wield power in fact have substantially changed throughout American history—and there is no adequate reason to suppose that the situation will alter in the future.

Furthermore, the thesis is predicated on the notion that the so-called new men of power—the technocrats—are not a monolithic group. Rather they tend to identify with other basic societal groups, with, that is, government and business in the main. The United States will continue to be a business-oriented nation. Businessmen might—likely will—change their modes of behavior with technological advance, but they will be able to call upon individuals of the technocratic segment, as well as those time-honored problem solvers, the lawyers, to keep the industrial machine going and, indeed, to keep the state itself viable. In short, even though the intellectual may be indispensable to the modern state, he is not dominant. [42] The technocrat, whether individual or institutional, will be the servant of the real power wielders in the polity. In the past, they have been the "rich and the super-rich," to use Lundberg's label.[43] That those people will easily give up positions of power and prestige just does not seem likely. They will "co-opt" the technocrats. Indeed, as Loren Baritz has argued, this has already taken place. [44]

The knowledge revolution and its personnel are minions of a power elite. A label for the development is "technocracy"—not the abortive political movement of the 1930s but technocracy as Jean Meynaud views it: "Technocracy [has] . . . dethroned the politician and replaced him by the technocrat," the person with intellectual skills. [45] During the past twenty years the machinery of government, says Meynaud, has been infiltrated by the "experts"; the consequence is that ever increasingly the problems of government are left to them. Real political power, to Meynaud, lies with the technocrat and not the politician (the elected representatives). Power, however, has never rested with the politician *save as formal authority*; that is, political officers are vested with the trappings of power. But this is not to say that ultimate control now, or in the past, lay in their hands. The base of real power in the United States is an elite structure drawn from wealth and family.[46] Both the technocrat and the politician, in this conception, are servants of power. The difference between them, among other things, is that the former asserts that he is objective and purportedly pursues knowledge for its own sake, whereas the latter is avowedly partisan and seeks selfish ends. Technocracy is coming—not by fiat but by recognition of the need for specialized knowledge. It grows by slow accretion.

It will readily be seen that we are suggesting the validity of a "ruling" or "governing" class hypothesis. In Chapter 4 that hypothesis was said to be at least as tenable as, if not more so than, any other in explaining the growth of the supercorporations. Power derived from ability—what Meynaud calls "the myth of the all-powerful technocrat . . . —the technocrat who can bring peace to society by organizing and distributing fairly a growing prosperity, basing his actions on the analysis of electronic brains"—is not necessarily going to replace traditional political systems. Compare, in this connection, two statements, the first by Meynaud, the second by Professor Victor V. Ferkiss:

[Meynaud:] The advent of industrial civilization is far from being the cause of the disappearance or even the decline of political activity in human societies. The thesis that politics must inevitably as absorbed into technics cannot really be supported. . . .

In other words, an examination of the forseeable future reveals there is no legitimate reason to assume that political relations will disappear: the important point is to ascertain who will be behind them and control them, and to whose advantage.

[Ferkiss:] Technicians, completely freed from the old ruling classes, may . . . form a managerial category of their own, with the material privileges normally attached to such positions. Burnham . . . puts forward this possibility as an absolute certainty and Djilas, speaking of Communist societies, describes the birth of a "new class." These are not very impressive commentators, intellectually speaking, but sociologists of sound scientific integrity like Gurvitch have made disturbing observations on the propensity of technicians to organize themselves as a group within the framework of a collectivized society.

The action of technicians has an inevitable social dimension. It seems permissible to suggest that, on average, this activity, even if carried on in an autonomous manner, tends to work in favor of that part of the system benefiting the ruling classes. [47]

There is, of course, no way in which such assertions can be proved or disproved. Only as the future unfolds will there be any conclusive evidence to buttress Meynaud's view—or the contrary as expressed by

Daniel Bell. Professor Ferkiss has examined Bell's thesis and rejected it. Speaking of the myth of a technical elite, he maintains that "the idea that the nation is coming under the control of a group of highly educated, well-paid technical experts must be severely qualified. Even insofar as they exist and play important roles, their standards do not predominate. Their economic position is controlled by the continuing dominance of the mores and laws of bourgeois man."[48] In other words, the technocrats serve the actual power holders.

No credible evidence exists to buttress the view that political relations will disappear in the future. Far from vanishing, politics today are not even on the decline. The thesis propounded by political scientist Robert Wood that an "apolitical" elite structure is arising within government cannot be supported.[49] Of course, so-called neutral technicians abound, and they act in purportedly objective and scientific ways, but their presence merely subtly shifts the question that political officers ask—"Can we do this?"—from one in which the ground rules are fixed by answering that persistent political question by asking, "Do the rules (i.e., the law) allow it?" to one in which the ground rules are set by asking, "Is it physically and politically possible?" Quite a different matter. Legal restraints are replaced by physical and political restraints. Historically the politician's tool kit looked like a lawyer's; it contained "bargaining skills, propaganda skills, and violence skills . . . . The political order obviously required leaders and advisors with the lawyer's special skill in value clarification, his verbal capacity, and his experience as an intellectual jobber and contractor who could make a strong case wherever one was required."[50]

Where Wood goes wrong is in overemphasizing the physical aspects of restraints on political behavior. He fails to see that the lawyer's question changed (perhaps less than he implies) from one based on an *interdictory* view of law—"Do the existing rules permit such a course of action?"—to an *instrumentalist* conception, that is, "How can law be employed to further the ends sought to be achieved?" With the advent of the Positive State, all law is coming to be seen as public law. That shift from a private-law oriented legal system has not been assimilated into legal theory. It is one of the more challenging intellectual problems of the day. We have already shown that during the past three decades the Constitution has been altered from one of limitations to one of powers. Discretion has become the norm. It is a poor lawyer indeed who cannot find a legal basis for almost any action a policymaker wishes to put into effect. Lawyers, in other words, are also technocrats; they have been "deprofessionalized." They are legal technicians, ready and willing to be servants of power—not all of them, to be sure, but the vast majority. And law has become politicized.

There is, in net, a subversion of scholarship. Both individual scholars and intellectual institutions are closely allied to the power structures of the supercorporations and the Positive State. Universities are service stations for industry and government. Baritz puts it this way: "Many industrial social scientists have put themselves on auction. The power elites of America, especially the industrial elite, have bought their services—which, when applied to areas of relative power, have restricted the freedom of millions of workers." The social scientists servicing industry, says Baritz, have been willing to serve power rather than pursue "the truth"; thus "they have been themselves a case study in manipulation by consent." [51] Baritz's point is that the power to control human behavior, now more and more possible, by social science techniques can be a fearful danger to human freedom when that power is placed at the disposal of industrial managers.

That the stream of scholarship has been polluted is difficult to gainsay. Perhaps it always has been so, but we are just now beginning to awaken to the dangers in such a situation. In *The Closed Corporation* James Ridgeway set forth numerous examples of how ostensibly objective scholars service industry and government. [52] The modern university, as Clark Kerr has said, all too often is the "federal grant university"—not all of them are, to be sure, but many of the most prestigious are closely tied to the federal government through contract and grants of financial aid. [53] What this means has been put by Ridgeway as follows: "In theory, the government gets the best independent scientific advice in this manner, but in fact, what happens is that the major universities become first captive and then active advocates for the military and paramilitary agencies of government in order to get more money for research." [54] Ostensibly private universities thus become public in fact; they are arms of the federal government.

The resulting structure of government-industry-university resembles a troika, or a triangular power system, with each part complementing and feeding on the others. Interlocked, the three characteristic institutions of the age present a form of corporativism in fact. The developing synthesis in the next chapter is toward ever closer interlocks. Business serves a special purpose—the businessman has "social responsibilities"—and so of course do the universities. The nation's young are educated for social ends; the universities provide a manpower pool for the corporations and for government.

There should be little wonder, then, that many today are questioning the gap between pretense and reality in the university. As professors have become entrepreneurs, either for themselves directly or as consultants for government and business; as universities have interlocked into the multibillion dollar research programs, many of which are for furthering America's capacity for violence; as social scientists learn to control the behavior of people—as all of these, and more, take place, a reaction has set in, a reaction that is at least endemic in many of the industrialized nations. What the result of that reappraisal will be cannot now be forecast, but surely it is already apparent that some restructuring will take place.

A main source of concern seems ultimately to be the fundamental hypocrisy of a nation that preaches one thing and does another. Neocolonial wars are fought in the name of freedom; millions of Americans live below the poverty line in "the affluent society"; black Americans are told by the Supreme Court and Presidents and Congress that they are first-class citizens, only to meet impenetrable roadblocks when they try to exercise the rights of citizenship; "America the beautiful" has become "America the polluted," as its rivers become open sewers, its air unfit to breathe, and its cities paved over to make way for that insatiable technological triumph, the internal combustion engine. All this and more breeds indifference and cynicism at best, a blind rage at worst, at a system that fails so miserably to live up to its ideals. The "last best hope of man" has become a hollow, unfunny mockery, as the politicians try to establish a global pax Americana, one in which technological goals are ends in themselves. The concern is deep-seated and did not vanish with the ending of the Vietnam conflict.

Scholarship has been perverted, more so in the modern age than historically, because the skills and knowledge of the scholars are much more important to the state. Zbigniew Brzezinski noted the change in an important essay. He perceives a "profound change" occurring in the intellectual community as "the largely humanist-oriented, occasionally ideologically-minded intellectual-dissenter, who sees his role largely in terms of proffering social critiques, is rapidly being displaced either by experts and specialists, who become involved in special governmental undertakings, or by the generalists-integrators, who become in effect house-ideologues for those in power, providing overall intellectual integration for disparate actions." [55] There is a knowledge revolution; a knowledge explosion is taking place; the storage and retrieval and communication of knowledge has become a major industry in itself, but the questions remain the same: In whose interests is that knowledge employed? Who exercises the power? Who makes the decisions and for what goals? In the synthesis that is developing in the United States, the subject of the next chapter, it will be seen that, while a new form of constitutional order is being produced, this does not mean that the actual power wielders have in fact changed.

The formal law of American constitutionalism bespeaks one type of reality, but it is strictly supposititious—a far cry from what the living law says. The Constitution, as written in 1787, is a facade. In order to know what the Constitution in fact is, as distinguished from what it purports to say, one must pierce that facade to see the underlying reality. That reality is a form of native corporativism.

6

THE DEVELOPING SYNTHESIS

> *. . . A substantial part of government in the United States has come under the influence or control of narrowly based and largely autonomous elites. These elites do not act cohesively with each other on many issues. They do not "rule" in the sense of commanding the entire nation. Quite the contrary, they tend to pursue a policy of non-involvement in the large issues of statemanship save where such issues touch their own particular concerns. . . .*
> *. . . The distinction between the public and the private has been compromised far more deeply than we like to acknowledge. . . . The very idea of constitutionalism sometimes seems to be placed in question.*

> —GRANT McCONNELL [1]

We have traced the growth of the supercorporations and the rise of the Positive State, and the rise of the "man of knowledge" to dizzy heights of power and influence, cast against the background of a concept of constitutional change. It is now time to pose the question—and to essay at least a tentative answer—of what these twentieth-century phenomena mean for the nature of American constitutionalism.

This may be done by stating a hypothesis: *the trend is toward the fusion of economic power (the supercorporations) and political power (the Positive State), both aided by the "knowledge industry"; the consequence is the creation of the "technocorporate" state.* In short, the living law of American constitutionalism is tending toward formation of a form of native corporativism. The corporate state, to be sure, is no new political invention. What does appear to be new is the manner in which the American form is coming into existence. Produced through the slow accretion of numberless transactions between government and business (and the centers of knowledge), layer by layer, it is developing like a coral reef rather than by a mighty volcanic explosion—that is, it is being created by custom, not by fiat. The development can be seen in economics and in politics and is reflected in law (both "private" and "public" law). This chapter outlines that synthesis and places it in historical context.

First, however, a basic point requires restatement for emphasis: the supercorporation is only one, though perhaps the most important, of the social groups of the United States. America is the organizational society par excellence. The basic unit of society has become—whatever it may have been in 1787—the pluralistic group. The Constitution (and its history) strongly suggests that the individual is the fundamental unit, but if that were ever true, it no longer is. The preamble still begins, "We, the people," but that should read, "We, the groups." The natural person (as compared with the artificial person known in law as corporations) receives importance and is significant in American society only as a member of some group (or groups). That assertion, though set forth baldly, seems to be irrefutable; it is particularly apparent in politics and in economics. In politics, the individual qua individual is nothing; he has power only to the extent that he can control wealth or property or can join some group that can exercise leverage. The United States is an organized democracy, one in which, as Jacques Ellul has said, "the normal way for a citizen to express himself is through his group. Each citizen must belong to one or several groups."[2]

The same may be said of economics, as John D. Rockefeller I, one of the chief robber barons, asserted about the turn of the century. Large-scale organization, he said, had "revolutionized the way of doing business"; this meant, he went on, that individualism was gone, never to return.[3] Willy Ley, the well-known scientist, echoed the same thought in 1967 when he asserted that "in a society based on technology, work must be done by many people together, and consequently every individual is destined to be part of a group, to say *we* instead of I."[4] The need, said Ley, is not for more Beethovens—people able to work by themselves—but for more Wernher Von Brauns, people whose genius talks in collective terms.

In short, the American ideal of individualism is dead. The core concept of the modern era is not independence but interdependence, even though the "autonomous man" has long been the American hero and people still yearn for the fancied glories of a long-vanished frontier. The autonomous man does not exist as such. The human being is important in an economic and political sense only insofar as he becomes part of a collectivity—a corporation, a labor union, a farmers' group, a consumers' cooperative, a veterans' legion. This is not, be it emphasized, to extol the development but merely to note its emergence. One may welcome it or rail against it; but it cannot be escaped from. Professor John William Ward made the point in somewhat more circumspect language: "Our society, like all modern industrial societies, is characterized by economic and social interdependence, specialization of activity, and large-scale organizations—social phenomena that pose troublesome problems for traditional American attitudes toward the relation of the individual to society."[5] The pervasiveness of private, voluntary associations meant that they must now be seen and acted on as the fundamental unit of society—although those organizations are neither very "private" nor really "voluntary."

Paradoxically, at the very time that the Supreme Court has been seeking to maximize the values of individualism—in effect, through the merger of the concepts of liberty and equality—the growth of corporate (and other) enterprise has produced a social milieu in which individual liberties or freedoms are not highly valued and cannot be realized except through the latter-day Thoreauvian ploy of "opting out." Uniformity, cultivated through national advertising and the astute use of the mass media, and conformity are much more prevalent. For that matter, one should remember that despite the myth to the contrary, Americans have never suffered nonconformists gladly. The true individualist has never been highly regarded in the United States. In the final analysis, furthermore, Americans seem to be more interested in materialism than in individualism. According to Professor William Withers, where they have had a choice or could make conscious decisions, "they chose the solution that led to greater material satisfaction, even at the sacrifice of individual freedom."[6]

We are postulating, then, a constitutional change of the greatest magnitude—the fusion of economic and political power into the corporate state, American style. Obviously this is so for those companies, some of the nation's largest, that are almost entirely dependent on government contracts for their livelihood. There private industry "on an enormous scale has become the agent of a fundamentally new economic system which at once resembles traditional private enterprise and the corporate state of fascism." [7] I am not suggesting that the emergent form of American corporativism is a repressive, totalitarian form of government. Not at present fascistic in nature, whether it will become so in the future cannot be answered at this time. (Corporativism—at least in theory—does not have to be fascistic.)

The fusion is also true for the other supercorporations and even for many smaller business corporations. The new slogan is "government-business partnership"—and that it is, an example of what can be termed a "public-law partnership." The relationship is symbiotic, not arms length. Business needs government—and government needs business. Neither could exist without the other; neither, more importantly, wants to exist without the other. They need each other (and perhaps they deserve each other).

That an interlocking partnership has developed is part of the accepted wisdom of the day; it need not be extensively documented. Witness, however, the statements of two prominent businessmen. In 1959, Melvin H. Baker, chairman of the board of National Gypsum Company, said: "Since the early part of this century we have been developing a new form of public-private society. . . . Call it what you will, the fact remains that this kind of government is here to stay, and those who would accomplish almost anything of public interest must work with the government. I say work 'with' it, not 'for' it." [8] That "new form of public-private society" is here called the techno-corporate state. Witness also the statement of Frank N. Ikard, president of the American Petroleum Institute, who said in 1966: "There is an old saying that facts have a way of out-running thoughts. The facts of today's world are such that the old attitudes of many businessmen toward government, and the old attitudes of many government people toward business, are no longer relevant. There can be no longer any question as to whether or not these two groups can or will work together. The vast changes that are sweeping our nation make cooperation a necessity." [9] Ikard maintained that "for the foreseeable future, the roles of business and government are indissolubly linked." Much earlier, Woodrow Wilson had noted the same tendency; in a prescient book published in 1913, he said, "One of the most alarming phenomena of the time—or rather it would be alarming if the nation had not awakened to it and shown its determination to control it—one of the most significant signs of the new social era is the degree to which government has become associated with business. I speak, for the moment, of the control over the government exercised by Big Business. Behind the whole subject, of course, is the truth that, in the new order, government and business must be associated closely."[10] Whether the determination to control business about which Wilson spoke exists today (or in the past) is dubious; it likely has been more apparent than real throughout American history.

The close linkage between the two most important entities of the era—government and business—can be seen in a number of areas: economics, politics, law, and public administration.

ECONOMICS

Evidence of the partnership between government and business is most clearly visible, perhaps, in the burgeoning system of American economic planning. The United States has, to use Michael Reagan's label,[11] a "managed economy"—with the management being done through cooperative action between the public bureaucracies of government and the private bureaucracies of the supercorporations.

To John Kenneth Galbraith, the supercorporation is the "basic planning unit" of the economy; in this respect, he says, there is little difference in the institutional structure of the economies of the U.S.S.R. and the United States. The difference between the two, a matter Galbraith, slights, lies in who controls the decisions made in planning. And he asserts that the technostructure, embracing "all who bring specialized knowledge, talent or experience to group decision-making," is in control—"the guiding intelligence of the enterprise."[12] That may not be true, as we have said in Chapter 5.

Economic planning, furthermore, is far from a new development. It has existed in some form or another throughout our history. What is new is the degree and the intensity of planning and also of some of the goals toward which it is aimed. Planning involves more than economics alone. Politics and law are also inevitably a part of the process. The only thing lacking from the relationship between business and government, to establish the corporate state in theory, is some formal legal link, such as contract or statute. That link exists by contract so far as the armaments industry is concerned; and we will see that contract is increasingly being used in other segments of the economy. Even without a legal link, however, the close economic relationship between government and business is a hard fact of life today.

One should be aware that the American system of planning bears different labels. Owing to a primitive fear of words that has had the consequence of clouding reality, and because of ideological considerations—by, amazingly, those avowed pragmatists, the hard-headed American businessmen—planning is hidden under a fog of more innocuous verbiage. Those who dislike the notion of planning seem to think that they can make it go away by not acknowledging it or by calling it something else. Of more importance, no modern institution or organization (or individual, for that matter) could long survive without some sort of planning, however obscured or denied. Examples of planning abound: tariffs and other subsidies, tax and monetary policies, "wars against poverty," and the like. The charter for the American system of planning is the Employment Act of 1946.

Basic to the developing synthesis, then, is a burgeoning system of economic planning. Not that this is a new notion. George Soule has said: "The United States Government has at all times followed plans of some sort that were directed toward the economic welfare of its citizens. The record goes back to Washington's first administration." [13] But it is markedly different today from the past.

If the rise of the modern corporation has undermined classical economic theory in much the same way that the quantum undermined classical theory in physics, so too has the rise of the Positive State, together with the supercorporations, undermined the preconceptions of traditional constitutional theory. No longer is it possible to think of atomistic individuals interacting in the market or of autonomous men acting as independent political actors. Something new is needed. That "something," in broadest terms, is the emergence of the corporate state.

Looking at the nature of American corporativism from a lesser degree of abstraction, planning is an organizing principle around which many of the activities of modern government can be arrayed. Embedded in the concept is the spectrum of relationships between government and business, the acceptance of responsibility by the federal government for the well-being of all the people, and the means by which a new form of social order is being constructed. Economic planning, always present in one form or another within the American scheme, has taken on new characteristics. Set forth here is a series of propositions about it as it now exists and as it will probably develop in the future.

1. The first inquiry must be to history, but only after a definition of planning is set forth. To Professor Neil W. Chamberlain, planning is the "systematic management of assets." [14] That sort of generalized definition can apply to any type of economic unit, from the individual to international communities or associations. At the level of the national economy, planning can be defined as "the systematic management of the nation's assets to achieve such objectives as may be sufficiently accepted, to provide a measure of executive authority in seeking them by means of such instruments and devices as similarly are permitted." Somewhat more precisely, George Soule speaks of planning in this manner: "Planning does not necessarily mean the abolition of market forces, or the outlawing of private profit as a stimulus to production of goods wanted by consumers. Rather, it means influencing existing economic habits and outlook by a program which serves needs not contemplated by, and not normally fulfilled by, the existing order. National planning looks at wider horizons or longer futures than do the daily decisions of the managers of individual firms or industries. And its goals, if sanctioned by the citizens, make use of foresights and capabilities developed by the 'organizing man,' in the domain of a whole society." [15]

These definitions will suffice for present purposes, particularly if it is noted that under both definitions emphasis is placed on the "organizing man" or the technician. Planning means widespread use of technical experts. Only through use of economists and other technocrats can any national plan—or, for that matter, any plan for a supercorporation—be effected.

Historically, planning mainly took the form of distributing government bounty to corporations and to others, plus such assistance to business enterprise as protective tariffs. A virgin continent made this possible. However, by the end of the nineteenth century the public's patrimony had been largely exhausted so far as tangible assets were concerned. There was little more free land, even though the federal government still owned about one-fourth of the total area of the nation. The frontier, as Frederick Jackson Turner so aptly said, had closed; the formative years of the American experience came to an end. During this time, it is true, some effort was made to control the supply of money and otherwise to manipulate the economy, but these controls were minimal. They may be taken as precursors of the present system.

By the time the nation entered World War I substantial efforts had been made to plan more systematically. The Supreme Court threw out early efforts to establish minimum wages and maximum hours. But the Sherman Antitrust Act (1890) stayed on the books, as did the Interstate Commerce Act establishing the Interstate Commerce Commission. The Federal Reserve system came early in the twentieth century, as did the Federal Trade Commission.

Most important of all, however, was the Sixteenth Amendment to the Constitution, permitting imposition of a federal income tax. Made necessary because a prior congressional statute had been invalidated by the Supreme Court, the amendment, and subsequent legislation, permitted a vast increase in federal tax revenue. With that came the slow realization, brought to fruition in the post-World War II period, that a new source of bounty was to be found. Largesse from the national government became a new form of property. [16] The national state became the welfare state.

2. During time of war, beginning with the Civil War and reaching a peak in the major wars of this century, overt economic planning was the norm. That was true in 1917 and 1918, during World War II, and even during the Korean conflict. Noteworthy about the Vietnam conflict, an undeclared war as was the Korean conflict, is that direct controls were not considered necessary. It is important to understand why. Two different reasons might be assigned: first, the economy had reached such a situation of strength that it could simultaneously function as a war economy and a peace economy, and second, planning had in fact—although (again) not in theory—become so prevalent by the 1960s that direct controls were not necessary.

Quite possibly, elements of both reasons are present. Certainly, it cannot be denied that the 1950s and 1960s were a period of unprecedented economic growth. But even more basic seems to be the second reason: no controls were necessary because some type of economic planning was already being conducted; and what is of equal importance, much of the growth of the economy came as a result of direct government expenditures (in armaments, in research and development, in space travel, etc.). In the mid 1970s, the bitter fruit of bad economic planning is being reaped in inflation and other economic ills.

3. Economic planning involves the use of business units [17] by government to achieve certain societal objectives. Under the terms of the Employment Act of 1946, those objectives are economic growth and maximum employment. These are the general goals. The specific goals are something else—weapons systems, trips to the moon, urban redevelopment.

4. Planning in the United States is noncoercive. Few direct controls are involved.

5. Planning is not centralized in the sense of having an overall plan for the *entire* nation and for the *entire* economy. Government uses social (corporate) groups to help effect planning. The centralization that exists is within specific areas or industries. It is true, however, that some aspects of planning, as in manipulation of fiscal and monetary matters, do affect the entire nation. Planning, in other words, tends to be along syndicalist lines (although it is not called that and it is far from the syndicalism theory), overlaid with aspects of centralization.

6. Planning, in the American sense, aids some more than others. Discussed below are three types of welfarism, which show that the rewards of planning are uneven. Egalitarianism, even though important, has not gone so far as to produce economic equality in fact.

7. Planning is not "redistributive." Rather, the goal is to create a bigger pie through more production so that more people can benefit from increases in material goods. The emphasis is on economic growth, not a different deal of the same cards. The rich still stay rich, both relatively and absolutely, but there are more with advanced levels of living and a promise that others can share.

8. Planning thus has the approval of a high number of the members of the "establishment" who have co-opted the notion in order at once to preserve their position and to stave off "socialism" or some other true redistributive scheme.

9. Planning, accordingly, does not engender intense political opposition. By and large, the American system is in accord with the political aspirations of the American people. Argument, when it comes (which is often), is over the details of planning, not over the basic idea. Save for a few unreconstructed Neanderthals, opposition to American planning is minimal.

10. With that degree of consensus, it is not at all astonishing to note that planning, American style, gets no opposition from the United States Supreme Court. Prior to 1937, it is true, the Court did try to establish itself as the ultimate arbiter of economic policy within the nation. Its success, which never was complete, terminated in 1937; and at the most, it lasted for about fifty years. Since 1937, the Justices have been content to leave final economic policy decisions in the hands of the political branches of government.

11. Planning (in the United States and in the Western world) tends to be multinational. The point has been well made by Michael Kidron in terms bridging national and multinational planning and also indicating how the corporations play a role: "The big corporations have particular reasons for pressing growth policies on their governments. Increasingly, their operations are international in scope, and their entry into foreign markets conditional on reciprocal liberalism at home. This would be difficult in the absence of rising domestic demand. Increasingly their ability to maintain competitiveness rests on freedom to shift resources across frontiers, which demands a fairly healthy balance of payments in the home country, which in turn depends on good growth performance from the economy as a whole." [18] Developed, industrialized nations are increasingly interdependent. Integration along economic and political lines makes it necessary for larger-than-national efforts at planning. Already examples of multinational planning can be seen in, for example, monetary matters and the regulation of certain commodities by international commodity agreements.

Furthermore, planning by world (geocentric) corporations may well run counter to political policies of nation-states. [19] To the extent that this is true—it cannot be measured at this time—the corporate giant might challenge the nation-state for dominance. Much more likely, however, is that corporations will use the political order (the nation-state) to achieve corporate ends.

12. One consequence of national planning, unless it becomes truly multi- or international, is the prospect of having entire economies competing with each other in an oligopolistic manner. Planning becomes necessary nationally for a variety of reasons, not least of which is international competition. Much as the supercorporations compete with each other within a national market, so nations (as planning economies) compete with each other in the world market.

13. National planning, despite the tendency toward multinationalism seen above (a tendency that might become much more necessary), tends to favor national or domestic integration or goals at the expense of international integration. Nations try to export their problems through various devices; unemployment is one example. [20]

14. Planning tends to become a technical problem to be dealt with by technicians—the technocrats—rather than by politicians. As government sees itself as a system (the economy or society are viewed as "systems"), then the supercorporations are subsystems. The problems arising are dealt with by technocrats, not ideologues and not politicians. This does not mean that the technocrats are neutral technicians. We have seen in Chapter 5 that they are not.

15. The early form of corporativism tried in the 1930s under the National Industrial Recovery Act proved, as we have seen, to be abortive. When the Supreme Court declared the act unconstitutional, few tears were shed. However, the practices begun under the NIRA—industry cooperation, in the main—continued under the tacit and at times overt approval of government.

16. The trend, finally, is toward more planning. Looked at historically, the tendency is toward increased intervention of government in business affairs and, at the same time, increasing use of government by business for its ends.

That listing of the characteristics of American planning is illustrative, not exhaustive. Perhaps, however, enough has been said to indicate the main contours of the concept. We now turn to another question, which can be dealt with summarily. That, in short, is the proposition that planning in the United States (and elsewhere) is far from perfect; it brings with it major problems—economic and political and eventually constitutional.

Planning brings unequal benefits to the people of a nation that is committed to equality (in the "equal protection of the laws" clause of the Fourteenth Amendment to the Constitution) and that has seen a steady movement toward egalitarianism over the nearly two centuries since its formation. There is, in other words, no adequate reason to suppose that planning will alter the basic composition of society or that it will substantially change the spread of wealth. The myth is to the contrary, of course. No doubt the United States is affluent (in its effluence, some would say); more people have a relatively higher level of living than ever before—and than in any other nation in history. That is attributable, or so it seems, to economies of scale and rising productivity levels attained by industry and agribusiness.

Neither a redistribution of wealth has taken place nor is it likely to occur. Approximately the same percentage of Americans control the same percentage of wealth as was the case forty or fifty years ago. [21] The New Deal wrought no revolution. It merely permitted the "governing classes" to absorb welfare programs in such a way as to quell discontent while simultaneously keeping the self-styled "upper" class in the topmost position. Accordingly President Franklin D. Roosevelt was a true conservative. Far from being "a traitor to his class," as so many unthinking wealthy Americans characterized him, his programs—the New Deal in general—permitted the system to be preserved practically intact. "Liberalism" in the modern sense was taken over by corporate leaders to control "free market" competitiveness and combat the growth of radicalism (socialism) as a political movement.

This is not to suggest that a conscious conspiracy took place but simply to say that corporate officials (and their minions in the legal profession) saw the need to counteract a rising tide of anticorporationism, including antibigness, and were keen enough to realize that their long-range interests lay in promoting at least minimal welfare programs. So it has worked—at least until the present. American welfare has been minimal; it still lags far behind that of some other nations. Medical care is an example; it exemplifies the very halting steps that have been taken to improve the health of Americans, steps that have been fought all along the line by entrenched medical groups and by the American elite, but nonetheless steps that are pitifully small as compared with those in some nations, Sweden for example.

At the same time, planning has continued in its time-honored manner of making a few either wealthy for the first time or wealthier. The "rich man's version of the welfare state" costs far more than does that of the poor man, but it is far less controversial. Enormous subsidies, either direct or indirect, plus contracts and grants, pour out from government to the favored groups. [22] The net result is that the rich get richer and the poor remain poor—both relatively and absolutely. In between the poor—who may total about 30 million Americans—and the rich are the middle classes, those who have some affluence but not much, who are not poor but nonetheless are closer to the poverty line than to the category of the rich and the super-rich.

Uneven economic benefits from planning are one of the prime causes of social unrest. Disadvantaged groups are demanding a larger share of the wealth. Their discontent is manifested in many ways—in the movement of blacks for a higher status, in the neopopulism of George Wallace and his "forgotten Americans," in the increasingly stiff demands for wage increases. It has not reached the point of conflict or rebellion, but a vast surge of disquietude is visible in the nation. Slowly but seemingly surely, millions of heretofore silent Americans are beginning to make their voices heard. One of the chief faults in the American system of planning is the inability to stem the tide of inflation while simultaneously maintaining full employment. The inflationary spiral in effect is a tax that falls especially hard on the people with small fixed incomes. Consumers' strikes and quite possibly price-control legislation are, accordingly, in the offing. In brief, the American people have been told for too long how rich the nation is. They now want to benefit from those riches.

Allied to the rich man's version of the welfare state is that of the intellectual. [23] Much of the several billion dollar annual federal expenditures for research and development falls into the third version, plus numerous other subsidies to intellectuals from the corporate sector. A major development of the past thirty years, it too is not controversial. Possibly this is because the sums thus expended tend to further the goals of the elite structures of the corporate state.

On the other hand, the poor are not only deprived, they are castigated for being in a lowly economic status. There is more than a remnant of something morally reprehensible in the minds of many people in this nation still infected with the Puritan ethic in being poor or "disadvantaged." What this ultimately means is that the poor are caught in a vicious circle of declining status vis-a-vis the affluent—what Gunnar Myrdal has termed the principle of cumulative social causation is at work: [24] the rich get richer, the poor remain poor or get poorer; "them as has, gits," in the old frontier slogan.

Myrdal's sociological principle is of particular importance as an insight not only into the United States domestically but also in the position of the nation compared with the Third World nations. The already industrialized nations of the North Atlantic littoral form a sort of rich man's club, with much of the remainder of the world in poverty.

POLITICS

As with economics, so with politics. There is a close and continuing relationship between the government and the governed (rather, ostensibly governed, for actual control of the ship of state may well be outside formal government). The business of America has always been business, in the past and now—and very probably, in the future, even if the society of the future is "postindustrial." (All that term can mean is that the type of business might change but the enterprise will remain an economic entity in basic thrust.) Whether in the legislature or in the public administration, and even in the courts, the business of government is business—not entirely, to be sure, but substantially or principally. The policymaking process in government is highly politicized; ours is truly a government of men and not of laws, and that is accurate whether those "men" are legislators or administrators or judges. The myth is to the contrary; it speaks in terms of a government of laws. Law as interdiction, as a set of normative commands, has little role to play in the higher reaches of the bureaucracies, public and private, and it has far less a role than is ordinarily realized in the lower rungs of the hierarchically controlled organizations (public and private) that dominate the nation.

Consider also the concept of "private governments." Suggested above is the idea that the American people live in a new *economic* order in which the most important segments are the supercorporations. Each of those enterprises, although a "person" in law, is in fact a collectivity, a federation of interests, a sociological community, a

private government, a *political* order. Taken together, they make up
the "corporate states of America"—a type of federalism that is of
fundamentally more importance than is the system of federalism (the
fifty states plus the national government) established by the Constitution. Their characteristics merit some attention.

When speaking of governments, the key question is one of power.
One of the more slippery terms in the lexicon of political and constitutional theory, power refers to the capacity or ability to make decisions affecting the values of others or of influencing significantly the
decisions that others make. The supercorporations both make
decisions affecting the values of others and greatly influence the
course of official decision making. Writing several years ago, Professor Carl Kaysen said it was a cliché that "a group of giant business
corporations, few in numbers but awesome in aggregate size, em-
bodies a significant and troublesome concentration of power." [25] He
went on to say that a few large corporations exert significant power
over others; "indeed, . . . over the whole of society with respect to many
choices, and over large segments of it with respect to others." Power to
Kaysen is "the scope of significant choice" open to "any actor on the
political stage." To that definition may be added that of Professors
Lasswell and Kaplan: "Power is participation in the making of decisions: G has power over H with respect to the values K if G par-
ticipates in the making of decisions affecting the K-policies of H." [26]
It will readily be seen from such definitions that the concept is not
easily reduced to a formula, but enough perhaps has been said to
point out the key factors: first, the focus is on important decisions
that, second, affect the values of Americans. Power can be exercised
with respect to one person only, as in the case of the discharge of an
employee of a corporation, or all or most persons, as in prices set for
goods or services sold.

How, then, do the private governments of the supercorporations exercise power? Several decisional categories can be suggested.

1. The supercorporations make decisions of national or societal
importance. They set national policy in significant areas of concern,
such as the allocation of resources, the direction and nature of investment, and so on. Alone or in concert with others, they set prices
(sometimes collusively, as in the "electric conspiracy" cases) [27] in
what is often a system of "administered" prices (prices set by cor-

porate fiat, not by the market), [28] carve up markets (often in concert with government, as with the airlines), [29] and even go so far as to
subsidize the arts and education.

2. Much of officially announced public policy is in fact an
amalgam of the interactions of private bureaucracies with public
officialdom. The supercorporations often can "veto" proposed public
policies, or at the very least delay them or substantially water them
down. In some instances, public policy, although enunciated by government, may actually have been set by corporate officials; the
supersonic transport, now jettisoned, might be one such example.
Compare, too, what happened when the Federal Trade Commission proposed to limit cigarette advertising, following a report of the
Surgeon General of the United States that smoking was dangerous,
with what happened when the Federal Communications Commission
sought to enact into administrative rule the code of ethics on commercials announced by the industry itself. In the first instance, the
tobacco industry went to Congress, found a number of complaisant
Senators and Congressmen, and was able to get legislation passed
requiring only an innocuous warning on cigarette packages—a
victory for the industry. For our purposes, it was a clear example of
how business power was exercised to get government policy. As for the
action of the FCC, the industry was able to "veto" the proposed rules
by a rather similar technique. Going to the House of Representatives, it was able to get a bill hurried through committee and over-
whelmingly passed by the House that would overturn the proposed
FCC action. Thereupon, the commission bowed to the inevitable and
rescinded the proposed rules. Power was exercised to stop a proposed public policy. [30]

Galbraith maintains that public policy often is a resultant of the
interactions of the technostructures of the supercorporations with
their counterparts in government. So it may be. Administration can
also be viewed as the marriage of politics and law. Policy is the
product of a parallelogram of conflicting group forces, with government often the broker among those groups but also having an interest
of its own to further. Many of the public agencies established for the
ostensible purpose of regulating industry or other facets of American
life act in fact as surrogates of the very activities purportedly controlled. The system transcends those agencies that were set up to

regulate business affairs. The Veterans Administration, for example, is to all practical effects an arm of the American Legion. And the Department of Agriculture often acts as spokesman for the Farm Bureau. The net result is that as Professor Grant McConnell says in the headnote to this chapter, "A substantial part of government in the United States has come under the influence or control of narrowly based and largely autonomous elites." Government *of* the people there is; government *by* the people there is not; and government *for* the people is present only in the sense that the people are not a monolithic whole. Commissioner Nicholas Johnson of the Federal Communications Commission put the matter succinctly in August 1969: "I think basically you have to start with a realization that the country is principally run by big business for the rich. Maybe you have to live in Washington to know that and maybe everyone in the country knows it intuitively. I don't know, but a government of the people, by the people, and for the people, has become, I think, a government of the people, certainly, but by the corporations and for the rich." [31]

The critical question that now obtrudes is whether this system can long last, whether, that is, the "American way" is doing its job. It will be suggested below that that question can be answered only in the negative. The present "system" cannot last, simply because it is becoming absurd. Democracy, in the sense of popular rule or even of true representative government, does not exist. Perhaps it never did, but the question now is whether even the attenuated democracy in the United States today can long endure. No answer to that question is given here. Merely posing it, however, indicates the depth of the problem.

3. The supercorporation is often an agency of administration for government. The federal government, faced with mounting responsibilities—the root cause of which is often science and technology—but not permitted to expand the formal civil service, farms out what Harlan Cleveland once described as "staggering" amounts of the public administration, of governing power, to private organizations. [32] Contracting out is particularly evident in research and development. However, there is scarcely an American governmental organ, including Congress, that does not participate in the system, a system that is creating an "external bureaucracy" in ostensibly private organizations. These organizations may be profit making, as

corporations, or "nonprofits," such as universities. It should be remembered when thinking about the delegation of administrative power to private organizations that, as Bishop Hoadly said in his sermon to the King in 1717, the true lawmaker is he who has power to interpret the laws (to administer) rather than the person(s) who first prescribed the norm.

4. The supercorporation is a private government because in its internal operations it is a political order. [33] The task of those who control the enterprise is to make a profit but not necessarily to maximize profits. Rather, profits may be "satisficed" as the oligarchs who control the firm (thereby exemplifying Michels' "iron law of oligarchy")[34] perforce balance the disparate interests of the corporate community.

5. The supercorporation, which, it will be recalled, includes the union, operates a form of private judiciaries. The system of industrial jurisprudence that has grown in this country since enactment (and validation by the Supreme Court) of the Wagner Labor Relations Act in effect transfers power to the corporate communities to settle their own affairs. It also encompasses a widespread system of arbitration of disputes that arise under the collective bargaining agreements. That system of arbitration is a private judiciary operating side by side with the public judiciary. Very little contact is made in any way between the two.

6. The supercorporation, alone or in concert with others, operates to legislate in the field of contract law; as contract developed in Anglo-American legal history, it was the analogue, if not the product, of free-enterprise capitalism, a system based on individual enterprise or, at most, small shops and firms. It is the legal concept appropriate to an economic system in which reliance is placed on exchange rather than tradition or custom or command for the distribution of resources. In an individualistic society, all law is ultimately based on contract, that is, derived from choices freely made by responsible individuals. However, the demise of laissez-faire and the rise of corporate combines have created a "new feudalism" in which contracts are not so much the result of bargains struck as of adherence to already established terms. Government contracts provide the classic illustration, but in the private sector most transactions still called contract are really "contracts of adhesion." The relationship

tends to be one of power, not of bargain, in which the group (often a corporation) dominates to set the terms and conditions under which agreements are made. Administered prices furnish the ready example; the contract of adhesion is the analogue of administered prices and price leadership. Freedom of contract, under the impact of the power of the supercorporations and the trade associations, has degenerated into the "freedom" to choose which agreement one will "adhere to." Standard-form contracts, in other words, are *legislative* prescriptions of the corporate communities and the trade associations. [35] (This is not to say that the law has fully recognized the development; here, as elsewhere, the melancholy fact is that law always limps along behind social developments, displaying a cultural lag.)

7. Finally, the supercorporation is a private government in those firms that control the mass media of communication. Again, they act in concert with government, particularly when a license is required (as in radio and television) but also, as Jacques Ellul maintains, because the media are employed by government in a pervasive system of propaganda that is so characteristic of the modern age. [36] This, it may be noted in passing, makes nonsense out of the Supreme Court's assertions about the validity of the "marketplace theory of truth." [37] In this time, as in the past, "the dictum that truth always triumphs over persecution is one of these pleasant falsehoods which men repeat one another till they pass into commonplace which all experience refutes." [38] When John Stuart Mill said that in 1874 in his famous essay *On Liberty*, the mass media had not yet come into existence. Today, with government secrecy policies, "managed" news, immensely complex public policies remote from a person's immediate experience, lack of candor by government officials, and other examples of pollution of the stream of information, the problem is enormously more difficult, the marketplace of truth a much more obvious fiction. In this connection, the argument by James Weinstein in *The Corporate Idea in the Liberal State, 1900-1918* that the social reforms associated with the liberal state—the New Deal, the Fair Deal, the New Frontier, the Great Society—were really developed and guided not by political "progressives" but by sophisticated leaders of the nation's largest corporations and financial institutions, is worth repetition. [39] The purpose was to control "free market" competitiveness and combat the growth of anticorporation radicalism (particu-

larly socialism) as a political movement. Weinstein does not base his argument on a conspiracy theory of history, but he does posit "a conscious and successful effort to guide the economic and social policies of federal, state, and municipal governments by various business groupings in their own long-range interest as they perceived it."

In many respects, the corporation with substantial involvement in world trade—the transnational or multinational firm— provides better illustration of the enterprise as an instrument of governance (even though it is difficult and often impossible to garner precise factual data about those companies). The point may best be made by summarizing some of the governmental (i.e., political) aspects of the firm domestically and then looking to the multinational corporation. Corporations are governments, we have seen, for a number of reasons: they develop and allocate resources, attract the loyalties of millions of individuals, and generally perform functions indispensable to the members of the American society. Although not so considered in orthodox constitutional theory, they perform and have performed vital public functions. This was recognized by a seminal thinker, Henry Carter Adams, who wrote in 1902 that every great industrial enterprise is clothed with a quasipublic interest. [40] Not only is the public (as consumers) interested in the administration of the economy, but, of more importance, a business organization is a depository of social power and for this reason cannot be properly administered independently of social considerations. Said Adams: "Corporations were originally regarded as agencies of the state. They were created for the purpose of enabling the public to realize some social or national end without involving the necessity of direct governmental administration. They were in reality arms of the state, and in order to secure efficient management, a local or private interest was created as a privilege or property of the corporation. A corporation, therefore, may be defined in the light of history as a body created by law for the purpose of attaining public ends through an appeal to private interests." Of course, since Adams wrote (and even before), the myth was to the contrary: the corporation was a property interest existing for the sole betterment of the shareholders.

Calling corporations private governments may be misleading in one respect, for they are not really private. Their function is public. But labeling them that way is helpful for distinguishing them from the avowedly public organs of government. If our thesis is valid, however, we will continue to witness the gradual growing together of the two sectors.

That the corporation *is* a government existing cheek by jowl with public government in a pluralistic system, and at the very least exercising economic sovereignty, has been asserted by a number of qualified observers in recent years, including Earl Latham, Richard Eells, Adolf A. Berle, Alexander M. Pekelis, Wolfgang Friedmann, Robert E. Hale, Peter F. Drucker, John K. Jessup, Justices of the United States Supreme Court, and judges on other federal and state courts. [41] Government by private groups is an operational reality in the United States. However, it is one thing to label the supercorporation a government so far as domestic affairs are concerned and quite another to conclude that a corporation is a private government internationally. General Motors or the Ford Motor Company or any other supercorporation, as centers of economic power, wield such influence and exercise such control over many segments of domestic life that it is difficult not to consider them to be governmental in nature. Turning, however, to external affairs, can it be said that the large corporation operating mostly or substantially externally (e.g., the Arabian-American Oil Company) is also a private government? The answer can only be affirmative. [42]

In fact, it may be easier to equate, in politico-legal theory, the international "private" corporation with government than it is for the domestic firm. Sigmund Timberg has described the situation well in an article discussing the corporation as a technique of international administration; says he:

England, Holland, and the other great trading powers of the seventeenth and eighteenth centuries were delegating *political* power to their foreign merchants, when they permitted those merchants to engage—collectively and under corporate aegis—in foreign trade. In Maitland's classic phrase, these were "the companies that became colonies, the companies that make war." The same proposition holds for the modern large corporation. The modern state undeniably delegates *political* power to large private corporations, as it does to the large labor unions with which the corporate behemoths deal. The authorization of collective activity has, at least since the time the early Christian and Jewish communities had their difficulties with the Roman Emperors, always been a state prerogative. Furthermore, the activities authorized for a large corporation involve such functions as price-fixing, the division of markets, the setting of wages, and the general development of local communities, functions which in a pre-Industrial Revolution era had been the primary responsibility of the State. It has been said of international cartels that some of the more powerful of them "are little empires in themselves, and their decisions are often more important than those of 'sovereign, political' entities like Holland, Denmark, or Portugal." The same could be said even more forcefully of the political strength of that more cohesive unit, the international combine; the notion that international combines and cartels are strong *political* entities is no longer a monopoly of the intuitively minded economist or political scientist. Judges have described international cartels as instruments of "private regulation," and have called an American subsidiary the "commercial legation" of its British parent. Even the counsel involved in drafting international cartel agreements speak of a trade area as "so-called neutral territory," or to put it another way as "spoils belonging to the British and ourselves as allies in the late war." Such a consistent use of political terms is more than a mere metaphor; it is a recognition of an underlying reality. 43

The multinational firm, in short, is a true instrument of government, even though it does not have the outward trappings of a political unit. Observers such as Adolf Berle and Peter Drucker maintain that these firms do a better job of governing their part of world affairs than do the nation-states. They pose a distinct threat to the dominance of the nation-state.

LAW

Seeing the large enterprise as an instrument of governance means that the question of sovereignty must eventually be faced. Here politics shades off into law—constitutional law. The ultimate question, at least in formalistic terms, is surely sovereignty—which is ultimate power. According to Bodin and others, sovereignty is indivisible. But does that accord with the facts of politico-economic life? Is there, in the terminology of Lord Bryce, a "practical" sovereign as well as a "legal" sovereign? [44] The answer to that question can only be yes; we are, however, suggesting in this book that the two sovereigns are fusing.

Corporations did not necessarily acquire sovereignty merely by being permitted to exist. After all, during the growth and heyday of nationalism corporations handled the nation's credit and its transportation, as well as performed other important functions. But "practical" sovereignty did flow to the enterprises, particularly in international affairs but also domestically, when the state, either through indifference or preoccupation with other matters or by being subtly "taken over" by the supercorporations, endowed them with new and significant characteristics. "These new attributes," says Timberg, "were irrevocable immortality, a very large area of immunity from supervision by the state, and an indifference to (at times even a conflict with) the general political aims of the state." [45] Another way of stating the matter would be to say that public government has formal authority by which it ostensibly rules economic affairs but that in fact corporations exercise effective control over much of the details of those relationships. Shared power over economic affairs does not mean that the power wielders operate wholly independently of each other. Quite the contrary. Often the *political* sovereignty—the formal authority— of public government is invoked to aid the *economic* sovereignty of the corporations. As Wolfgang Friedmann has said, "Public and private activities, and with them, public and private law, are today increasingly intermingled." [46] The consequence is clear and unmistakable: *a constitutional change of major dimensions has taken place.*

Some of the ramifications on law and the legal system, including the private legislation in contract matters and the system of industrial jurisprudence that has grown up during the past three decades, have been noted above. Other changes in law are evident.

At the highest level—that of constitutional law— is the series of Supreme Court decisions that legitimized the government-business partnership—and that also have had the significant consequence of progressively blurring the line between public and private. No longer does the Court make final economic policy decisions, as it did prior to

1937. Now it accords a high degree of deference to the political branches of government. Of equal importance, its economic decisions are always subject to second-guessing by Congress, which has not been reluctant to use that power of "review."

A handful of decisions, federal and state, impose constitutional norms on private enterprise. Noteworthy in this development are the so-called white primary cases, under which political parties are not permitted to discriminate in primary elections on the basis of race. But, even more, there are those decisions relating also to racial segregation that have in large part erased the line between public and private so far as any business holding itself out to serve the public is concerned. However, here Congress has also entered the field, as in the Civil Rights Act of 1964, so that norms of a constitutional nature have been legislatively placed on business concerns. Businesses cannot now discriminate on the basis of race, color, creed, or national origin.

Of perhaps even greater importance is the group of cases, of which *Marsh* v. *Alabama* (1946) is the landmark, that place constitutional limitations on corporate activity outside the area of race relations. [47] In *Marsh*, a person convicted for trespass on the streets of a "company town" while trying to proselytize for her religion had that conviction overturned by the Supreme Court. The *Marsh* case was extended, perhaps significantly, in 1968: in *Logan Valley Plaza, Inc.* v. *Amalgamated Food Employees Union*, [48] members of a labor union successfully argued that the First Amendment should be read to permit picketing on the private property of a shopping center. To these cases can be added statements in scattered other decisions, federal and state, and some state court holdings that applied the Constitution directly to labor unions. The net conclusion seems clear: the constitutional line between public and private is being—perhaps, has been—broken down by the impact of such decisions. That is another way of saying that a form of corporativism is coming into existence. In addition to the system of industrial jurisprudence that has grown up around the institution of collective bargaining and the legislative character of contracts of adhesion, both of which have already been mentioned, noteworthy also is the growing body of government contract law governing the system of federal procurement, through which operations of many of the supercorporations are tied closely to government. In effect, although not yet in theory, these firms are "arms of the state." Government contract law not only regulates the transactions in government procurement but also has had and is having a considerable impact on "private" contract law. An aspect of government contract law is what can be termed "substantive" administrative law—and that makes up another category.

Administrative law—public law in general—is becoming dominant in the legal system. It is making massive inroads on traditional law—the private law of individuals. Contract is only one category. The law of civil wrongs—of torts, in legal parlance—is also being affected by the governmental dimension. So, too, with property law, which has been drastically altered in recent years insofar as it was a body of law based largely on possession of tangible real or personal things (land and chattels) and insofar as power flowed from being that type of property holder. The important type of property now is intangible, largely made up of some sort of promises:—contract rights, stock holdings, government benefits, and the like. [49] (And economic power, as Berle has said, is often exercised by those who in fact control little property, of whatever type.)

For law, the consequence of developments such as these is its politicization. Law no longer is viewed as a set of normative commands, a system of "thou shalt nots." Ever increasingly, it is becoming instrumental, for the American "democracy" has taken on the immense task of not only saying what the law is but what it should be. The "ought" element in law involves its inevitable mixture with politics. More important, perhaps, it requires the development of new theory to explain the twin demands on law—as a set of interdictory commands and as a system through which the values of the American people are translated into operational reality. No one has as yet produced that theory; it is a pressing requirement of the age. The role of law in social affairs, oddly enough, is still very much terra incognita. Our knowledge is primitive indeed; it is prescientific and far from precise.

The sum and substance of what has been said about the developing synthesis between economic and political power was aptly summed up several years ago by Professor Marver Bernstein: [50]

The fraternity of political scientists and public administration experts has increasingly accepted the finding that regulation is a political process. "Politics" is now rightly viewed not only as un-avoidable, but as essential to the formulation of policies that bear some rational relation to economic and technological con-ditions. As one scholarly study concludes: "The mentality which disdains 'politics' and strives for a neutral and technical perfec-tion rejects the very solvents that would reduce the obstruc-tions."

The synthesis leading toward the emergence of the technocorporate state can be seen throughout American society—in economics and politics and law and sociology. The organization is dominant; the individual is submerged. Corporativism has arrived in America. Even so, this should not be taken to mean that there is no merit in the new constitutional order. Indeed there is. Quite probably, it is only through the cooperation of government and business that the material wants of all Americans can be satisfied. (The wants of the mass of humans who live below the "poverty line" throughout the world surely cannot be satisfied, if they ever are, without some sort of mass production.) It is possible, of course, that what Americans want on a mass scale may not be satisfied, for it is by no means certain that the proper decisions will be made to spread the equality principle that far or that the environment will continue to suffer grievous blows. What does seem to be certain is that it will take the full and con-tinuing cooperation of the two dominant entities of the day to do the job, if it is to be done.

THE LIVING LAW

To demonstrate in legal theory that a "corporate state" exists, one must show a nexus between government and the corporations (and other economic social groups). Historically (mainly in Europe) that connection has been established by statute or by fiat. In the United States, however, other than the abortive experiment in corporativism in the early days of the New Deal—the National Recovery Act of 1933 (invalidated by the Supreme Court)—no such overt legal instrument is discernible. The only present-day exception is the arms industry, principally those companies that owe their livelihood to federal contracts and that accordingly have the legal instrument of contract as a connector between state and enterprise.

Statutes, executive fiat, and contracts are elements of the "positive law," a body or aggregate of known legal precepts or rules. But since Eugen Ehrlich published his *Grundlegung der Sociologie des Rechts* in 1912 (translated in 1936 and published as *Fundamental Principles of the Sociology of Law*)[51] the postulate of analytical jurisprudence (positive law), that all legal norms derive ultimately from the authority of a politically organized society, that is, from the "sovereign," has been known to be at variance with reality. Not that analytical jurisprudence is not followed; it still is the prevailing ideology of the American legal profession, as Judith Shklar showed in her 1964 volume, *Legalism*.[52] But that may be attributable to the well nigh infinite capacity of the human mind to delude itself, as well as to the difficulty to exorcise partially exploded beliefs.

The difference is between the "law in books" and "the law in action." If one looks only to the former, then corporativism cannot be demonstrated. By considering the latter, a different picture emerges. "The significant feature of Ehrlich's thinking," Roscoe Pound said, "is in its looking at the legal order, at the body of norms of conduct and at particular legal precepts functionally, and in marking the limited function of the norm for decision. He thinks of society, not as an aggregate of isolated abstract individuals, but as the sum of human associations having relations with each other. The inner order of the associations and relations which make up a society is ultimately translated into the positive law. Anything not soundly anchored in the living law stands little chance of surviving as an enforceable or enforced precept."[53]

If Ehrlichian jurisprudence is applied to the problem under discussion, then it is necessary: (1) to focus upon the important societal decisions and ask the question, *Who* makes those decisions, *how*, and with what *effects*? (2) to make a distinction between those who exercise formal authority to make such decisions and those who exercise effective control over them; (3) to have a knowledge of the factors that influence or control given decisions; and (4) to have an appreciation of what difference decisions make in the social structure.

These are large and difficult questions that can only be outlined here. The basic thought has already been suggested: that important societal decisions tend more and more to be made by an amalgam of the interactions of public and private bureaucracies. Often those decisions are put into official form through the formal authority of government officials—usually administrative or legislative but at times even judicial. Equally often—although neither area is quantifiable—corporate managers make those decisions; but corporations, we have said, are created for public purposes and as arms of the state; the managers thus have an express or tacit delegation of authority from the state. The flow of decisions, both those of overriding importance—the "high visibility" decisions—and the myriad routine "low visibility" decisions—constitutes the living law. That law, as Ehrlich maintained, is in contrast to that in force merely in the courts and with the officials. The living law is that law not imprisoned in rules of law, but which dominates life itself. The sources of its knowledge are above all the modern documents, and also immediate study of life itself, of commerce, of customs and usage, and of all sorts of organizations, including those recognized by the law and those disapproved by the law. [54] The living law, in other words, is the flow of decisions important to Americans. Some are made by private officers, some by public officials. Some, but far from all, are formalized in administrative rule, legislative act, or judicial decision. Many of those privately made are of national significance. Furthermore, many of those made by public officials are in fact influenced, not to say controlled, by outside forces, of which the giant corporation (and its managers) is the most important.

Law, then, is far more than the "command of the sovereign" or a corpus of known rules. As much or more unwritten than written, it is what the important societal decision makers actually do; it is a process, not a static system. The black-letter rules are important and necessary, but they are only part of the picture. The myriad routine transactions between the two characteristic institutions of the day—big government and big business—make up a body of living law of American corporativism.

A system of law exists in the United States consisting of the informal transactions between government and the corporations (and other pluralistic social groups). This system of law is the nexus that makes the corporate state a reality in legal theory. At times the system is formalized, but more often it exists as a set of working rules that are understood by the participants but that seldom receive formal cognizance. The system is not necessarily cohesive and consistent; it is a series of laws rather than a logical whole.

The complex web of informal interactions between economic entity and government is law because power can be exercised through its operation. Not codified or entombed in the musty volumes of law libraries, the living law of American corporativism is "invisible" law— something akin to John R. Commons's "working rules" of going concerns. [55] Commons spoke of a corporation's charter as a

> group of promises and commands which the state makes in the form of working rules indicating how the officials of the state shall act in the future in matters affecting the association, the members of the association, and the persons not members. It is these promises and commands, or working rules, of officials which constitute the charter and determine the status of the association . . . . This collective, intangible living process of individuals, the functionaries of the state find already in a trembling existence and then proceed "artificially" to guide the individuals concerned and give it a safer existence. The guidance is made through promising them a certain line of behavior on the part of public officials, which sets forth the limits on their private behavior and the assistance they may expect on the part of officials.

The suggestion is not that Commons openly embraced Ehrlichian jurisprudence, but surely his "working rules" seem to parallel the "living law."

This discussion of the theoretical basis for the legal connection between corporation and the state is but an adumbration—but certainly a compelling case can be made that it is valid. It does not have to refer to the corporate charter as the legal connection between government and corporation, although all corporations were so created. Lax, in fact nonexistent, enforcement of chartering laws and the possible visatorial rights accorded to state officials makes the charter merely an incident, albeit an indispensable one, in the life of a corporation. More is needed to demonstrate the necessary nexus in law. That can only come through scrutiny of the living law. Allen Schick has summarized the net consequence: "It is no longer possible to tell where private ends and the public begins as public and private funds and workers flow and work side by side in SST development, job training, and countless other programs. In the basic social accounts, the public-private distinction no longer is significant; more and more, the accounts concentrate on the aggregate social input and output, regardless of its public or private character." [56] We have, in sum, a new social order. A silent constitutional revolution has occurred.

In this chapter the fusion of the economic power of the corporations with the political power of the government has been discussed. That ends the argument of the book. We now turn to a discussion of the constitutional problems and consequences of the development.

part III

The argument analyzed

The development of a native form of corporativism has major implications for the American constitutional order. It warps the traditional Constitution. And it brings a host of problems with it, problems far from solved or even recognized. In Part III, these consequences and problems are discussed. The principal idea is to suggest that the immensity of the changes that have come, unbidden and without fanfare, involve the very capacity of government to govern adequately in the scientific-technological age. The Constitution remains a living instrument of governance— but is it adequate to present and future needs?

7

CONSTITUTIONAL PROBLEMS

> *The new partnership [between government and business]*
> *is emerging at the same time that a vast conglomerate*
> *merger movement concentrates a larger portion of our na-*
> *tional wealth in the hands of a smaller group of corpora-*
> *tions. The two forces accentuate each other, producing a*
> *unique brand of corporate state in which the government*
> *and private sectors threaten to coalesce in a way that could*
> *be antithetical to democracy itself. Countervailing forces*
> *—in industry, government, and even in organized labor—*
> *are meshing in power alliances that can signify the forma-*
> *tion of an elitist group with the power to determine the*
> *course it wishes to follow quite independent of the cus-*
> *tomary processes of popular democratic participation.*
>
> —RICHARD J. BARBER [1]

No substantial doubt can exist that a new socioeconomic order has appeared in the United States, one with profound constitutional consequences. Disputes are merely over the details of the type of social structure that is being built. Richard J. Barber, a former law professor who at one time was counsel to the Senate Antitrust Subcommittee and a Deputy Assistant Secretary in the Department of Transportation, tends to agree with our analysis—as the quotation reproduced in the headnote to this chapter reveals. In his recent book, *The American Corporation*, [2] he set forth many of the factual data underlying the thesis that we have stated above. Although Barber suggests that the corporate state presents many challenges to the political order, he does not develop them. No exposition of corporativism, however, can be complete without reference to and discussion of the problems, present and emergent, that Americans are called upon to face. In this chapter, some of them are outlined, with some indication of possible ways to overcome them.

The beginning, however, must be with two elementary propositions. First, it is likely that not many—perhaps only a few—will agree with the analysis in this book. To cite Richard Barber only does not prove anything; the proof of social effects is much more complicated than that. [3] The essential point was made some years ago by Professor Robert Dahl in an essay concerning the American business system. Discussing "corporate legitimacy," a topic to which we will return in this chapter, Dahl said that "as with most public 'issues' the role of business in American life is a matter of immediate concern only to a minority. It is extremely doubtful whether the problem of the 'legitimacy' of the power of the large corporation in American life is meaningful to anyone outside a tiny group of perceptive observers like A. A. Berle." [4] But that tiny group of social commentators is growing so that one may forecast with confidence that corporativism—the interlocking relationships between government and business—will be in the forefront of scrutiny by constitutional scholars and others in the future. That is so for no other reason than there is growing evidence of a deepset perturbation about the performance of American business. [5]

The second proposition is in the form of a question: What is a problem? That is, how are social problems recognized (and dealt with)? How are given situations considered to be problems? This may appear to be too elementary for mention, but it is not. If many scoff at the thesis of the corporate state, the same may be said about the problems listed below. Many will see them not as true problems but as "right" or "proper" situations, to be applauded rather than deplored. How, then, do we identify a problem? The question is important, if for no other reason than that the means and criteria of determining them may well control the result that is reached. As Theodore Sorensen, close advisor to President Kennedy said in a discussion of presidential decision making, "A President's decision may vary according to how the question is formulated and even according to who presents it," [6] a position that echoes what Justice Felix Frankfurter asserted in 1943, "In law also the right answer usually depends on putting the right question." [7]

Identification of problems is no easy task. The business community expends considerable effort to awaken people to the idea that they have problems, for which the businessman (as advertiser) has answers. "Sometimes we simply do not recognize that we have alternatives from which to choose, and opportunities to act. One purpose of advertising, for example, is to make people aware of decision opportunities that they did not previously know about." [8] We posit in this book that the emergence of corporativism poses a problem of considerable magnitude to the American people. How can that be demonstrated?

The concept of problem can be illustrated in several ways. For the individual, it might be represented simply by an unanswered question or as a measure of dissatisfaction or an unattained objective. Within society generally, a problem may reflect a dispute arising from conflicting claims of influential interest groups or by a situation where available resources cannot meet competing demands. Conflict, wherever found, is frequently equated with the concept of problem; Sorensen again provides apt quotation: "If I were to name the one quality that characterizes most issues likely to be brought to the President, I would say that it was conflict—conflict between departments, between the views of various advisers, between the Administration and Congress, between the United States and another nation, or between groups within the country." [9]

What all of these situations have in common is a situation involving an unsatisfactory present condition when measured against desired goals or objectives. This, in short, means that a problem arises when a person or group perceives a gap between expectations and demands. That, of course, says nothing about the ability to close the gap. Indeed, some problems may not be solvable. For example, human violence has been known throughout human history and shows no signs of abating, even though most people would probably call it a problem worth solving. If one is to believe the ethologists (such as Konrad Lorenz in his book *On Aggression*) [10] and others (such as Arthur Koestler in his *The Ghost in the Machine*), [11] there may be something inherent in the human psyche that makes violence unavoidable. In some problem situations, then, the persons involved may have no recourse but to suffer the deprivations either of deteriorating circumstances or of a continuation of the same adverse condition.

Usually a problem can be visualized as (a) a situation in which a person (or a group) knows that a loss in personal, group, or institutional net value position is probable unless some action is taken to try to correct that loss; and (b) a situation in which a desired gain in net value position is considered possible if a deliberately chosen course of action is taken to achieve a specified goal. This, to be sure, involves a knowledge of what a problem is and a thought-out set of goals on the part of the person or group. The latter, however, is by no means a common attribute of persons or nations. The job of the person or group under those two circumstances is to determine possible alternatives of action that will either minimize loss or maximize gain in net value position and then to make a choice or choices from among those alternatives.

Perceived that way, the concept of problem obviously is one of considerable difficulty. The existence or size of a specific problem is not always clear. For many years, even decades, overpopulation and the quality of the environment have been seen by some as major problems facing mankind, but it is only in very recent years that both have penetrated into the consciousness of enough people (in the United States) to make them acknowledged problems. A problem must be perceived before adequate response can be made (if such response is indeed possible): "The selection of problems which need solution is a creative act of the highest order. But it is a facility which does not require methodological expertise, as witnessed by the work of Aristotle, Karl Marx, and others." [12] Kenneth E. Boulding, economist and philosopher, put the point aptly:

> The perception of divergence between the perceived real value and the ideal value of any important psychological variable— that is, of any variable which is strongly related to utility or general satisfaction—may be labelled *discontent.* In this sense, discontent can be regarded as the prime mover of man to action provided that his image of cause and effect permits him to believe himself capable of such action as to reduce the divergence between the perceived real and ideal. We may notice a point here, the importance of which will be clearer later. The divergence between the real and ideal may be reduced by acting so as to manipulate the real. But it may also be reduced by adjusting the ideal. This is the way of renunciation—of wanting what you

get, rather than getting what you want. It is traditionally associated with Eastern philosophies, and if adopted it is a powerful deterrent to rapid change. [13]

What this means, in present context, is this: the problems listed below, although real and fundamental enough, may not be adequately met either through lack of desire (such as a failure to see them as problems) or by an inability to grapple effectively with perceived problems. If that occurs, then "adjusting the ideal" will indeed have to take place—in this case, the renunciation of some of the traditional values of American constitutionalism.

The implication is that the basic values Americans cherish will ultimately determine whether they will face up to problems brought by incessant, rapid change and the rise of corporativism. Whether this will be done is by no means clear at this time. Americans may persist in desiring material affluence, even though the gains will be short-term at best.

The final aspect of this too brief discussion of the concept of problem is this: it should be constantly borne in mind that human problems are never finally solved. [14] They merely get temporary resolutions, usually ad hoc, "pragmatic" adjustments of an incremental nature. As Lawrence Durrell says, "Nothing is ever solved finally. In every age . . . we are facing the same set of natural phenomena, moonlight, death, religion, laughter, fear. We make idolatrous attempts to enclose them in a conceptual frame, and all the time they change under our very noses." The most that *any* resolution of a social problem does, Alvin Weinberg tells us, is to buy some time. [15] Seldom, if ever, are true revolutionary measures taken; and even if they are, they merely create a new set of problems. John Dewey once said, "As special problems are resolved, new ones tend to emerge. There is no such thing as a final settlement, because every settlement introduces the conditions of some degree of a new unsettling." [16]

What, then, are the problems, present and emergent, of American corporativism? The following demand resolution if the ideals of American constitutionalism are to be attained.

THE PROBLEMS

The first problem is philosophic: the need for a new way of thinking, of approaching public policy questions, because change or motion has become epidemic in the United States and because of this nation's pervasive influence throughout the world. The problem, in simplest terms, is this: change must be managed if constitutional ideals are to be preserved ("achieved" is probably a better word). Science and technology, together with centers of decentralized power, must be brought under social controls that at once permit the urgent tasks of government to be performed and secure—nay, enhance—the values of humanism. Donald A. Schon has called this "the problem of the development of an ethic of change":

> The concept of an ethic of change very nearly appears as a contradiction in terms. Our norms are precisely norms for stability. We hold on to our norms and objectives, stand fast by them, keep them, and because we do, maintain a steady course which enables us to dispense with an ethic of change. Our moral heroes . . . are generally those who stand firm in the face of challenge . . . . We are apt to see change of objectives and norms, when it occurs, as inconstancy.
>
> And yet the problem of the development of an ethic of change now confronts individuals, organizations (companies and others), and our society as a whole. The individual asks, How shall I act when the foundations of my self (and the roots of my action) are disappearing? The company asks, How can we find our way into the future and maintain our integrity when it is no longer clear what business we are in? . . . Our society asks, How are we to guide our course now that the instrument of technology has eroded our objectives and we are deprived of the illusion of a stable state toward which we are headed? [17]

The notion is truistic, to be sure, but nonetheless one that is too little acted upon. Mankind still drifts, seemingly willy-nilly, without attempting that careful management of change so necessary to create the sort of social order that will maximize national ideals. That situation cannot last; more and more it is being seen as inadequate. We are in the midst of one of the most profound revolutions in history. On the one hand, total industrialization throughout the world is rapidly replacing the agrarian societies of the past (that "past," even in the United States, is not more than 100 years distant). The agricultural revolution, lost in prehistory, is the only comparable alteration, and then only in amount but not in speed of change. On the other hand, and speaking only of known history, within the past 500 years the human mind and psyche has been shaken as never before—and it is now on the verge of another enormous upheaval.

About 400 years ago Copernicus and others shattered the Ptolemaic conception of an anthropocentric universe. Not only is the earth not the center of the universe, it is not even central to the solar system. Man at that time began his known journey on "spaceship earth." The intellectual discoveries led John Donne to wail, "Tis all in peeces, all cohaerence gone." So it was and is—and the human animal has still not recovered from the shock. That blow was equaled by Darwin's views on the origin of species and natural selection. No longer was homo sapiens on a pedestal in God's creative scheme; he was just another mammal in the long process of evolution. The foundations of conventional religion were torn apart. Religion still remains, outwardly strong, but built on quicksand. Then came Sigmund Freud to plumb the depths of the subconscious and to show the hollow nature of the ideas of the Age of Rationalism and the ideals of the Enlightenment. The irrational side of man was revealed, another trauma that was even more intellectually upsetting when the published views of the ethologists (like Konrad Lorenz) on the inherently aggressive nature of man were added to the somber picture. Simultaneously another mental jolt struck—the idea of relativity, the view that there are no absolutes. Man was truly all alone and afraid in a world he never made.

If that was not enough—in fact, it was more than enough—we are now faced with still another intellectual ordeal. This one may be even more humbling, if that is possible. It takes the form of a paradox: just at the time that man's technical competence permits him to create whatever future he might want, he is faced with the ecological revolution. That intellectual cataclysm, in short, means that humans must give up their assumed status as masters of the earth and earth's creatures with the divine right to plunder, pollute, and treat those creatures as *things*. Instead we must recognize their needs and values and become their partners; we cannot continue to dominate but must willingly cooperate in an ecological cycle that, when broken, becomes irreparable. This must be done, and soon, but we have little time. Perhaps time has already run out. Perhaps the social and ecological ice age cometh.

This is not a matter of sentiment but one of basic survival. It poses in starkest terms the intellectual problem of the corporate state. Man has learned to harness the elements and to bend them to his will, but in so doing he has so plundered the earth that he is making it unlivable. Growing pressures of population on resources (it is the rich who pollute the earth), accompanied by ecological outrages (such as air, water, and land pollution) plus adverse effects of technological "progress" on the environment, have now reached the point where a conscious choice must be made to resurrect and preserve ecosystems that have sustained life for untold millennia. There is not much time—and that presents the truly fundamental problem of managing inevitable change. To stop ravaging the earth will require thought-out public policies that are designed to curb population and to preserve (and recreate) a balance with nature that will sustain life. The industrialization of the planet, now coming to its zenith (nadir may be a better word) with the operations of the twin gargantua of state and corporation harnessed together, has enabled man to plunder the earth, and, in so doing, to bring him to the edge of disaster.

Strangely enough, American corporation executives, who supposedly are hard-headed pragmatists and who pay little attention to ideology, are in fact among the most prominent who adhere to a new way of thinking. The large business enterprise must and does plan on a routine basis. It could not operate otherwise. It is government—"society" as a whole—that is derelict in the planning process, although, as we have seen, governmental action to manage the economy is taken in the halls of modern government. Government still tends to be ad hoc, hit and miss, of the "putting out fires" variety rather than the long-range, thought-out plan. Perhaps this is the way the industrial partners want it. As the basic planning unit within America, the corporations can thus have it both ways: they can plan and know what they want while simultaneously calling on government for any assistance they desire from time to time. By keeping government splintered, furthermore, special interests can be furthered without interference. It works well for individual interests—for example, the petroleum industry, which can get favorable policies promulgated without having to worry about some other agency vetoing them. This leaves the "public interest" largely unguarded and unprotected, swept away in that Theodore Lowi calls "interest-group liberalism."[18] In other words, the planning that government does, in which some halting steps are taken from the dead center of pragmatism, is often for the furtherance of what corporate managers want in individual situations. And that, in sum, is the essence of corporativism. The new type of thinking alluded to above does exist, thus, but in the wrong places and often for the wrong purposes.

A quarter-century ago, Morton White in an incisive book, *Social Thought in America: The Revolt Against Formalism*,[19] traced the influence of several seminal thinkers on American thought patterns: Holmes (law), Dewey (philosophy), and Veblen (economics), among others. Their essential message was aptly summed up in the title of his book: "formalism" in American thought was rejected in favor of fluidity, of pragmatism, of emphasis on means rather than ends. As is typical of the United States, which is characterized by violent changes in temper and thought, that revolt went much too far; the intellectual pendulum swung sharply to the other side. We are now confronted with the need, highly more important simply because the many abrasive problems of the human condition have created what biophysicist John Platt calls "the crisis of crises,"[20] of remedying that violent surge and recapturing if not some of the formalism, at least some of the sense of the ends and purposes of what is needed and wanted in the political and legal orders. (Platt's "crisis of crises" refers to the coalescing human problems of overpopulation, pollution, poverty, and peace, all of which now seem to have merged and come to a head, so much so that they have produced a social carbuncle that is in danger of imminent eruption.) The essence of the problem is to recapture the beneficial aspects of formalism while simultaneously permitting flexibility and fluidity of intellectual choice. Not an easy task, that. It requires adherence to external standards of judgment while at the same time not allowing those standards to be calcified into rigid dogma. Dogma is intellectual death.

That poses the dimensions of the problem. Let no one think that it will be easily or quickly resolved—or even that it will ever be. Although a growing number of social analysts perceive the need as stated here—an example is Professor Theodore Lowi in his 1969 *The End of Liberalism*[21]—the situation is far more susceptible of description than prescription. Intellectual habits die hard; even the mori-

bund formalism that White wrote about still persists in its old form in
many quarters. There is even a marked reluctance to admit that the
problem exists. But exist it does, ever more pressing, and until it is
realized and acted upon, many of the other problems of corporativism will lie unmet and unresolved.

No useful purpose would be served to classify all of the problems
brought by corporativism. Essentially they involve public policy questions, or, perhaps more accurately, constitutional matters, and thus
ran the gamut from law through politics and economics to philosophy and sociology and psychology. Nor should it be thought that they
are novel to the new type of state that has come into existence. Most
are ancient; they are the age-old problems of human governance that
have plagued man (and political theorists) since the beginnings of
known history. But they are cast in a different form so they tend to be
new to the American experience. Only in recent years have the people
of this country had to face problems that have been epidemic in other
lands for centuries, even millennia. That realization, just now being
driven deep into the consciousness of Americans, is reflected in a
wholly new phenomenon—the loss (or lack) of confidence by Americans in their institutions. Our age of innocence died; it was dealt a
mortal blow by World War I but it lingered on until after World War
II. Becoming all too clear is the hard fact that what not long ago was
glorified as "the American way" has serious shortcomings, not to say
faults. One of the sobering lessons here is the fact that of several dozen
new nations created since 1945, not one has modeled itself after the
United States.

THE STATE AS A "GROUP-PERSON"

The Positive State, as a collectivity, is the hypostatization of the
public interest—and the public interest is greater than the arithmetical sum of the private interests of the nation. That in briefest
form is a statement of the architectonic problem of American corporativism. Government in the modern era has to some degree taken
on a momentum of its own, separate from and greater than the individual interests of the nation.

As has been noted previously, President John F. Kennedy put the
thought in express terms in 1962 in the context of a prior assertion by

the Secretary of Labor concerning an alleged public interest in collective bargaining negotiations. In response to a question at a press conference, the President said: "These [steel] companies are free and the unions are free. All we [the executive] can try to do is to indicate the public interest which is there. After all, the public interest is the sum of the private interests, or perhaps it's even sometimes a little more. In fact, it is a little more." With those words, the President articulated a view of government basically different from that which historically existed (at least in theory). Within the confines of the public interest as so stated by the President can be found both the essence of positive government and many of the problems inherent in the new posture of officialdom vis-à-vis the persons and groups of American society. It also posed directly the question of who is senior or dominant in the government-business partnership.

That President Kennedy's press-conference statement was no accident, or no aberration in his thinking, can be discerned by referring to his oft-quoted demand in his inaugural address: "Ask not what your country can do for you; ask what you can do for your country." That starkly states a philosophy of group dominance over the individual. This is not to say that President Kennedy consciously espoused a philosophy of corporativism; but it seems clear, if one takes the two statements just quoted and adds to them actions that he took as President (escalating the Vietnam conflict, the Cuban missile crisis, and his imbroglio with the steel companies in 1962), the conclusion seems unavoidable. President Kennedy thought in terms of a transcendent "public interest," one that he as President had the duty and responsibility to enforce. President Johnson echoed that holistic conception of the nation not only in the Vietnam conflict but also when he sent 20,000 troops to the Dominican Republic. On at least two occasions, Johnson publicly maintained his constitutional right to commit more than 500,000 troops to Vietnam without regard to any congressional authorization.[22] President Richard Nixon and his administration repeated the pattern. They asserted an inherent right to tap telephones,[23] without either congressional or judicial authorization, and Nixon insisted that he had the power to wind down the Vietnam conflict in his own way and at his own pace.

In net, then, slowly but subtly a new conception of government has become the norm. Only in times of extreme emergency (Lincoln in the

Civil War is an apt example) did previous Presidents assert such powers. [24] In other words, the slow aggrandizement of power in the presidency, a process that has been going on for decades, has now reached
the point where it is tacitly recognized that the President is dominant
in government and can enforce a conception of the national interest
that overrides the prerogatives of the other branches of government—
and can go to the point of the ultimate (waging war, with a consequent
loss of life of tens of thousands of Americans). President Kennedy in
the Cuban missile crisis brought the nation, and thus the world, to
the very brink of nuclear war, a war that could have resulted in
hundreds of millions of deaths. An awesome power, that, dread in its
implications.

Speaking of the state as a group-person in that way transcends, of
course, the economic sphere. It is a statement of the concept of constitutional raison d'état, with the state as an entity with drives and
purposes of its own and with interests that dominate those of the populace, individual and group. That concept—"constitutional reason of
state"[25]—means that the state (in the American system, the President) can take actions to protect the integrity and viability of the
nation even if those actions would in other circumstances be morally
repugnant. Anything that will help insure survival of the nation as determined by the President is valid under this conception—a notion, it
should be noted, that the Supreme Court has approved (although not
in express terms of raison d'état). This makes, says Amaury de Riencourt, the President "the most powerful individual human being in
the world today." Reincourt, a European commentator, believes that
the President of the United States in time will become a "full-fledged
Caesar," for today he wears a number of hats—"as Head of State,
Chief Executive. Minister of Foreign Affairs, Chief Legislator, Head
of the Party, Tribune of the People, Ultimate Arbitrator of Social
Justice, Guardian of Economic Prosperity, and World Leader of
Western Civilization." [26] Quite a load, to be sure, but the character-
ization has at least a ring of validity.

The state as group-person is not a mere collection of separate
human beings, plus the pluralistic social groups that those individuals have formed. Rather, "it is an entity in its own right, endowed with
a life of its own, a collective life greater and far more lasting than the
lives of the separate individuals who belong to it." [27] To that state-

ment by Riencourt might be added the perplexing question of whether the state as group-person has or will have a life greater and more lasting than that of the supercorporation. We have noted above that some commentators believe the corporation is posing a distinct threat to the nation-state, struggling for domination, and that it may prevail. Our thesis, however, is somewhat different—that the corporation and the state are entering into tacit (sometimes, overt) alliances that will preserve the appearance—the facade—of the political order with the underlying socioeconomic reality being far different. It is in this latter sense that we speak here of the state as a group-person, the state being the corporate state. Seen that way, then there appears to be validity in what Riencourt says and also in what Sidney Webb, the Fabian Socialist theorist, said: "A society is something more than an aggregate of components. . . . Its life transcends that of any of its members. . . . The individual is now created by the social organism of which he forms a part." [28]

The blurring of public and private or the corporate state as group-person are two ways of speaking about the same phenomenon. It is the fourth leg of our definition of American corporativism.

The Positive State, as a collectivity, reifies the "public" or "national" interest—and those interests are greater than the arithmetical sum of the private interests of the nation. In the modern era, government—an amalgam of public and private organizations—has taken on a momentum of its own, separate from and greater than the individual interests of the nation.

The state has become a group-person in the way that Otto von Gierke used that term. To Gierke, "groups were real persons—real 'unitary' persons, existing over and above the multiple individual persons of which they were composed." He was convinced that "the group really and truly *is* a person," but he was not convinced that it was "an organism, but only that it [was] like an organism." Said Gierke: "Properly understood, the analogy [to real persons] only suggests that we find in the social body a unity of life, belonging to a whole composed of different parts, such as otherwise we can only perceive in natural organisms. We do not forget that the inner structure of a Whole whose parts are men must be of a character for which the natural Whole affords no analogy; that here there is a spiritual connection, which is created and developed, actuated and dissolved, by

action that proceeds from psychological motives; that here the realm
of natural science ends, and the realm of the science of the mind begins." [29] Gierke drew upon biological and psychological analogies to
buttress his "assumption of a real corporeal and spiritual unity in
human groups." [30] However, he relied very little upon psychology. As
his chief translator, Ernest Barker, put it, "The group which he
[Gierke] has in mind, with its group-personality and its group-will, is
not a psychological tissue, connecting the threads of individual
minds: it is a sort of high reality, of a transcendental order, which
stands out as something distinct from, and something superior to, the
separate reality of the individual." [31]

If one applies Gierke's analysis to the nature of American corporativism, it is readily evident that he appears to be talking about the
nature of human groups other than the nation-state. But his analysis,
particularly the notion of a transcendental order, is applicable to the
present discussion. A substantial segment of American constitutional
law is concerned with the rights of a never-defined entity called "society." [32] In litigation before the Supreme Court, the rights of individuals are said by the Justices to be "balanced" against the rights of
society. Save in marginally significant cases where no great societal
impact is discernible by the Court, the balance is struck on the side of
society. The Constitution may speak in seemingly absolute terms, but
the law is different. [33] Whether they realize it or not (they probably do
not), the Justices are espousing Gierke's notions of a mystical entity
called society, which they have reified into a group-person, when they
balance the interests of individuals against the collectivity.

Group personality, then, exists, expressly articulated by recent
Presidents and inferentially by the Supreme Court. The same can be
said for the supercorporations when they are considered as separate
entities. One should view them holistically, with the totality being
greater than the sum of the individual parts. "The" corporation has
become a group-person—in Earl Latham's label, "an anthropomorphic superperson whose reality is as real as that of human
beings." [34] One must seek to penetrate beneath the shell of both state
and corporation (and corporate state) and find its inner core. "We
must," Ernest Barker said in 1933, "not talk of 'fictions' which hover
in a shadowy and unreal existence above a number of real individuals; we must not talk of 'collections' or 'brackets' or contractual nets,

flung over so many individuals to bind them one to another in the bonds of an impersonal nexus."[35] In other words, what is to be seen are two group-persons, corporation and state, and their marriage into one overriding social organism. When President Kennedy said that the public interest was more than the arithmetical sum of the private interests of the nation, he was recognizing the state as group-person. Whenever actions are taken and justified "in the national interest" without delineation of the reasons therefor, but merely "on faith," further tacit recognition is given to the idea.

There is a great danger in viewing the state as a group-person. We can do no better than to use the words of Ernest Barker: "If we make groups real persons, we shall make the national State a real person. If we make the State a real person, with a real will, we make it indeed a Leviathan—a Leviathan which is not an automaton, like the Leviathan of Hobbes, but a living reality. When its will collides with other wills, it may claim that, being the greatest, it must and shall carry the day; and its supreme will may thus become a supreme force. If and when that happens, not only may the State become the one real person and the one true group, which eliminates and assimilates others; it may also become a mere personal power which eliminates its own true nature as a specific purpose directed to Law or Right." [36] That, in short, is corporativism. One need not probe very far into actions of American Presidents and courts to determine how deeply that view has been assimilated in the American polity.

Corporativism, of course, is to be distinguished from syndicalism, which is a doctrine relating to the autonomy (or sovereignty) of groups, particularly economic groups. [37] Of French origin, in its more extreme form syndicalism would eliminate the state entirely, replacing it with a congeries of economic groups, predicated on the notion that such groups are anterior, and should be superior, to political organization. More moderately, syndicalism is a theory of condominium between the state and groups based on a view that sovereignty is plural rather than unitary. Writing in 1913, J. N. Figgis, in his well-known *Churches in the Modern State*, postulated such a moderate form of syndicalism. [38] He viewed the nation as a large hierarchy of interrelated societies, each alive, each personal, and tried to vindicate for each what he called "the necessary independence of a self-developing personality." Figgis was mainly interested in the church, but he also sought to link its cause with the cause of groups in general. He rejected the idea of the position "of *corporate groups in the State*"; he thought that to be false, contrary to the facts. "It makes," said he, "the world consist of a mass of self-existing individuals on the one hand and an absolute State on the other; whereas it is perfectly plain to anybody who truly sees the world that the real world is composed of several communities, large and small, and that a community is something more than the sum of persons composing it—in other words, it has a real personality, not a fictitious one. This is the essence of what is true in modern nationalism, and in the claims for the rights of Churches and of Trade Unions." In other words, Figgis pleaded for recognition of the need for strong social groups to counteract the overweening power of the state.

Accordingly, if groups, such as corporations, have a "real personality," that could lead to syndicalism. But the far more likely result is corporativism. What Gierke and Figgis and Barker, among others, have not noted is that corporativism emanates from the fact that groups have found it useful to merge their power with that of the state in an interlocking series of relationships that allow groups not only to retain sovereignty in fact—economic power, that is—but also to call upon the political sovereign for aid and assistance when needed. The intermesh in the United States is neither pure syndicalism nor pure corporativism. The latter, as Barker intimates, postulates the state as "the one real person and the one true group." The "corporate state, American style" is a new entity, the result of a merger of the economic power of groups and the political power of the state. And it is being built by inadvertence—by slow accretion—not ordered by fiat. The difference from historical corporativism can be seen by comparing a statement of Benito Mussolini, who personified Barker's fear of totalitarianism: "The higher personality (*personalita superiore*) is that of the Nation. . . . The Fascist State, synthesis and unity of all values, interprets, develops and actuates the whole of the life of the People. . . . For Fascism the State is an absolute, in whose presence individuals and groups are the relative. . . . It is *anima dell'anima. . . realta etica. . . volunta etica universale.*"[39] In the United States, the fusion between group and state has produced something new in the manner in which humans order their affairs. It resembles corporativism but makes it unnecessary to answer the fundamental question of who is senior or dominant in the partnership. The emerging entity is a politico-economic organism that is sui generis, a "super-group-person" at once larger than both the state and the corporations.

The answer as to which is in control, in Mussolini's terms, which is the "absolute," is this: *neither the corporation nor the state is dominant in America, but both, working together, are dominant in the nation (and perhaps in the world).* And they work together and for each other much more than they conflict. Each needs the other and uses the other. The benefits tend to flow more toward than away from the corporations. What is required is a new label, not syndicalism and not corporativism, but something that combines both. In this book we have adopted corporativism as that label. However, a more precise term would at least by hyphenated—perhaps something like syndo-corporativism or corpo-syndicalism. But since labels are unimportant, we will continue to use the term as in previous chapters, emphasizing once again that no neat political theory fits the American model. The modern state is something new under the constitutional sun, not only for the United States but for other countries as well.

WHO DETERMINES THE "NATIONAL INTEREST"?

The modern state is also the managed state in the sense that a system of planning exists (as we have seen), particularly in economic matters. The American system of economic planning by the super-corporations, often, perhaps usually, in concert with their surrogates in government, can accord with constitutional principles only if the totality of the resulting decisions can be equated with the public interest (or, synonymously, the national interest). This poses fundamental questions for American constitutionalism. Who is to determine that public or national interest? How? By what criteria? Is it the President? The Congress? Both working together? Where does the Supreme Court fit into the pattern (if at all)?

These questions are far more easily stated than answered. American corporativism is distinctly *not* a unitary state. It is a series of *vertical* relationships between state and group. Only occasionally, and then usually in time of emergency, can the state, acting through government, enforce *horizontal*—that is, true public-interest—decisions.

This is the meaning to be given to Professor Grant McConnell's conclusion, quoted before, that a substantial part of governing power in the United States has come under the control of narrowly based elites, who are interested only in matters that directly touch and concern them. [40] At the most, the public interest or the national interest is what a government official (such as the President) or an organization (such as Congress) says it is: it has no substantive content, but it is a procedural matter. In other words, when the proper governmental ritual has been followed, then the decisions that result are said to be in the public interest. Or when the President says that the national interest requires, say, sending 20,000 troups to the Dominican Republic, the National interest is there by definition.

Obviously that is not enough, as Walter Lippmann pointed out several years ago in *The Public Philosophy*. Something more is needed; the concept must be given substantive content over and above the decisions that tumble from governmental decision-making spigots. But a definition is not easily come by. Lippmann's, for example, is so nebulous as to be useless: "The public interest may be presumed to be what men in the end would choose if they saw clearly, thought rationally, acted disinterestedly and benevolently." [41] To operationalize the term in more precise and less abstract language is difficult, perhaps impossible. Professor Stephen K. Bailey believes that the true test of the public interest is "the freedom of the individual men and women who constitute society"; more, he says, it is "the central concept of a civilized polity." Further:

> The phrase "the public interest" is the decision maker's anchor rationalization for policy-caused pain. Without such a concept, most presidents, congressmen, governors, commissioners, managers, and mayors—and, I should hazard, commissars, premiers and generals—would become unnerved. The moral buffer between social gains and losses consequent upon public decisions would disappear. The wounds incurred in the strife of policy battles would fester and rankle. Retaliations would become certain in their uncertainties.
>
> There is perhaps no better example in all language of the utility of myth than the phrase "the public interest." It is balm for the official conscience. It is oil on the troubled waters of public

discontent. It is one of society's most effective analgesics. But to have this phrase serve this purpose over time, public servants must be able to give it a rational content anchored in widely shared value commitments. The more that a society is built upon consent rather than upon threat and constraint the more this is true. [42]

How, then, to give the concept "rational content"? No one has been successful so far, even though attempts have been made for decades. The American constitutional order historically equated procedure with the public interest but we are now seeing that such a notion is hollow.

If, however, we are unable to say what the public interest or the national interest is, is it possible to postulate what it is not? Can it be said that the interests of narrowly based elites are contrary to the public interest? Quite obviously, the answer must be no. As a matter of logic, the private interest of such an elite can be either (a) in accord with the public interest or (b) contrary to the public interest—provided that the concept is given generalized attributes, that is, that it can be stated relatively briefly in a manner that encompasses government (or the state) comprehensively. We are driven, when all is said and done, to a view that no substantive content can or will be put into the concept unless and until the basic goals or values of Americans are articulated with clarity and precision sufficient for them to serve as a set of standards by which decisions can be evaluated to determine whether they coincide with the public interest. Unhappily, however, as we have previously said in the discussion about the perils of pragmatism, that is exactly what is lacking in the United States today.

This discussion of one of the truly basic problems of the corporate state must, then, end with a repetition of the plea already uttered—of substituting a new way of thinking for what now passes for thought in the making of public policy. To be somewhat more precise, however, these statements can be made:

1. What is good for General Motors *may* be good for the country—but not necessarily so.
2. What any government official or organization decides *may* be in the public interest—but not necessarily so.

3. Professor Bailey's assertion that individual freedom is to be equated with the public interest *may* be valid—but not necessarily so. It may well be that many, perhaps most, individuals would opt for something other than freedom—for materialism, for the warmth of the herd, for being something other than alone and afraid, alienated and insecure, in a world they never made. If so, if the majority chooses not to be free, then where is the public interest?

4. To be meaningful at all, the public interest must be more than a procedural concept. It must have substantive content. But that is an enormously difficult task.

Whatever conclusions one draws on such matters, nevertheless, the question is one of the most persistent in the modern state.

LEGITIMACY

The supercorporation has only a thin claim to legitimacy in the constitutional order. Power, to be legitimate under the Constitution, must ultimately be responsible and accountable and must be derived from the consent of the governed. In English history, corporate legitimacy came from recognition by the sovereign. But the same cannot validly be said for the supercorporation in the United States. Its power, as we have seen, is so great that it challenges government itself for dominance when the two institutions are viewed separately. When considered as a fusion of economic and political power in the corporate state, then the concept of legitimacy becomes crucial. It is an unanswered question.

Power always exists in human societies, the only questions being *who* exercises it and *how*, not *whether* it exists. As a new form of social order, the corporate state requires legitimization. The question is difficult, for it encompasses finding the "right or title to rule," which is the definition of legitimacy not only for officials in public government but also for the officers in the private governments of the land (the corporate executive). In this discussion, we focus first on the supercorporations and then show the relevance of that discussion to corporativism.

In the past, legitimacy has been founded on a number of beliefs, which in turn are based on a range of religious and metaphysical notions. These include a magical belief in descent from the gods, blood descent which equates rule with the right of property, the divine right, custom and tradition, and by those being ruled expressing a preference for the ruler (or the rule) by voting for him or her (or it). [43] The ruler in the American system achieves legitimacy because he has been voted into office.

Note, however, that this differs from the exercise of naked power. La Cosa Nostra—the Mafia—may have power to rule in certain situations and may, undoubtedly does, exercise it. But no one would say that the organization has constitutional legitimacy. The same can be said for the corporate oligarchs of the supercorporations, those who vote themselves into office, who are self-appointed and self-perpetuating, much like college boards of trustees. (Perhaps I should emphasize that I am not equating the Mafia leaders with corporate executives. What I am saying is that both have a large amount of uncontrolled power.) Harvard's Dean Edward S. Mason said it well: "Who selected these men, if not to rule over us, at least to exercise vast authority, and to whom are they responsible? The answer to the first question is quite clearly: they selected themselves. The answer to the second is, at best, nebulous. This, in a nutshell, constitutes the problem of legitimacy." [44] Now, as Dean Mason says, "some of our best people are oligarchs," but that merely means we are ruled by benevolent despots—not a very desirable practice in a nation that calls itself democratic.

The Positive State attained legitimacy because it was approved by the elective branches of government and stamped with the constitutional imprimatur by the Supreme Court. For the supercorporation, that status can only be because of long-continued usage and by a tacit recognition in law that these overmighty economic sovereignties are necessary, and thus desirable, for the attainment of the goals of the Positive State. The recognition in law comes both in private law (the "contracts of adhesion" discussed previously) and, of probable greater importance, in public law. In addition to the acceptance by the Supreme Court that the corporation is a constitutional person, that tribunal has held in a series of decisions that bigness is no violation of the antitrust laws. (That is possibly what Galbraith had in mind when he called those laws "a charade." Certainly corporations are far larger now and wield far more power than the "trusts" against which the legislation was aimed.) The political branches of government, not excluding the Antitrust Division of the Department of Justice, treat the corporation as an accepted fact and seek to employ it, not to change it. (Antitrust administration is noteworthy for proceeding against the inconsequential.) The corporation is considered necessary for the Positive State, indispensable for national security, and a tool adaptable for new uses (as in the Communications Satellite Corporation). Despite the antitrust laws, if the supercorporation did not exist, it would probably have to be invented. It is the American substitute for nationalization of industry; it preserves the facade and presumably the benefits of privateness without the detriments of the supposedly "dead hand" of government but with the benefits of subsidies and of the legal system. [45]

An intellectual foundation for the giant business firm has been provided by a number of commentators. Writing in the mid-1950s, Morton Baratz maintained that such writers as David E. Lilienthal, J.A. Schumpeter, J. K. Galbraith, and A. D. H. Kaplan, in their various writings, did just that: To them, "The activities of the giant business firm tend to bring about a more optimum allocation of resources, raise the level and reduce inequality in the distribution of income, and promote secular rise in output." [46] Those writers were concerned with efficiency, not legitimacy, and clearly point up the fact that a unidimensional—in this case, economic—analysis is not enough. If we are to understand the supercorporation, it will require putting economics and law, political science and psychology, sociology and philosophy, into a common vessel and distilling the essence, not only of legitimacy but of all of the hard questions about those titans.

Legitimacy, furthermore, is one of those nebulous concepts that academics argue about but that gets little attention from the practical men of action. The pragmatic bent in American thought, both in government and in business, accepts the corporation and bigness without even raising questions about them. Those men may, as Keynes once said, be intellectual prisoners of some defunct academicians, [47] but that does not seem to worry them. The system has evolved not in response to any precise or logical model, but as needs and opportunities developed. Academics and other scribblers, after the fact, try to find order and system in what has transpired. We may, however, be moving into a new era, one of "total planning"; if that is so, then future evolution would have to follow some type of preconceived model.

The questions of enterprise legitimacy must be faced, even more so as the American people seek consciously to guide the future and to create the social conditions permitting constitutional ideals to be maximized. As Dean Mason has put it, "a satisfactory contemporary apologetic [for the supercorporation] is still to be created,"[48] even though the intellectual (and political) attack on the capitalist apologetic of yesteryear was successful. In this task, he asserts, economists will have little to contribute, and it will be "the psychologists, the sociologists, and, possibly the political scientists who will be the main contributors. It is high time they were called to their job." Mason ignores the lawyers, illustrating the melancholy fact that most members of that profession have little or nothing to contribute to the necessary intellectual task.

Legitimacy is a problem for the domestic corporation, and even more so for the firm in world business. As Kenneth E. Boulding has said, "The international corporation faces a peculiarly difficult problem in establishing its universal legitimacy. Within a nation, the corporation achieves a certain legitimacy simply from the fact that it is incorporated by some public body. . . . The international corporations do not have even this shred of legitimacy, simply because there is no international body to charter them. The international corporation, that is, operates in a kind of governmental vacuum, and it has to depend for its survival on legitimacies which are derived from special skill, from bargaining power, or from the prestige of the national government with which it is most closely associated."[49] The economic sovereignty of the multinational corporation permits it to take action with few constraints, action that can and does have significant consequences, direct and indirect, on peoples in many nations. What cannot be determined, save on the basis of custom (as Boulding says), is where it got that right to rule. A further question is to whom and for what are the officers of the supercorporations (domestic and multinational) accountable? That question cuts across that of legitimacy; it raises further constitutional problems of the highest order.

Enough has been shown to reveal the depth of the problem of legitimacy, a problem that is far from solved. Perhaps it will never finally be, even though the corporations will doubtless continue to exist. Even so, until recently economists (and others) tend to accept or ignore the question. Witness Robert Heilbroner, writing in 1966: "The position of business within society was never more solidly entrenched. By this I mean that its legitimacy is now virtually complete, its acceptance without question. For perhaps the first time in American history there is no longer any substantial intellectual opposition to the system of business nor any serious questioning of its economic privileges and benefits."[50] Perhaps he would not be so dogmatic today. He wrote in the context of an analysis of the supercorporations and appears to equate absence of dissent with consent—which may or may not be valid. Even more important, however, since the publication of his book, *The Limits of American Capitalism,* many studies have been published that, although they do not oppose business as such, nevertheless raise serious questions about it and its privileges.[51] As of today, it is not accurate to say that legitimacy of business is "virtually complete." There is intellectual opposition—how substantial cannot be measured—to the business system. Whether the serious questioning of the "privileges and benefits" adhering to the businessman will long continue cannot be forecast with precision.

We have considered the problem of legitimacy thus far solely from the standpoint of the corporation. Difficult and knotty, it is far overshadowed by the further, more important, question of the legitimacy of the corporate state. Those who have the actual power to rule in modern United States must be accountable if their power is to be thought legitimate; they theoretically cannot exercise discretionary power uncontrolled by known external standards—uncontrolled, that is, by law. But that is precisely what the problem is for the supercorporations, for the bureaucracies of the public administration, and thus for the corporate state, American style. This is not to say that officials in those private and public bureaucracies are acting illegally—that is, against known interdictory rules of law—but it is to say that they operate within a legal system so flexible and so loose that their power for all practical purposes is unlimited. More precisely, it is circumscribed only by an inability knowingly to engage in acts that would be so outrageous that they would shock the conscience of the nation. The American government, it cannot be emphasized too much, is one of men and not of laws, if one uses the term "law" to mean a set of known external rules that substantially interdict official behavior. The same can be said—even more so—for the corporate manager (and the union leader). All act within a framework of "public law," which by definition is as much or more instrumental than interdictory.

Insofar as the policies of American corporativism are enunciated officially, they have been "constitutionalized," and thus legitimized, by a series of governmental pronouncements, congressional and presidential, which have in turn been upheld by the Supreme Court. That tribunal, acting as a spokesman for constitutional theory, has said that the Constitution permits the Positive State. It has also said, of course, that the Constitution permits the supercorporation. What it has not said, at least expressly, is that the two may merge into the corporate state. Its approbation can be gleaned only from the interstices of its decisions, as much from what it refuses to do (by rejecting many appeals) as from what it has done affirmatively.

Certainly the Court has constitutionalized the "administrative state"—the massive delegations of legislative power to the public administration—and has not stood in the way of further delegation (via contracting out) to private organizations. But the Justices have not seen fit to attempt to ameliorate the excesses of interest-group liberalism—Theodore Lowi's term for corporativism—and no one has seriously challenged that system in the courts. Lowi's prescription of "juridical democracy," set out in *The End of Liberalism*, might be said to be a plea for such action; but the recommendation is fuzzy and not susceptible of careful analysis or explication. The essential point is that the corporate state has not yet been expressly fitted into constitutional theory. There is growing opposition to it just as there is increasing disapproval of some of the practices of the supercorporations. That discontent may grow or it may cease or it may stay endemic in the American polity; but as long as it lasts, legitimacy will be a problem. Adherence to Ehrlich's "living law" theory may provide the legal nexus between state and enterprise, but that does not make it a part of American constitutionalism—not before considerably more intellectual effort is expended.[52]

ACCOUNTABILITY

If legitimacy is unsolved in the corporate state, then accountability is much more so. Accountability—the requirement "to answer in another place" for decisions and actions—is central to American constitutionalism. Again the problem is twofold; it refers to both corporate officers and government officials. Legitimacy means the right or title to rule, and accountability has to do with the details of how that exercise of governing power is actually carried out.

At least two levels of subproblems to accountability exist—first, the means by which true public-interest decisions emanate from the corporate state. We have alluded to the question above and will expand on the issue now. It is the basic problem of how to translate private greed into public good, when those who pursue their own ends have in effect co-opted government. In the discussion here, we will speak of the "politicization" of law and the legal process. The second level of the subproblem is insuring that corporate decision makers act properly, that is, in accordance with constitutional ideals of fair play with members of all of the segments of the corporate community, plus those who for some reason wish to become a part of the corporation (as an employee). This part of the discussion will focus on application of the constitutional precept of due process of law to the corporate entity.

To postulate a growing politicization of law is to assume that a different state of affairs existed in the past. But that assumption may not be valid; what may be seen now, in the political nature of law, is something that probably always was present but was so shrouded in myth and fiction that its true nature was obscured. The shibboleth that the American government is one of laws, not of men hides the hard reality that is diametrically opposed; it cannot be repeated too often that ours is emphatically a government of men, not of laws. Put another way, a high degree of discretion characterizes the activities of the corporate state, American style. Discretion is not "illegal" in and of itself; it may in fact entirely accord with statutes that have been validated by the Supreme Court. What discretion means is that those who are decision makers are bound in the main by the limits of the political process, not by those external standards of judgment that are interdictory law.[53]

When such ideas as "the rule of law" or a "government of laws, not of men" are talked about in their historical or ideal sense, the only meaning that can be given to them is that those who exercise power in America do so under the restraint of known external rules that circumscribe their behavior in definite ways. That is the traditional conception of law. But such a government has never existed in any absolute sense, certainly not in this country and obviously not at the present time.

To repeat: there is a rule of law today, but law should be seen as mainly *instrumental, not interdictory.* It is a tool for achieving desired results rather than a set of prohibitions. Statutes are law, the Constitution is law, the agencies of government make administrative law wholesale, and even the private governments of the nation make law—the latter in the "living law" sense espoused by Eugen Ehrlich. Public law, in other words, is the law of the corporate state, and that law is the marriage of an instrumental conception of law and politics. American legal theorists have not yet produced a useful analysis or explication of the role and nature of public law in the modern state; it remains one of the great intellectual challenges of the time. When a political theorist like Theodore Lowi says that the "new public philosophy is hostile to law," he affirms our assertions of the politicization of law. Lowi calls "liberal jurisprudence" a contradiction in terms; he asserts that liberalism is antithetical to law, even though it may be motivated by the highest social sentiments and even though "it favors the positive state only because the positive state is the presumptive instrument for achieving social good."

Lowi has a superb description of the faults of the present-day system of governance. His prescription, however, is only that of something he calls "juridical democracy," a fuzzy concept at best, which he seems to equate with the "rule of law." But he never defines law, save to assert that interest-group liberalism "has little place for law because laws interfere with the political process":

> The political process is stymied by abrupt changes in the rules of the game. The political process is not perfectly self-correcting if it is not allowed to correct itself. Laws change the rules of the game. Laws make government an institution apart; *a government of laws is not a simple expression of the political process.* A good clear statute puts the government on one side as opposed to other sides, it redistributes advantages and disadvantages, it slants and redefines the terms of bargaining. . . . Laws set priorities. Laws deliberately set some goals and values above others. [54]

Professor Lowi seems to be thinking of law in terms of a set of rules that would circumscribe the behavior of governmental officials. That is the ancient (and repudiated) idea of law, espoused by Blackstone and others, that there can be some sort of dichotomy made between "law" and "policy."

By thus failing to define law rigorously—and to see that it encompasses, now as in the past, both rules and policy—Lowi flaws an otherwise brilliant discussion. (He also indicates how much easier it is to say what is wrong than to put forth prescriptions of what should be done to remedy present ills.) One who speaks of law must, at the very least, ask further questions: *Which* law? *What* content is there in the rules? What criteria should guide an evaluation of those rules? For there are rules, but they are loose and flexible and they permit, as we have said, a maximum of discretion. The historical (Blackstone) juristic order has been forever shattered. Its relics lie all around us, intellectual artifacts from a bygone age, much like the way in which the marble columns of the Roman Forum still remain as physical remains of the Roman empire. What Lowi does not like is the flexibility, the ambit of discretion permitted the administrators of the corporate state.

In this position he echoes the complaint of federal Judge Henry J. Friendly, who in 1962 maintained that "the basic deficiency, which underlies and accounts for the most serious troubles of the agencies, is the failure to 'make law' within the broad confines of the agencies' charters" and that "once this basic deficiency is remedied, other ills will largely cure themselves; and that shadows and miseries will long be with the agencies if it is not." [55] Judge Friendly's point was that much of the "justified dissatisfaction" with the public administration is the failure of administrators and others "to develop standards sufficiently definite to permit decisions to be fairly predictable and the reasons for them understood." His indictment, as with Lowi's, is sound but his prescription is similarly faulty. He would make the administrative agencies look like idealized versions of the courts; he would judicialize the public administration. Further, he speaks mainly of procedure and does not get around to the substance of the standards he would like to see. That as we have said about Lowi, is precisely the problem. The procedure is there, the substance is absent; and it will not do to call for definite standards unless one is prepared to go on and make suggestions about what those standards should be. That Judge Friendly does not do. Accountability cannot be effected, in other words, within the corporate state unless and until there are *both* procedural rules making it necessary for officials to answer in another place for their actions and substantive rules that would insure that desired goals are maximized.

The problem is one of staggering immensity. It calls not only for restructuring government but for articulating national goals so that they can serve as the "definite standards" that Judge Friendly espouses. Take public economic policy as an example. Insofar as it is determined administratively, it tends to be the outcome of the conflicts of political forces. Government institutions are at once the object of that struggle and one of the participants in the contest. The aim is to control the flow of public policy decisions. Particularistic interests, such as the supercorporations, energize political forces and battle for influence in that process. Regulation and administration, especially in the higher echelons, tend thus to be a process of bargaining, of politics. Law there is: the decisions that emanate are law, "public law." But it is law that reflects bargains struck rather than adherence to established doctrines. This, to repeat, is not to say that the situation is new or novel to the American experience; likely it has always been present in reality, but not the myth. What is new is the size of government—the number of decisions it makes, the influences it has, its entire posture vis-à-vis the citizenry—which has expanded exponentially in recent decades.

The point is fundamental—and profoundly significant. Law increasingly has become visible as a purposive tool for the furtherance of goals desired by the bargaining process of politics rather than a set of inhibitory commands limiting the discretion of administrators or even canalizing their decisions. If administration is politics, the received notions, the conventional wisdom about the nature of law, become suspect and require thorough reexamination and reappraisal. Scholars must accomplish that task if ever a philosophical reconciliation of law and politics is to be forthcoming and if ever the administrative process both receives legitimacy and is made accountable in the light of the ideals of the historical Constitution.

We can move on into a rough transition to the second aspect of the problem of accountability—that of limiting the power of corporate executives—by noting the rise of elite structures in government and out. These elites interact routinely in the corporate state.

As elites, they exemplify what German sociologist Robert Michels

called "the iron law of oligarchy": "It is organization which gives
birth to the dominion of the elected over the electors, of the manda-
taries over the mandators, of the delegates over the delegators. *Who
says organization says oligarchy.*" [56] Michels wrote in 1911; his is the
major argument against popular democracy, against majoritarian-
ism, against the central threads of both democratic and socialist
theory. According to Seymour Martin Lipset, "Michels argued that
the malfunctioning of existing democracy, in particular the domin-
nation by the leadership of the society and popular organizations,
was not primarily a phenomenon which resulted from a low level of
social and economic development, inadequate education, or capitalist control of the opinion-forming media and other power resources, but rather was characteristic of any complex social system.
Oligarchy, the control of a society or an organization by those at the
top, is an intrinsic part of bureaucracy or large-scale organization.
Modern man . . . is faced with an unresolvable dilemma: he cannot
have large institutions such as nation-states, trade unions, political
parties, or churches, without turning over effective power to the few
who are at the summit of these institutions." [57]

Even so, Michels' formulation, even if we accept it, is not a sufficient description of many organizations. Some of them, of course, but
not all illustrate that "effective power" always rests in "the few who
are at the summit" of the organizations. In other words, there may be
considerable validity in Galbraith's observation in *The New Industrial State* about the power of the technostructure—the power, that is,
of lower echelon personnel, both line and staff, who can in large part
determine what the few at the summit see and can guide the manner
in which it is presented to them. The power of the bureaucracy, of
entrenched organizational modes of behavior, may be sufficiently
great to prevail over those ostensibly in charge. True, those at the top
have the formal authority to make the decisions; but the question,
often unanswered, is who has effective control over those decisions.
No answer that would cover the situation in general is possible.

However, this does not mean that the corporate state is not oligarchic. Indeed it is; the only question is who governs, not if the major
institutions are democratically controlled. A careful study of trade
unions led three sociologists to this conclusion: "The experience of
most people as well as the studies of social scientists concerned with

the problem of organization would tend to confirm Michels' generalization. In their trade unions, professional societies, business associations, and cooperatives—in the myriad nominally democratic voluntary organizations—men have learned, and learn again every day, that the clauses in the constitution which set forth the machinery for translating membership interests and sentiments into organizational purpose and action bear little relationship to the actual political processes which determine what their organizations do. At the head of most private organizations stands a small group of men most of whom have held high office in the organization's government for a long time, and whose tenure and control is rarely threatened by a serious organized internal opposition. In such organizations, regardless of whether the membership has a nominal right to control through regular elections or conventions, the real and often permanent power rests with the men who hold the highest positions."[58] The myth to the contrary notwithstanding, the "popular rule" model of government, whether public or private, does not reflect reality. Michels' insight into the governance of organizations is valid. This means that some sort of elite structure in fact exercises real power in the modern state.

That elite need not perforce be cohesive, a class apart, one in which the individuals of the class identify with each other. But it would likely tend to have loose working relationships among members of the elite. Certainly those who are on top of the heap in the several vertical power pyramids of the nation have more in common with each other than they do with the small businessman, the farmer, the worker, or the typical college professor.

If we apply the conception of the elite to the corporate state, American style, one major problem is immediately apparent. Speaking quite generally, students of the American political order have not developed data adequate to substantiate generalizations about how the managers of the supercorporations relate to government. Only in very recent years, and then only in broad generalities, have studies appeared. The point has been made by Arnold Rose in his *The Power Structure:*

This assertion [that the economic elite controls government] might have a degree of plausibility if empirically supported ex-

planations were offered as to the means of linking the conspiracy to the observable facts of power. But the conspiracy theorists who adopt the economic-elite-dominance hypothesis do not
offer such explanations as far as the observable facts of political power are concerned. . . .

I understand these and other statements by Mills to mean
that the economic elite has taken over control of the Executive
branch of the government. But just exactly how they have done
that, he does not say.[59]

Rose's reference to Mills is to the latter's well-known *The Power
Elite*, published in 1956, which postulated control of the key decisions in the United States by a loose combination of corporate
managers, high military officers, and political officials. The criticism
of Mills is a fair one, for his volume is notable for a paucity of empirical data. But studies since 1956 show the close interlocking relationship between business and government and the devices by which
business is able to exercise, if not total control, then certainly great
influence over governmental decisions. Professor G. William
Domhoff of the University of California has noted six major links between big business and government: (1) continuing organizations
such as the Council on Foreign Relations, the Business Council, the
National Planning Association, and the Committee for Economic
Development, which routinely advise government agencies and have
close working relationships with them; (2) presidential task forces
and commissions, the members of which tend to be drawn from a
small, narrowly based group of people; (3) special committees of
executive agencies, described by Professor Grant McConnell as "a
direct 'pipeline' to government for businessmen"; (4) appointments
in the executive branch, which tend to come from a rather small
group of "upper class" people; (5) political campaign funds, which
often tend to be camouflaged but which come from the corporate
rich (the cost of campaigns having skyrocketed in recent years, politicians are all the more beholden to the donors of contributions); and
(6) lobbying.[60]

How much influence businessmen exercise, and in what way, are
questions not yet answered by careful students of the political process. Just why this is so is an interesting question: why haven't po-

litical scientists taken up the task of finding out "who governs" in fact? Professor Robert Dahl has made that point: "The difficulty . . . is that we do not have anything like enough carefully formulated case studies of the roles of the businessmen in politics. To be sure, library shelves sag with cases in law, business and public administration. But few if any of these cases are useful for testing hypotheses about influence, for the relevant questions were not in the minds of the authors." [61]

Elitism is prevalent in both public and private government. Noted above has been the proposition that law, in its historical sense, usually does not interdict what the elite wishes to do. Law is used as a purposive tool to effect desired policies. Lawyers are the specialists who are able to find that given policy alternatives have a basis in law. [62] This does not mean, it should be noted, that *no* interdictory rules exist. Of course some do, but only in broad generality and principally in areas that have little to do with what official policymakers wish to do. In other words, if government officials agree that a given policy is desirable, there is little in the corpus of law to stop them. Furthermore the Supreme Court will not erect any barriers. The problems of governance tend to be "political" rather than "legal" (in its historical sense).

When one views the corporate officer, much the same pattern emerges. Some rules of law may be discerned, rules that curb his behavior, but nothing of a truly significant nature. "The need to answer in another place" may be central to American constitutionalism, but it is a need unfulfilled for many power holders. Just as there has been a loss of "citizen" sovereignty insofar as the elite structure of public government is concerned, so there has been a loss of "consumer" sovereignty with respect to the corporate giant—as well as the sovereignty of other groups within the corporate community. [63] The power of corporate managers, John F. A. Taylor has said, "is arbitrary quite independently of the motives which guide them in their performances. Nothing is gained by supposing the modern captain of industry wicked or malevolent. Unread in the arts of Machiavelli, he could school philosophers and princes in the real conditioning of power." [64]

The corporate elite exercises power that knows few bounds so far as law is concerned. But here again, they are not acting "illegally,"

for the general framework of law permits an immensely wide discretion. The law is less a system of prohibitory commands than a
broad dispensation to rule—insofar as the other groups in the corporate community (noted in Chapter 3) permit them to do so and
within the amorphous confines of the regulatory proscriptions of
government. Corporate officers have much flexibility and freedom of
maneuver. And they use lawyers as "ambassadors" to leaders of
other power centers as well as sources of suggestions that permit
them to achieve objectives within the law, and without running afoul
of any express prohibition. The lawyer, in other words, is a power
broker for the corporate leader.

If one were to believe the classical economists (and their present-
day disciples), the businessman really does not have to be concerned
with ethical or legal behavior. Acting as the personification of "economic man," bent ceaselessly on maximizing profit, he is considered
to be controlled by the "market." Market forces, or as it is sometimes put, consumer sovereignty, supposedly operates to control
antisocial behavior. The intervention of external command (law) or
government is not necessary because an "invisible hand" magically
translates the pursuit of selfish gain into the overall public good. The
market, in short, is said to operate as an external standard. By
merely being, it performs a vital societal function.

That this model of politico-economic activity no longer is adequate is quite clear. Quite likely it never was, save in the published
lucubrations of economists who sat secure in their ivory aeries taking an Olympian and magisterial view of human affairs. Something
else is needed in an economy dominated by corporate giants, operating in the corporate state. That "something" traditionally has
been the law. In some limited degree, law does operate to limit corporate decision making. For example, the antitrust laws set boundaries, admittedly very broad, beyond which corporations cannot
openly go; labor laws require bargaining in good faith with the union
over a range of disputes; and the restraints of law operate to some
extent to protect the public (pure food and drug laws, automobile
safety standards, etc.) against the more outrageous examples of corporate greed. However, it seems clear that in the higher reaches of
corporate activity, and certainly in the basic decisions that mean so
much to Americans (such as investment decisions), law plays little or
no part.

The problem that this poses is twofold: how can accountability be effected with respect to (1) the internal units of the corporate community and (2) the external segments, including the public at large? In essence, the first is a matter of due process of law, to use constitutional language; and the second is a question of how to insure that true "public interest" decisions are made. It will be recalled that the supercorporation has been defined as a federation of interests: internally, the security holders, the corporate managers, the rank-and-file employees, the technostructure, and the union managers or leaders, and externally, the suppliers, the dealers, the consumers, and the public generally. The fundamental concept of due process of law can be used to apply to all elements of both segments, save the largest and most nebulous (the public at large).

To pose the question, Should corporations adhere to due process norms? is another way of stating the question, If the Constitution were to be rewritten today, what would be said in it about the supercorporation? The labor union? The suggestion here is that because the corporate giants (as defined) are truly governments, albeit private governments, constitutional precepts should be held applicable to them. Of those principles, due process is the most fundamental. We can begin with a statement of sociologist William M. Evan:

> There is a growing awareness of the need for restricting the powers of the corporation. In particular, it is being argued that the courts and legislatures should extend constitutional guarantees of procedural due process to the corporation or that corporations should develop their own "supplementary constitutional systems." The venerable doctrine of due process . . . includes a complex of procedural safeguards, against the exercise of arbitrary and unlimited power. These norms seek to insure that disputes are resolved impartially and fairly. This complex of norms includes the right of all parties to be heard, the right to confront witnesses, to cross-examine them, and to introduce evidence in one's behalf.[65]

In other words, if a corporation takes action adverse to any member of the corporate community, it should be in accordance with the standards of fairness that sum up the concept of due process of law.

Those decisions that touch and concern members of the corporate
community directly should not be left to the whim or caprice of the
corporate oligarch. Included among those protected, if such a concept were to be applied, are employees, suppliers, and dealers. Some,
of course, are already safeguarded; for example, members of the
union are by legislative mandate. But the question that is posed by
the problem of accountability is much broader. Should due process
become a constitutional command directed at corporate managers
and should it be imposed judicially?

Taking those questions in reverse order, whatever due process
does exist within the corporate community has by and large been the
result of legislative commands—labor laws, and the Automobile
Dealers Day in Court Act, to cite two examples.[66] That is a limited
coverage. Labor laws do apply wherever collective bargaining agreements are in effect—in, that is, the basic industries—but their provisions apply only to members of the union. Other groups within the
corporation do not enjoy such protection—not the white collar worker, not the supplier, and not the dealer. An exception to the last category is the automobile industry, where a statute does exist purportedly giving franchise dealers of auto manufacturers their "day in
court" under their agreements with the manufacturers. That statute
is a congressional intervention into the corporate community, one in
which an attempt was made to redress some of the arbitrary practices inflicted on local auto dealers. Its success has been minimal at
best.

Other than such relatively insignificant applications of the due
process concept, little has been done, save in one area: civil rights.
There, the Civil Rights Act of 1964 represents an effort to redress
some of the wrongs black Americans have suffered for so many
years. Among other things, it provides for an Equal Employment
Opportunity Commission, which has as its mission the enforcement
of the provisions of nondiscrimination in employment practices by
industries covered by the act. But the EEOC has not been effective
and other federal agencies have not made any sustained effort to
make the nondiscrimination principle stick. Even the federal contractor, which since 1942 has been under a promissory obligation not
to discriminate in hiring practices, falls far short of the desired end.
If due process can be equated, in a rough sense, with fairness and

decency, then these political attempts (by Congress and the President) to enforce nondiscrimination can be termed due process of law. However, here again the aim exceeds the grasp.

What, then, should be done, not only for black Americans but for all other individuals in the neofeudalistic entities called the supercorporations? Professor Evan suggests the extension of the due process principle, but he does not indicate in detail how that might be done. Should it come by more legislation, followed by strong and affirmative enforcement by the executive? Or should federal courts set the norm, establishing thereby a standard and leaving it up to the political branches to enforce?

Ideally, all branches of government would cooperate in making the rules and insuring that they are followed. There are reasons, however, for asserting that the judiciary is the one organ of government that most likely can and should take the lead. So to argue of course calls for an enlarged role for the federal courts, particularly the Supreme Court, at the precise time when that Court is under heavy attack and is receding from some of the advanced positions that it took during the twenty-year period between about 1948 and the departure of Chief Justice Earl Warren in 1969. No doubt many students of American government would maintain that it would place too large a burden on the courts and that it would be otherwise improper to ask them to do more, to take on a larger jurisdiction—that of the units of private governance, the supercorporations. [67]

That argument has merit, but it can be countered, even overcome. On the negative side, Congress (and the public administration) seems to be too closely allied with the supercorporations to be in a position to put more effective restraints on their behavior. True, Congress did enact the Automobile Dealers Day in Court Act, but the record of both legislative and administrative regulation of industry is so dismal that one would be ill advised to look in that direction for the type of legal breakthrough that is so vitally necessary. And on the affirmative side, the courts have been used as instruments by pressure groups within the nation during recent years, perhaps at an accelerated pace. The classic example is that of the black, who when he found that neither the legislature nor the executive (state or federal) was responsive to his long-repeated demands finally turned to the courts for relief. Haltingly at first, but then with a rush, the courts responded. The consequence is the elimination of official racial discrimination throughout the nation—no mean achievement, even though the norm that was erected is far from the social reality. The point, however, is clear: the courts, if judges take an expanded view of their role in society, could help to bring due process of law—and thus accountability—to the corporate community. We have seen in Chapter 4 that the Supreme Court in recent years has embarked on a new path, that of implanting a "concept of constitutional duty" in a few doctrinal areas on the units of public governance within the nation. The problem, then, becomes one of transferring an already existing approach to what are purportedly private entities.

If the sovereign state of Delaware is subject to the limitations of the Fourteenth Amendment's due process clause, and thus cannot deprive any person of life, liberty, or property without due process of law, and if it further must adhere to the same amendment's principle that it must give "equal protection of the laws" to all persons within its jurisdiction, then why should not the "corporate state" of DuPont or General Motors or United States Steel be similarly limited? By applying the Constitution to such enterprises—by "constitutionalizing" the supercorporation—might it not be possible to retain some of the benefits flowing from private ownership of business while simultaneously attaining a higher degree of fairness in the social order? A colorable case can be made for such a proposition. Requiring that the supercorporation, which we have defined to include the labor unions, follow due process standards may help maintain a wall of separation between the state and the corporation. Legislation would probably tend to crumble that wall, simply because it has to be broader and more all encompassing. If our hypothesis that the corporate state (with the state as group-person) is being created has validity, the imposition of accountability on the corporations through legislation would further that development, whereas the more limited, narrowly imposed judicial activity would not. More action by the courts might even slow down the seemingly ineluctable movement of events toward American corporativism simply because it could help to preserve the distinction between public and private.

To do so, however, requires a major constitutional leap—the concept of "state" or "governmental" action under the Constitution would have to be rewritten (in effect) by the Supreme Court. Not only would the concept of private governance have to be recognized, but a distinction would have to be drawn between official and private government. The first may be easier than the second, for if private governments are made subject to some of the Constitution's provisions, it would be quite difficult to differentiate them in fact from public governance. But the ingenuity of lawyers and judges should be up to the task.

Could the concept of state or governmental action be reinterpreted so as to include the enormous, overmighty economic entities called supercorporations? The short answer is yes; in fact, it already has been in at least two cases (as well as a number of analogous decisions). Since at least 1883, and doubtless before even though the case was never squarely presented to the Supreme Court, the Constitution has been said to run against governments only. The seminal decision came in the *Civil Rights Cases* (1883), [68] which effectively nullified post-Civil War legislation to enhance the status of Negroes. Said the Court: "It is state action of a particular character that is prohibited. Individual invasion of individual rights is not the subject-matter of the [Fourteenth] Amendment." Therefore, Congress had no power to enact legislation banning racial discrimination by innkeepers and owners of other places serving the public. Since that time the notion of what constitutes "state action" has been progressively broadened. This is not the place to trace the development in detail; however, some highlights may be given.

The *Civil Rights Cases* antedated recognition by the Supreme Court that the corporation is a person within the terms of the Fourteenth Amendment and thus is entitled to its protections. [69] That came in 1886 in what is surely one of the most important decisions in American constitutional history. The essential question, yet to be fully acknowledged by the Court, is whether a "corporate person" that has constitutional protections also has duties to adhere to the norms of the fundamental law. This is not to ask whether the natural person, the human being, has such duties, but whether the Court will recognize the transparency of the fiction that equates General Motors with an individual. That it should is the thrust of the argument here; and that it is can be seen from a series of Court decisions that find it edging ever closer to acceptance of the idea that giant corporations are private governments.

The first breakthrough into the realm of ostensibly private organizations being held to constitutional norms is a series of cases dealing with racial discrimination in voting in Democratic primary elections. After first holding that a political party could not be subjected to the Constitution, the Supreme Court in 1944 held in the landmark case of *Smith* v. *Allwright* that Negroes had a constitutional right to vote in primary elections. Immediately efforts at systematic and sophistication evasion of that decree were developed; for example, whites established a small group that designated candidates for the Democratic primary and then permitted Negroes to vote in the primary. But that scheme was negated in 1953 when in *Terry* v. *Adams* the Court held that the Jaybird Party, which had been set up to evade the *Smith* v. *Allwright* decision, [70] could not be foreclosed to Negro voting. Political parties, ostensibly private, had become so public-ized that they were held to be within the ambit of the state action concept. Their function was so fundamental, so basic to the workings of the American governmental system that the law, as Justice Frankfurter once said, would reach sophisticated as well as simpleminded schemes of avoidance. For present purposes, a "private," "voluntary" association has been "constitutionalized."

Of more direct importance is a pair of decisions a generation apart, *Marsh* v. *Alabama* (1946) and *Amalgamated Food Employees Union* v. *Logan Valley Plaza, Inc.* (1968), [71] both of which enforced the Constitution against business corporations. In the *Marsh* case, a member of a religious sect was arrested for trespassing on the private property of the Gulf Shipbuilding Company, which wholly owned the town of Chickasaw, Alabama. Chickasaw, a suburb of Mobile, looked like a typical American town. Mrs. Marsh wished to proselytize for her religion in the residential section of the town. Warned off by officials, she refused to leave, was arrested and convicted for trespass. But she argued that her right to freedom of religion, protected by the First Amendment, was violated by the conviction. Even though private property, she said, Chickasaw should be treated as any other American town; if she could constitutionally prospect for converts elsewhere, then she should be permitted to do so there. A majority of the Court agreed. For the first time in American constitutional history, a corporation had been limited by a specific constitutional provision.

That of course is freedom of religion and not due process of law. Nonetheless the decision rests as a time bomb ticking away in the Court reports ready for use. That that time may be approaching is a possible conclusion from the spate of recent civil-rights decisions relating to sit-ins in restaurants and other places of accommodation. In those cases the Court all but erased the state action concept, this time to find that privately owned places of business were so protected by state law and custom that they should be considered within the broad reach of governmental action. Again, the reasoning was not on "due process of law"; rather, it was first on state action and then on finding an invidious discrimination by businesses holding themselves out to serve the public.

The signal from the Supreme Court helped to trigger so much social pressure that by 1964 Congress passed the Civil Rights Act. It was promptly upheld by the Court. Technically, that act (and the cases validating the public accommodations section) did not reverse the ancient holding in the *Civil Rights Cases* of 1883, for the act applies only to businesses within the reach of the power of Congress to regulate interstate commerce. But what businesses are in interstate commerce has been so broadly and loosely interpreted by the Supreme Court that almost any organization—restaurant, motel, hotel, etc.—that serves the public and that has even a tenuous tie with commerce (by way of customers, food served, etc.) is within the reach of the act. In effect, then, if not in theory, the *Civil Rights Cases* of 1883 have been overruled; by a combination of political action and judicial approbation, the Constitution now applies to private businesses—at least insofar as Negro rights are concerned. Accountability—in law, although perhaps not in societal acceptance—had come to the corporation.

Other provisions of the Civil Rights Act apply to employment by businesses in interstate commerce, and the nondiscrimination clause has been a part of federal contracts for almost four decades. Here again political action is forcing constitutional norms on private businesses. "State action," long considered to be a barrier, was neatly sidestepped by using congressional power to regulate in commercial affairs.

Finally, the 1968 decision in the *Logan Valley Plaza* case held once again that a private company was subject to the First Amendment—this time the freedom of speech provision was at issue. Members of a labor union were arrested for picketing on the property of a shopping center. Their conviction for trespass was reversed by the Supreme Court, with the majority of Justices relying on the 1946 decision in *Marsh* v. *Alabama*. The *Marsh* time bomb had exploded—not entirely, to be sure, but enough to indicate that the 1946 decision was no mere one-shot aberration.

Some other judicial decisions exist, but none that call the corporation sufficiently like a government to bring the Constitution into play. In a few state courts, notably Kansas and California, labor unions at times have been held subject to constitutional limitations when they had closed-shop agreements. And there are scattered statements in some Supreme Court decisions to the same effect. Perhaps the other outstanding decision was one in which that Court assumed that the Constitution would apply to a private company (in this instance, a street-car line), but held on the merits that it had not violated rights of riders who had complained about music, news, and commercials being piped through the street cars to "captive" audiences. [72]

It should not be inferred that corporate "constitutionalization" has gone very far or has even been recognized as valid by many commentators. But the concept is far from dead, as the foregoing discussion reveals, even though it has more potential than actuality. However, it is an idea whose time has come, and one need not be thought overly rash to predict that this—and surely the next—generation of constitutional lawyers will increasingly be concerned with private governments. Corporate due process, within a broadly defined corporate community, will be central to that concern. Individuals directly involved with the supercorporation and who are subjected to some type of corporate sanction—loss of a franchise, failure to be accorded fair treatment in personnel policies, arbitrary action of any type—will, it seems likely, seek to invoke constitutional precepts. Possibly some plaintiff will even get a court to agree that he has a right to a decent environment—to be free from pollution—and get relief from what has become the newest American commonplace: the rapid "deprovement" of the planet.

The trend toward constitutionalization of the corporation has, however, been halted, at least temporarily, by some more recent

Supreme Court decisions. Although these decisions do not over-rule *Marsh* and *Logan Valley*, nevertheless they have not expanded the application of the Constitution to corporations. In fact, in the most recent, *Jackson* v. *Metropolitan Edison, Co.,*[73] the Court ex-pressly held that a public utility was not within the ambit of the state-action concept and hence could not be held amenable to due process standards. The case involved termination of a utility's ser-vice to a customer without notice and without a hearing. The lower courts had held that a hearing ("procedural due process") was re-quired, but the Supreme Court reversed. Some other recent deci-sions are of the same tenor.[74]

Nevertheless, there are no solid reasons for not making the super-corporations amenable to the Constitution. Certainly their power overshadows even (public) government itself in many instances. Nothing quite like the corporate giant has been known in human history. The growth of the living Constitution could—in my mind, should—be in that direction. That document should reach *all* in-struments of American governance, not merely those historically recognized. Eventually even the Supreme Court will perceive that need.

8

CONSTITUTIONAL CONSEQUENCES

> *A corporation is government through and through. . . .*
> *Certain technical methods which political government*
> *uses, as, for instance, hanging, are not used by corpora-*
> *tions, generally speaking, but that is a detail.*
>
> —ARTHUR BENTLEY[1]

That the rise of private governments has definite, even enormous, consequences for the American constitutional order should be obvious. The document of 1787 has been changed by Supreme Court interpretation; but more importantly, the social basis underlying the eighteenth-century words has long since been completely altered. This chapter outlines some of the more fundamental of the constitutional consequences.

HUMAN FREEDOM

Corporativism has ominous portents for the nature of human freedom. In a society dominated by a fusion of big government and big business, freedom means the attenuated liberty to decide which group to join—and not much more. We have already discussed the decline of individualism in this nation, including the individualistic basis of law, and the rise of the social group to dominance as the basic societal unit. In this brief discussion of liberty in the modern state, several propositions (in addition to the one just mentioned) will be advanced: (a) the values of materialism prevail over liberty; (b) people generally, instead of wanting to be free, seem to wish to belong (the herd instinct is dominant); (c) there is an American aristocracy of wealth (and of talent), an aristocracy that tends also to be hereditary; (d) this means that many Americans, particularly blacks, do not even have the attenuated freedom to join the group they wish; (e) citizen sovereignty in political matters (as has been previously said) is a myth; (f) the First Amendment's protection of freedoms of speech and of the press is hollow because its underlying assumption (of the "marketplace theory of truth") is invalid; and (g) repression, even totalitarianism, could result either through external threat or by the elite's feeling itself threatened from within, or both.

If, as we have said, the quintessential unit in American society is the group and not the individual human person, many of the other characteristics listed above follow as a matter of logic. Others, not so evident, require more discussion. Take the first proposition as an example: Americans honor liberty more in the abstract than in the actuality. If they have a choice, as often they do, between a higher degree of freedom and greater material wealth, they tend almost invariably to take the economic gain. A half-century or more ago when the unions were struggling for power during the heyday of primitive capitalism, all but the willfully blind or uncaring could see that necessitous men were not free men. The power of the state was used to countervail the power of the corporations and to permit the wage bargain to be balanced. Now, however, fewer are necessitous (some are, of course, even millions, but the point is valid for the majority), and the aphorism can be altered: men want neither to be free nor to be necessitous; rather, they want to be affluent. They are willing to trade a measure of liberty for the silken chains of high wages, fringe benefits, and pension funds. They opt for security. This is not to denigrate them, for the desire to be secure, physically and economically and ultimately psychically, is surely a primordial drive. Only the unthinking and those who already have it decry its attraction for others. Our point, however, is that freedom is not equally basic: it is cultural and likely is limited to a short period of time in a small corner of the earth (the last 300 to 400 years and the nations of the North Atlantic littoral).

The values of individualism and liberty are evanescent and transient, confined in time and space—values that in the future will be viewed as historical oddities. Join up or drop out are the *only* choices, and the former will prevail. There is little evidence of any countervailing tendencies, now that the "counterculture" has died.[2] The counterrevolution against material comfort and the middle-class values propagated by the corporate state was an aberration; it was the revolt of affluent youth against the very affluence that they have been given without effort on their part. The counterculture movement was not a true social mutation, with high survival value. Social rewards likely will continue to go to those who have the skills and techniques necessary to fulfillment of the complex mechanisms of the corporate state. A major reversal to a nonurbanized, nonindustrialized type of polity is not remotely probable. Other than some of the young—those James Michener called drifters—no evidence indicates that most people will choose anything other than greater or adequate material well-being.[3] True, the attainment of that status may prove to be hollow, but that will not deter those who do not have it. Should that statement be doubted, one has only to ask a black what he thinks of the great middle-class "revolt" against environmental pollution; blacks tend to see it as a threat to *their* chances to reach that plateau of middle-class affluence that so many whites have reached. Black smoke from chimneys means jobs—the greatest need for black Americans.

If people want materialism more than freedom, perhaps it is valid to suggest the rejection of freedom itself—or what Erich Fromm, in discussing the Europe of a generation ago, called "the fear of freedom."[4] Fromm, a psychoanalyst, said that people wanted to "escape from freedom." This to him explained adherence to Nazi and fascist movements in European nations.

One need not go as far as Fromm to be able to postulate that there does seem to be a marked herd instinct. One of the major human drives is the desire to belong; a person escapes from loneliness by becoming a member of groups. That tendency was chronicled in America more than a century ago by Alexis de Tocqueville.[5] Rather than being "autonomous men," people are "other-directed." They may still be anomic, in "the lonely crowd," as David Riesman has said;[6] but the clear tendency is visible nonetheless. Human freedom in the organizational society is indeed the attenuated freedom to decide which group to join—and people generally would not have it otherwise.

Our third point is that there is an American aristocracy in fact, one based on both wealth and family. It has become hereditary as well. Little doubt exists that wealth is concentrated in a tiny number of individuals. Recent studies have shown that, even with the alleged wealth redistribution schemes of the New Deal, that concentration today is about the same as it was before F. D. Roosevelt. [7] The aristocracy—read "elite structure"—is one of talent also; we have seen that the corporate rich co-opt members of other classes who are able to perform the technical tasks to run the machinery of the technocorporate state.

If this analysis is valid, then the direct consequence is clear—and of great importance to human freedom: the ground rules (the law) that set the framework within which individuals act in the United States tend to reflect the values and preferences of the American aristocracy. Important decision makers in both public and private government are drawn from the elite structure; and their decisions institutionalize what that elite wants. That seems to be accurate for judges, legislators, and administrators, as well as for corporate officials (and union officers). And what the elite cannot itself supply by way of manpower, it reaches into other classes to snare individuals with special skills and intelligence.

With the elite solidifying into an aristocratic caste, freedom for many Americans has been so reduced that they do not have even the liberty to join the group that they wish. True enough, some "new wealth" can be seen, and those who display talent early enough can go to the "correct" schools, get the "correct" education, and thus become minions of the aristocracy. The corporate rich can, in that way, replenish its intellectual talent, so much needed if the complex machinery of corporativism is to be kept viable. The legal profession provides perhaps the best illustration. It has long been used as a means of upward social mobility by members of the poorer strata of society. Lawyers are among the indispensable technocrats of the modern state, men of power but—and this is to be emphasized and reemphasized—only to the extent that they are allied with the real pools of power. A lawyer representing only himself is nothing when he approaches a governmental decision maker. Unless he speaks for a major group, such as a trade association (for example, the American Medical Association) or a supercorporation, his influence—his very ability to be heard by the decision makers—is nil. Lawyers, in other words, are important not because of intrinsic merit but because they have joined or represent a special group.

Unless one has the intellectual skills valued by the corporate elite, one has little chance of becoming important in a group or of even joining a group. The apt example is the inability of blacks to become members of some unions. Despite Supreme Court decisions, congressional statutes, and presidential proclamations, blacks in the United States still find it difficult, at times impossible, to be employed or even to join certain unions. Their freedom is hollow indeed, a mere shade of the ideal. If unions were to be recognized as what they are—private governments—then a possible constitutional remedy would be available, one that in time could change the pattern of exclusion, but little activity toward that end is evident.[8]

For a nation that prides itself as the main bastion of the "free world," that purportedly is built on principles of liberty, that ostensibly values the autonomous man, the yawning gap between the ideal and reality is dismal indeed. The dreary actuality can be traced in part to corporativism, a system that highly rewards certain intellectual attributes but which has little place for those who do not have them. In other words, the first industrial revolution by and large eliminated the need for much manual labor, by those who are called unskilled; the second industrial revolution, now in process, has rendered those who perform menial mental tasks obsolescent.[9] The computerization of industry ultimately means that a substantial part of the available work force is simply not required to run the corporations. Oblique recognition of that has come in the proposals for a guaranteed annual income and other schemes for socializing the human costs of corporativism, which should be seen as attempts to buy off discontent by providing a minimal level of economic well-being. No number of "make work" efforts, such as those to find jobs for the hard-core unemployed, will succeed in the technical environment that the giant corporations and government have created. The end result is not difficult to foresee: a large mass of unemployed and unemployable, a lumpenproletariat that may approximate the "proles" of Aldous Huxley's prescient *Brave New World*.

That such a situation will in turn breed frustration and despair and that it could, as a consequence, result in violence against the established order is only too evident. That is already seen in militancy among black Americans, those who have been foiled by the gap between actuality and the American creed. If blacks are joined by others left out of the mainstream of economic rewards in the corporate state, then one would be unwise indeed to predict anything other than a continuation of intensified tension throughout the nation—and indeed the world—as the ill fed, ill clothed, and ill housed among the poverty rows of the world see immense affluence in the North Atlantic community. Just as within the nation a situation of relative poverty will in time create situations of bitterness and frustration that will probably erupt in violence, so in the world, where those reactions will be even more intense. Lincoln said that the United States could not remain "half-slave and half-free"; the point is that it cannot remain with top-heavy affluence and a high degree of poverty nor can it long stave off the onslaught of those from the Third World who want to get a larger share of the economic pie.

But, more basically, social mobility, save for a few, no longer exists in this nation. In all probability, it was more mythical than real in history, Horatio Alger to the contrary notwithstanding. A lumpenproletariat crammed into a few megalopoli is one of the more explosive social conditions in the United States today. The same may be seen when the United States is compared with the Third World, where bleak conditions and hopeless masses are the norm.

It follows from what has been said, and from previous discussion of the decisional process within the modern state, that citizen sovereignty in political matters is in large part a myth. More, it is an unattainable ideal—now surely, but it was probably so in the past. In modern conditions, with the complexity of public-policy issues that are also usually quite remote from the immediate experience of individual Americans, with government secrecy policies coupled with manipulation of the news in a vast system of covert propaganda, with the private bureaucracies of the supercorporations mostly hidden from scrutiny by all except the few, with the proliferation of reading material (and radio and television) to the extent that it is impossible for any one person to assimilate or even know about what is published, it is unarguable that the social base of the ideal of citizen sovereignty has been forever shattered. Even for those who want to know and have the capacity to learn, the same situation prevails, although in a somewhat lesser degree. The lumpenproletariat, which may consist of the mass of Americans, is the manipulated object in the corporate state, necessary to its viability but not to its decisional processes. [10]

Saying that means, of course, that representative democracy has become a mockery. The principal function of its institutions is to formalize decisions taken by the elite. Congressmen, for instance, do not "represent" the constitituents who elected them, save only in the broadest sense; rather, they represent—are surrogates for—the elite structure among their constituency (and elsewhere in the nation). The corporate state could not function otherwise.

If this is valid, it should not be thought that the silent majority— what H. L. Mencken called the "great unwashed"—are unhappy with that state of affairs. Quite the contrary: they are not. As long as government continues to be a gigantic siphon that sucks wealth into its coffers and disburses it in the various versions of the welfare state previously mentioned, there is not likely to be any serious opposition to the death of citizen sovereignty. No one should think that the constitutional revolution that brought American corporativism into being meets with any substantial opposition from the people generally. Those who oppose are a few intellectuals, some remaining members of the counterculture of the youth, and the rising lumpenproletariat. The crowning irony, of course, is that while invisible chains tend ever more to shackle Americans, they think they are free. They are told that in an endless stream of propaganda that pours from government and from the mass media, which when coupled with the well-nigh infinite capacity of the human mind to hide harsh realities, enables them to hold inconsistent ideas in their minds. A strange paradox, that: Americans think they are free but at the same time apparently do not want to be free. (Perhaps that is an example of what F. Scott Fitzgerald meant when he said in that it is the mark of a first-rate intelligence to believe mutually inconsistent ideas at the same time and still function. [11] Perhaps, too, Americans might be likened to those Germans prior to World War

II, who, as Milton Mayer has chronicled in *They Thought They Were Free,* indeed did not realize that their liberties had vanished.)[12]

The mythical nature of citizen sovereignty also means that the theoretical basis of the First Amendment's freedoms of expression has been shattered (if, indeed, it ever existed). Not only does government employ the mass media in a pervasive system of propaganda (as Jacques Ellul has said),[13] but the Supreme Court's "marketplace theory of truth" is at best a romantic notion, one not pertinent in the present day.[14] There is, furthermore, a tendency toward monopoly control of the media, which the "media barons" having the final decision over what the people read and see. Compare a statement by English legal theorist Dennis Lloyd:

> In the complex web of our social and economic structure, which tends to place the vital organs of expression and public opinion in the hands of a few individuals or of the public authorities themselves, there is constant need to ensure that the essence of democratic values is not eroded at its very source. Is it really practicable to create a climate of genuinely free opinion and discussion within a framework of control retained by a tiny minority of powerful individuals and groups? As Lord Radcliffe has recently remarked, "Censors will be very powerful but will not even be identified as censors," for what may be permitted to emerge in these various organs of opinion may depend upon what the owners and publishers of newspapers and the producers of broadcast programs consider as suitable for the public eye or ear. Hence, in the future, the idea of law must not confine itself to grappling with the technical problem of giving effect to human values through legal machinery, but must take thought as to what means may be devised for ensuring that the stream of free thought does not dry up at its source, by virtue of monopoly control.[15]

Lloyd's plea may be another instance of calling for remedial action after the deed is done and probably irreversibly, for the stream of free thought may long ago have become a trickle at best. Politicians have become expert in manipulating public opinion, with the media barons as willing allies. As communication techniques have

improved and as learning and literacy have spread far beyond what
was true in eighteenth-century American, there has come a concomitant need that communication be managed so that the values of
the governing class—the corporate rich—will be furthered. Hence, all
but a tiny portion of the respectable press is establishment oriented, and the broadcasters seldom run counter to the official line.
This is not to say that they are "bought"; as said above about the
citizenry, they think they are free, but they are not. The managers of
the corporate state would not have it otherwise.

We come finally to the idea that repression will result if the elite
feels itself sufficiently threatened. When (and if) it does come, no
doubt it will travel under the banner of freedom; or as Huey Long
once said, if fascism ever comes to the United States it will be in the
name of antifascism. The elite has never been reluctant to use violence when considered necessary to stamp out threats, internal or
external. Internally the history of the labor movement, particularly
that of the IWW, provides impressive testimony of the point. [16]

Externally, the pattern is even more apparent. Not only is American history one of territorial aggrandizement, [17] it is a long chronicle of the use of military force to accomplish given ends. One need
look no farther than the Caribbean, where Marines were used for
decades to enforce America's fiat as law within that area. Dollar
diplomacy, backed up by gunboats, has not vanished, as the 1965
Dominican Republic episode evidences. Furthermore, once this nation gets into a war, it tends to wage it in a "total" manner, savagely
and brutally with little regard for the niceties of distinctions between combatants and noncombatants. War for America has been
"socialized." (The same can be said, of course, for other nations; the
point here is that a purportedly free counry can act in an uncom-
monly repressive fashion once war begins.)

In net, then, the conclusion is clear and incontrovertible: freedom in the corporate state is more ostensible than real.

THE CAPACITY OF GOVERNMENT TO GOVERN
ADEQUATELY

Next in this list of the consequences of the modern corporate state is
the apparently increasingly marasmic condition of government itself. Government cannot govern "adequately," that is, in accordance

with the ideals of the American Constitution. More precisely, it is incapable of coping with the manifold problems of an urbanized, highly industrialized, technological nation. It has become obvious that the 1787 Constitution has serious flaws.

One such shortcoming is the sheer inability of any government of any nation to control the corporations, particularly those with multinational characteristics. The political order simply does not have the resources sufficient to the need; even more, that order has become, if not the captive, then the surrogate for the economic order.[18] There is no real desire to place meaningful controls on corporate activity. That there should be has already been stated. That there will not be is highly probable. Little evidence exists that the structure of the emergent corporate state will be substantially altered. Some stirring in the direction of "participatory democracy" may be dismissed as a modern version of the age-old longing to return to a fancied golden age. The centralizing propensities of modern states will not be reversed. In all probability, they will become even more evident. There may be a revolt against authority in this nation, but the net result of that result will probably be to exchange one set of masters for another.

If that is valid, then a series of lesser problems show no immediate likelihood of rational resolution. Abrasive questions of race, deterioration of cities, technology continued as an end in itself, the need for an "optimum" population, environmental pollution in its varied forms—all these, and more, have pyramided into a social condition biophysicist John Platt has described as "the crisis of crises." Writing in *Science* magazine Platt discussed overpopulation, pollution, and nuclear war; he said: "The next decade is likely to see continued crises of legitimacy of all of our overloaded administrations, from universities and unions to cities and national governments. Everywhere there is protest and refusal to accept the solutions handed down by some central elite. The student revolutions circle the globe. Suburbs protest as well as ghettoes. Right as well as left. There are many new sources of collision and protest, but it is clear that the general problem is in large part structural rather than political. Our traditional methods of election and management no longer give administrations the skill and capacity they need to handle their complex new burdens and decisions. They become swollen, unresponsive—and repudiated."[19]

This statement, he says, "may seem uncertain and excessively dramatic. But is there any scientist who would make a much more optimistic estimate after considering all the different sources of danger and how they are increasing? The shortness of the time is due to the exponential and multiplying character of our problems and not to what particular numbers or guesses we put in. Anyone who feels more hopeful about getting past the nightmares of the 1970s has only to look beyond them to the monsters of pollution and population rising up in the 1980s and 1990s. Whether we have 10 years or more like 20 or 30, unless we systematically find large-scale solutions, we are in the gravest danger of destroying our society, our world, and ourselves in any of a number of different ways well before the end of this century." [20] Our juristic order, our political order, and our social order have been shattered by the crisis of crises: population and pollution, poverty and peace.

Doubtless it will be hard, even now, for some to accept that government cannot govern adequately. But surely the burden of proof is not on those who assert that proposition; the evidence is too numerous and prevalent to permit a contrary conclusion. This is not to argue that the conditions cannot be alleviated. Perhaps they can—and will. Only a glandular optimist will feel that they can be solved without hard and unremitting effort, an effort that thus far has been minimal at best.

Another set of problems, again traceable to the fundamental capability of government, is more economic than political. Inflation is one, a tendency toward autarchy another. Nations committed to goals of maximum employment, as in the United States, have been unable thus far to stem the tide of creeping—at times, galloping—inflation. Programs designed by government to create employment opportunities, to stimulate economic growth, to better the economic situation generally have had an invariable concomitant of spiraling prices. Efforts to halt or at least slow down that insidious movement have not been successful. Inflation is at least endemic, perhaps epidemic, in the United States (and other nations of the Western world).

At the same time, American programs designed to alleviate economic distress within the country tend to be at the expense of other nations. We prosper by "exporting" unemployment, by being able to provide more employment and high economic growth rates through the erection of barriers to the free movement of goods, services, and people across national boundaries. As some economists—for example, Gunnar Myrdal—put it, internal economic integration in the United States is accomplished at the expense of external disintegration.[21]

Our point now is that inflation and a tendency toward autarchy characterize the corporate state. Again, they reveal basic flaws in the system of government; they call for structural change at the very least. (What seems quite probable is that an imposed system of price and wage controls will be instituted within the United States in the near future.)

WARPING THE CONSTITUTION

We have suggested the rise of the technocorporate state and a system of overt economic planning, the constitutional consequence of the close connection between the supercorporations and the Positive State. The industrial system will be considered separate from government not much longer. Even with some judicial resistance,[22] it will be seen as half of the entity that includes both the giant corporations (and other decentralized power centers) and the state. Already the major federal contractors—those firms whose livelihood is dependent on government largesse—are a seminationalized branch of the economy, and already the railroads are public enterprises.[23] But firms that have a smaller proportion of sales to the government are more dependent on it for the regulation of aggregate demand and not much less so for the stabilization of wages and prices, the underwriting of especially expensive technology, and the supply of trained and educated manpower. That relationship cannot be denied or ignored indefinitely, even by lawyer-judges. Increasingly it will be perceived that the corporations are tightly locked into the administrative state. Already the line between the two is rapidly blurring; eventually will disappear. Americans then will no longer have to pretend that General Motors and U. S. Steel and AT&T are private businesses.

That renders time-honored political and economic theories irrelevant. The consequences for American constitutionalism are several and serious. Traditional constitutional forms have been warped; new problems have arisen. The corporate state, American style, has so altered the "living" or "practical" Constitution that the document written in 1787 has now been outmoded in basic particulars. These may be given in relatively brief, outline form.

FEDERALISM

Perhaps the most evident of the constitutional changes is within the federal system. The new patterns can be seen in three trends: (a) from dual to national federalism within the structure of "formal" federalism; (b) the burgeoning of "functional" federalism, that is, the growth of the supercorporations within the American polity; and (c) the advent of "federalism by contract."

Federalism is based on the assumption that the jobs of the state can be split and placed into separate pigeonholes, largely distinct one from the other. In the United States, at least, it grew to fruition when the prevailing notion was that of a strictly limited government. Since the change from the negative to the affirmative state, the original conception has undergone marked changes, not the least of which is the apparent necessity for one of the two governments to be dominant.

Whatever the intention of the framers of the Constitution, the two governments—national and state—were roughly co-equal in power during the formative years of the nation. Even though a series of seminal constitutional decisions by the Supreme Court gave early legal sanction for a broadly conceived exercise of national power,[24] the central government was reluctant to intervene in social and economic affairs. The first really important change in this attitude came with the Civil War, but it was not until the late nineteenth century that national intervention of a nonemergency nature took place in individual activities. Until the turn of the century, then, the federal system was correctly termed "dual" federalism. The jobs of government were few in number and could be split without undue difficulty between the two systems. Since 1900, however, the trend has been away from that conception. Although the myth still operates to indicate otherwise, in actual fact the structure of federalism has been greatly altered. Dual federalism has become "national federalism," or better, "national cooperative federalism." The formal structure of decision making under the Constitution, in other words, has been altered so that the national government is dominant in the federal system. [25]

The reasons for this fundamental alteration are not difficult to locate. They are the well-known changes that have taken place in the social and economic structure of the United States, largely since 1900: the industrialization and urbanization of American society, the growth of rapid transportation and communication, the impact of two world wars and the depression of the 1930s, the advent of the federal income tax with the result that the bulk of the tax dollars flows to the national treasury, and the lack of fiscal independence of state governments, with their consequent inability to fulfill the demands of their constituents and still remain financially viable. These and other similar factors have coalesced to bring about the demise of dual federalism and the establishment of the new model of formal federalism.

Law follows society and cannot run contrary to the mainstreams of societal impulse and belief. Even the Supreme Court recognized this in the late 1930s. Reluctant at first, refusing to believe that changes in American society meant inevitable concomitant changes in all law, including constitutional law, the Court finally gave its imprimatur to the unifying forces of American society in a series of landmark decisions. The leading cases, as has been seen, are those concerning labor relations and those that upheld the provisions of the Social Security Act (both old age survivors insurance and unemployment compensation). [26] These decisions gave final constitutional approval to the outlines of cooperative federalism. Once breached, the dam has never been repaired; the trickle became a stream and then a flood. The result is that today the federal grant-in-aid is the principal means of financing the new activities of state governments and an ever increasing segment of the traditional functions. State taxation systems take higher portions of the tax dollars, but federal grants or subsidies are looked upon as the main source of funds. The advent of the federal income tax in the Sixteenth Amendment, and subsequent legislation, has had enormous consequences for the nature of American federalism.

So far as the traditional federal system is concerned, the implications of the change are clear. Chief among them is that, to a large extent, states today operate not as autonomous units but as administrative districts for policies established centrally by both public and private government. No doubt it is inaccurate to think of them as hollow political shells, but it is true that the once-powerful state governments are being (or have been) bypassed by the movement of history. Save for "housekeeping" functions, they have little concern with the main flow of important decisions. When new problems arise, eyes swivel to Washington, not to the state capitol—where eyes also turn to the banks of the Potomac.

States still exercise a great deal of control over individuals—much more than in the nineteenth century—but that control tends to be in matters of relatively minor or purely local importance; or, more significantly, that power is exercised in the administration of policies emanating from Washington or the corporate headquarters. The transcendent issues get national attention and national resolution. In areas of major public concern the decision-making process has been nationalized so far as formal authority is concerned, the American people apparently not being willing to tolerate fragmentation of policy in those areas. The problems of government today—broadly, social service domestically and national security externally—are believed to be beyond the powers of the individual states to grapple with effectively. The demands that the American people are making today can be satisfied (if at all) only through the promulgation of policies uniform throughout the nation, and that means that the national government must be the chief policymaking organ of formal government; it must be the one to promulgate and place the official stamp of officiality upon decisions of more than local importance. Such an argument gives short shrift to recent ideas of "participatory democracy." Whatever that means, it seems highly probable that policies will be national, even though administration is local.

The basic alteration in formal federalism was noted by Harold Laski in the late 1930s. The federal form, he said, "is unsuitable to the age of economic and social development that America has reached." He asserted that the "epoch of federalism" was over.[27] Since that prescient observation was made, it has become clear that federalism as traditionally known has declined. There may be a strength of tradition, of the sentimental values of yesteryear, of a yearning for a long-vanished frontier, but the economic imperatives of the age of science and technology require uniform, even unified, policies throughout the entire nation and do not permit the kind of economic (and political) fragmentation that goes with truly effective member-state sovereignties. Some, to be sure, still appear to find elements of strength in federalism, and a movement arose in the 1960s for the development of what was called "creative" federalism—which apparently meant some sort of cooperative arrangements largely financed by the federal treasury. But these assertions and attempts belong more to the category of pious hope or yearning for a bygone age than statements of fact. Federalism in the sense of true dual government is no longer possible in the age of the supercorporations and the Positive State. The formal structure of government will likely remain but only as a facade behind which the great changes that have taken place are hidden. For that matter, it is by no means self-evident that the United States should remain divided into fifty states, a national capital, and assorted possessions. The time may well have come when some sort of actual regionalism—of the combination of contiguous states along natural lines and boundaries—should be seriously considered. Why should there be more than about ten or twelve states?

The fundamental changes in formal federalism are only part of the division of power between governments. In addition, and probably of far greater long-range importance, is the concurrent growth of "functional federalism." This, in short, encompasses the dimension of the systems of private governments existing within the United States.

Orthodox constitutional theory and doctrine recognize the existence of but two entities: government and the individual person. Nothing intermediate is envisaged. The Constitution limits government in favor of individuals, a notion based on the unstated assumption that individuals live and act as autonomous units. Not even the political party is mentioned in the Constitution, and it is only through a sometimes disputed construction that artificial persons are included within the scope of the constitutional individual. That concept, as we have seen, is a reflection of the philosophical ideas current in the eighteenth century, ideas of both a political and an economic nature that can be usefully summed up in what has been called the Protestant Ethic. Max Weber's hypothesis, popularized to some extent by Tawney, [28] of the close connection between the rise of capitalism and the burgeoning of Protestantism is the classic statement of the Protestant Ethic. A basic tenet of this concept is that of individualism, both political and economic, an individualism that later got its prophets (and apologists) in such writers as Adam Smith, Ricardo, Locke, John Stuart Mill, William Graham Summer, and Herbert Spencer, among others. As outlined by these and other commentators, the Protestant Ethic extolled the sacredness of property, decried the spiritually debilitating effects of security, and asserted the supreme virtues of hard work, thrift, and independence.

Constitutional theory should now recognize an entity intermediate between the individual and the state: the group—the basic unit of functional federalism, the wielder of effective control in fact over large parts of the American power system. The late John R. Commons once observed, in a statement relevant to the idea of functional federalism, that "the 'modern state,' or 'political power' . . . is increasingly focused upon the delegation of power to administrative commissions whose members are officials of government, while the 'new economic state,' or 'economic power,' is the corresponding delegation of power to private corporations whose officials are the boards of directors." [29] We speak now of power in the sense of making myriad decisions necessary to spell out a preexisting policy established by superior authority. We speak thus of administered capitalism, to use Adolf Berle's concept, [30] or of the delegated power of command, to cite Karl Renner, [31] and our attention is on the organs to which the state has entrusted the performance of some of its essential functions. The focus is upon the recipient of economic power—the large corporate enterprise or factory community—the most important of the pluralistic groups in American society. These are the functional units of economic federalism and the basic units of a system of private governments.

Just as the national government must entrust the administration of many of its national economic and social programs to the state and local officials, so it can be said that private entities are entrusted with the performance of their important societal functions. This can be called a delegation of power without doing undue violence to normal terminology or established doctrine. Historically it can be said that this was recognized in constitutional law in the concept of businesses "affected with a public interest."[32] But the label placed on it is unimportant. What is important is the existence of the factory community as an entity (in Kenneth Carlston's term, a "structure of social action"[33]) which, ostensibly private, in fact performs functions of a public governmental nature.

In an industrial society the most important units of local government are the supercorporations. The decay of American local governments, especially of town, city, and county, is primarily the result of a shift of focus to the giant firms. Compare the following observations: "The corporation is now, essentially, a nonstatist political institution, and its directors are in the same boat with public officer-holders."[34] "Even in 1787 Hamilton called the states a mere administrative convenience. Today they are not so much a sanctuary of sovereignty as a source of Senators. . . . Business is erecting a new basis of economic power that is beyond the reach of government. It is thereby helping to preserve freedom."[35] This system of private governments makes up the structure of economic federalism, or of functional federalism, as distinguished from formal (political) federalism. In 1908 Woodrow Wilson maintained that "the question of the relation of the states to the federal government is the cardinal question of our constitutional system."[36] Today that question has largely been settled, and the cardinal questions now for constitutional law are, internally, the relations of individuals and of the state to the other centers of power, and externally, the relation of the nation to the remainder of the planet.

That the state qua state does not exercise a monopoly of power is clear. Sovereignty is not unitary, Bodin to the contrary notwithstanding. Pluralism is the operative political fact of American society. "Many of the concrete functions of government are coming to be carried on 'outside of the pale and oversight of the state under the supervision of various specialized committees and functional associations,' e.g., neighborhood groups and labor unions. The legislature is not the only group enacting legislation; whoever makes policy is legislating. We are dealing here with functions, regardless of the structures—governmental or otherwise—which fulfills these functions."[37] This is the American brand of collectivism. The pluralism, in addition, can be thought of as pluralism of elites—the leaders of the groups that make up society and exercise sovereignty. Taking the factory community as the most important of these groups, the impact that community makes upon the allocation of resources, the level and distribution of income, the rate of economic development, and the price system has been examined by a growing number of analysts. In addition, a number of observers have remarked on the essentially governmental character of the activities carried on by the factory community. [38]

Further: "The law of corporations . . . might well be considered as a potential constitutional law for the new economic state; while business practice assumes many of the aspects of administrative government." [39] The factory community operates to perform important societal functions: economic development, production of essential goods and services, distribution—in short, the allocation of resources within the United States. In economics, it is the hub around which the economy revolves. Not the individual, but a collectivity that by legal legerdemain is considered in law to be an individual, is the basis of the national economic structure. The abstraction to replace economic man is the modern factory community. Peter Drucker puts it this way: "The abdication of individual property rights as a basis of social power is the central institutional change of our times." [40] He went on to say that the representative social phenomena of the industrial system of our time are the mass-production plant and the corporation.

No fanciful mental gymnastics are required to say that the factory community operates as the recipient of delegated power to carry out important societal functions. It is the economic counterpart—and superior, be it said—of the unit of political federalism, the fifty state governments. It is the basic unit of functional federalism. It is a private governmental system, performing some of the jobs of government. "As far as we can observe," says Berle, "the power system emerging is in essence federalist. It contemplates autonomous economic organizations—corporations. It engenders loose relationships between these organizations, usually for the purpose of stabilizing or apportioning the markets." [41]

Economic federalism thus exists as a patent fact of modern American political life. Of course the units of this system are not as clearly defined as are the units of political federalism. They are not geographically delimited; they are functionally organized. They are far more amorphous than the units of political federalism, and they call for focus on the decisions made by the group in order to ascertain their importance. They are the decision makers for a decentralized system of decision making. They are the units of "neofeudalism." As such, they tend to be far more viable and autonomous than are the states, which by and large follow the lead set out by central authority. And they raise real problems about their relationship to and influence on the state, problems of control, problems of how to limit the exercise of power.

Another form of federalism and other constitutional changes wrought by the rise of the technocorporate state demand attention. Writing in 1954, Dean Don K. Price called attention to what he termed "federalism by contract."[42] By that he meant the pervasive system of contracting out much of the public administration by a number of government agencies, principally the Department of Defense, the Atomic Energy Commission, and the National Aeronautics and Space Administration. Taking place is a delegation of authority to "private" organizations, profit making and nonprofit, to administer federal programs. It could be called "administration by contract." However labeled, the system is a significant alteration in time-honored ways of conducting public affairs as well as a marked illustration of a growing partnership between public and private organizations to accomplish important social matters. Welded together with the legal instruments of contracts and grants, the scientific community in America is in fact a triangular partnership of the federal government, business, and the universities. Billions of dollars spent annally for research development are not expended "in house," that is, with civil service personnel doing the work, but are farmed out on contract and grant. It is a system that enables government to get some urgent business done without the purportedly hampering effect of bureaucracy and the civil service laws.

Federalism by contract is comparable to cooperative federalism, for both entail power sharing with the national government. In the former, private entities are used to administer national public policies, whereas in the latter the purportedly sovereign states do so. The net result is the creation of a corps of personnel who receive their livelihood indirectly from the national treasury, but whose paychecks come from private organizations and state and local governments. Both exist as an external bureaucracy to the actual bureaucracy in Washington and the regional offices of federal agencies.

Private organizations often are functionally a part of the national government, whether in administration of (say) weapons systems for the Pentagon or by being influential over policies made by the formal bureaucracy (e.g., such organizations as the RAND Corporation). In substance as well as form, governmental policy in contracting out for services resembles public governmental activity. "Government, faced with public expectation that it will expand its functions but not expand its bureaucracy, freely farms out to private organizations staggering proportions of the public business."[43] Two consequences may be noted. First, public and private functions have become so intertwined that business often is no longer merely a supplier but is also a participant in the management and administration of a public functions. The line between public and private has been broken down. Second, a "feedback" of personnel between public government and private organizations having substantial contacts (or contracts) with government takes place. Harlan Cleveland made the point aptly:

> To get the expanding volume of decisions made, new social forms are developing. They tend to be large, complex webs of tensions, with power so diffused within them that the term "decision-making," which has been used and abused by a whole generation of political scientists is now quite misleading. Each "decision" about public affairs is now a complex process of multilateral brokerage both inside and outside the organizations primarily concerned. They are manned, these new style public/private organizations, by a relatively new breed of modern man, which I will call the Public Executive.[44]

Perhaps another term for this "new breed of modern man" would be the "technocrat."

In any event, the scientific-technological revolution, exemplified in the supercorporations and the Positive State, is having the effect of superimposing a third layer of federalism upon the constitutional structure. What began as dual federalism in 1789 eventually became cooperative federalism. At the same time, the growth of the supercorporations produced the system of functional federalism. In recent years, federalism by contract has become prominent. A growing body of constitutional, statutory, administrative, and judge-made law is developing to weld this complex, possibly unwieldy, system together.

SEPARATION OF POWERS

Americans have the most complicated government in history. Its complexity is nowhere better seen than in the federal system, formal and actual. But it can also be seen in the division of power of the national government—the misnamed separation of powers (for it is not that, but separate institutions exercising similar powers, quite a different thing).

If for purposes of this discussion we equate the state with the formal structure of the national government, then it is obvious that massive changes have taken place and will probably continue to take place in the manner in which decisions are made within government. The state illustrates the same differences between formal authority and effective control in the exercise of power that were outlined above in the discussion of modern federalism. The Constitution sets up a government system, but the hard logic of events has necessitated major departures from the original model. The 1789 model of a tripartite division of governmental powers has been giving way to what approaches a bipartite division and what threatens to become even more streamlined. Both the judiciary and the legislature have waned in their positions of relative power. That loss of power has been accompanied by a corresponding growth of relative power in the executive (including the administrative) branch of government. The changes can be summed up in five propositions:

1. The role of the Supreme Court in the national government has undergone a marked change in the past thirty years. The thrust of its powers is more in interpretation of the legislative and executive will than as an aristocratic censor through constitutional construction.
2. The bureaucracy has taken on a much more important position in the power hierarchy than it held historically. It is in fact a fourth branch of government.

3. Basic policy decisions are made outside the formal, constitutional allocation of governmental powers.
4. The executive—the President and his immediate office—
has taken an increasingly important role in the formulation
of state policy.
5. A "new" separation of powers has been created in the giant
corporations.

Each of these changes merits brief discussion.

Today the Supreme Court and the relative position of the third
branch of government have declined markedly in power vis-à-vis
both Congress and, particularly, the President. In questions of political economy and social welfare, the basic policy prescription is
legislative; the judiciary fills the interstices left by Congress in its
enactments. The spate of civil-libertarian decisions in the past thirty
years indicates, however, that the Supreme Court is something more
than an adjunct of Congress. With the change in governmental
posture from laissez-faire to affirmative intervention into societal affairs has come the change in role of the Supreme Court. It no longer
occupies the lofty position of aristocratic censor of the passions of
the multitude; within the national government, much of its work
deals with statutory, not constitutional, interpretation. Outside the
central government, however, with respect to the relationships of the
federal system and in enlarging the zone of officiality, the Court's
traditional role is more manifest.

In many of its relations to Congress, the executive, and the bureaucracy, the Supreme Court's ostensible power of judicial control
now must be exerted through less obvious channels—when it is done
at all. The occasional cases, such as *United States* v. *Nixon* [45] dealing with the presidential privilege of confidentiality, are more aber-
rations than the norm. That norm, despite the contrary conventional
wisdom, is of judicial deference; it likely will continue. Even the rash
of recent civil-liberties and civil-rights decisions is a last effort of a
once-powerful governmental organ before it, too, succumbs to the
pressing exigencies of the Positive State, which is now, and will continue to be, dominated by the President. There are some commentators who maintain that the alleged loss of power by the Court is il-
lusory. To these observers, the Court is and will continue to be far

more than a mere conduit through which pass the policies of the other branches of government. Moreover, as Professor Willard Hurst once said, "The really important area of judicial contribution to policy-making is in the field of the interpretation of statutes." [46] With the American power process as it is, with the state qua state not supremely dominant but locked into a fusion with corporate groups, those interpretations are ever increasingly subject to being overruled by Congress or ignored by the bureaucracy.

Ultimate power in policy formation rests outside the judiciary; the Supreme Court today operates in narrower, more canalized areas than it did historically. So far as civil-libertarian matters are concerned, the Court's surge of activism under Chief Justice Earl Warren did not set a permanent pattern. In other words, it is increasingly clear that a welfare state, in an age of mass "democracy," will not permit an essentially oligarchic institution to set basic policy. [47]

In final analysis, the role of the Supreme Court vis-à-vis other branches of the central government will be to effect an adjustment between the deliberately broad statements of policy enunciated by the state (in this case, Congress) and the infinitely detailed realities of industrial and community life. Examples of this role would include the federal labor laws and the antitrust laws, which can be viewed as legislative prescriptions of broad generality, which establish fundamental policy but which leave to the federal courts the responsibility for spelling them out and applying them to particular factual situations. In this status, possibly the Court is the most continuously active and influential faculty of political theory in the country. [48]

Even so, it is far overshadowed by the public administration. The second and fourth characteristics of the modern version of separation of powers are analogues of the first: the rise of the executive and the bureaucracy to positions of greater relative power. The growth of these two branches of government has characterized the rise of the Positive State.

Whether governed by Parkinson's Law, the bureaucracy has proliferated in quantity and has become far more powerful than ever before. Within the executive branch proper, and within the "headless fourth branch of government," [49] is located the nerve center of the American state today. The vast bulk of governmental decisions are made administratively, including many of great importance. Operating on broad delegations of authority from Congress, the administrators exercise a high degree of flexibility with only nominal supervision from other branches of government. Deference to the legislature by the Supreme Court has included deference to the creatures of Congress: the administrative agency and the government department. Some restraints exist in the threat of judicial review, but it is a fact that only a microscopic number of administrative decisions are reviewed by the federal courts. Even fewer are overturned. So far as Congress is concerned, the pattern is equally clear; congressional supervision of administrative decision is nominal at best, nonexistent in many instances. And with regard to the President, his is not a position of power dominance over the bureaucracy, even though he certainly exercises great influence over some of its decisions. The fourth branch of government, headless or not, is in its seemingly infinite complexity a fact of life today and an exerciser of considerable power in the governmental decision-making process.

Whatever was originally visualized as the office of the presidency, the chief executive is emerging as the strongest of the three traditional branches of government. As Edward S. Corwin put it, "Taken by and large, the history of the Presidency is a history of aggrandizement, but the story is a highly discontinuous one."[50] Try as some might to avoid the tasks of governing and of leadership, today's insistent problems do not allow it. One can even agree with Justice Black's poorly conceived opinion in the *Steel Seizure Case* (invalidating President Truman's takeover of the steel industry during the Korean War),[51] and say that only Congress can set policy, but even so, this does not eliminate the need for presidential leadership. The schoolboy version of government, recent talk about the "imperial presidency" to the contrary notwithstanding,[52] does not meet the pressing needs of the mid-twentieth century. A nation catapulted into world leadership and beset by continuing crises requires a government that takes affirmative steps to meet those crises. To do that, leadership is necessary, leadership that in the constitutional system only the President can furnish. A tripartite division of constitutional power into three roughly equal branches has had to give way to the demands of an industrial society and a shrinking planet.

Separation of powers and the formal structure of policymaking within the national government have been supplanted by an informal system cutting across the executive, administrative, and legislative branches. The picture is blurred and is difficult to get into focus, but it is obvious that the really important decisions made within the government are made by a relatively small group of men: the President and his closest advisers; the leaders of Congress, particularly the Senate; and the administrators directly interested in the decision to be made. This is decision making by a high-level committee with a shifting membership. Were it not so invidious in its connotations, such a committee might be called a supraconstitutional camarilla or junta. To some extent, this group has been given a legal basis in the creation of the National Security Council, with the "Forty Committee" acting in intelligence matters. Foreign-policy decisions find the President and Secretary of State often only formally the decision makers; informal committees of high officials have great influence, perhaps even control, over these decisions.[53] At some point, congressional leaders are brought into the picture and their advice sought, the lesson of Henry Cabot Lodge and his "little group of wilful men" and the League of Nations having driven home to the administrators the vital necessity of not eliminating the legislature from participation. The congressional leaders, in addition, are able to assess and report on the temper of their colleagues in the legislature, who will in turn have assessed the temper of the influential groups in American society, for the decision, when made, often requires subsequent ratification by Congress. Only Congress can make a law or a policy, or so the Constitution says and so the Supreme Court would have us believe. So the matter goes to "The Hill" for the ritual of discussion and final affixing of the imprimatur of officiality. The form is preserved, while at the same time allowing for the urgent business of government to get done. The result is that despite constitutional provision to the contrary, the broad official statements of national policy in the field of economic and social affairs, as in external relations, are often made by a small group of men acting as a unit superimposed on the constitutional system. A strong case can be made for the proposition that government by junta is a cardinal fact of late-twentieth century America.

Much like the "new" federalism is the "new" separation of powers. The rise of pluralistic social groups to prominence and even domination, largely within this century, means that a system of "private" governments has been created. Of them, the giant business corporation is by far the most significant. These corporations are the planning system of the American economy and are, as has been seen, a species of political order that is as important as—perhaps more so than—the organs of public government. When viewed in their totality, they exercise more influence over the way Americans (and others) live than does, say, the Supreme Court of the United States. It is high time, then, that the repositories of economic sovereignty— the giant corporations and their financial allies—be recognized in constitutional theory and in our thinking about the nature of separation of powers today. [54]

This is not the place to argue the point in any comprehensive way. It is beyond dispute that the corporations (and other prominent groups) are governments in fact. The question is how to relate that proposition to the orthodox conception of separation of powers. At least three statements can be made. First, the economic power of the corporate giants results in further disintegration of an already badly splintered concept of national sovereignty. Second, and paradoxically, there is dawning recognition, in law and otherwise, of the close interlocks between the social groups and the units of public government. Previously it has been suggested that those interlocks are creating the fusion of economic and political power, or, in other words, the development of an indigenous form of corporativism. If that is valid, then a truly new form of constitutional order is being created. Finally, great danger to human liberty results from the control of more than one department of public government by one social class. If substantial segments of both Congress and the executive are dominated by, say, units of economic sovereignty, then powers are no longer truly separated and the consequent concentration has portentous, even ominous, meaning for freedom. (The courts need not be excluded from such an analysis. They, too, are "political" and should be seen as the target of interest groups.)

Jacques Ellul maintains that "the organs of representative democracy no longer have any other purpose than to endorse decisions prepared by experts and pressure groups" and thereby dismisses the power of modern legislatures as an "illusion."[55] Certainly there is little evidence to the contrary. Congress, to speak only of the United States, has neither the will nor the staying power to reassert lost powers or to become a truly effective instrument of governance. Perhaps it could and, to speak normatively, perhaps it should; but despite much recent huffing and puffing, at a time when the presidency under Richard Nixon was (to use Stewart Alsop's unfortunate label) "paraplegic," little of substance or of permanence emerged from Capitol Hill. After having been largely instrumental in creating the Frankenstein that is the modern executive branch, Congress's reaction is more hortatory than significant. [56]

It will do little good to argue that if Congress is an illusion, then the populace, as an entity, can look to the chief executive to represent them. The executive is also the target of interest groups. Here, as with Congress, the entire branch is not conquered; instead, as Professor Grant McConnell has said, "control of significant parts of [government] may be established by particular business interests." [57] The interests of the presidency are not necessarily coterminous with the interests of the "public" (if, indeed, that entity exists at all). The executive pursues his own ends, defining the public interest as anything that he says it is. In such a situation, McConnell's observation "that a substantial part of government in the United States has come under the influence or control of narrowly based and largely autonomous elites" [58] becomes particularly apposite. If he is correct—his argument is accepted, in different terminology, by leading commentators—then historical separation of powers has indeed broken down.

The important separation thus has become one between public and private governments—and their interlocks. If narrowly based elites control a substantial part of government, to what avail the classical American doctrine of the separation of powers? The question is only raised here. The pressing need is for research to determine the extent to which different social groups control the three branches of government—if at all. In other words, there must be a sociological basis to the separation doctrine, something that Bentham saw. [59] The constitutional principle of separated powers must be paralleled by the sociological principle of balanced social forces. The latter does not exist in America today.

It is not enough to expect the largely autonomous elites to cancel each other out so that the net result is maximization of human liberty. Quite the contrary. As Madison clearly foresaw, the rise of faction could have pronounced dangers to freedom. [60] Furthermore, almost by definition the public interest—however defined, perhaps a hopeless task—cannot emanate from the system in the sense of the overall common good. [61] Most economists have long since given up on Adam Smith, and even Galbraith no longer talks about "countervailing power" as a substitute. In politics, laissez-faire is even less adequate, simply because social groups, which have risen to prominence, have replaced the individual as the basic societal unit. Law follows—or reflects—the political economy. "Separation of powers" theory today must take "private" power into consideration.

If federalism has been greatly altered and if the division of powers in the national government displays equally significant changes, much the same is true for other constitutional consequences. Three can be mentioned, one of which is of fundamental importance: the desuetude of representative or popular government. Others include a trend toward a larger-than-national resolution—toward multi-nationalism—of public policies; and, as has been seen, the progressive blurring of the line between public and private in America.

MARASMIC REPRESENTATIVE GOVERNMENT

Perhaps the most portentous change is that relating to the decline of the theory and practice of representative government in the United States. Jacques Ellul said in 1965: "The idea that the citizen should control the state rests on the assumption that, within the state, Parliament effectively directs the political body, the administrative organs, and the technicians. But this is a plain illusion."[62] In the corporate state, control by the citizenry is not possible. Nor, for that matter, is control of the apparatus of the state by legislative organs. In the democratic ideology, citizen control is made possible through election of the legislatures. But in the modern state, the legislature—we will take Congress as our model—has become a part of the governing structure of the state. Legislators act less as a check on the bureaucracy than as a part of the decisional process. In so doing, they do not represent the citizens of the nation; they by and large reflect the desires and ends of the interest groups with which they are allied. The appropriate label is "functional representation."[63]

A belief that constitutions can change the situation to bring about control by the citizenry is naive. There is some importance, to be sure, in juridical processes, and the rule of law is not unimportant. But that merely means that the democratic state is not the same thing as the authoritarian state. In briefest terms, just as there has been a loss of consumer sovereignty in the economy, the citizen has lost sovereignty in the political order.

The intellectual need is for a model of decision making within government and for a conception of the state and of the bureaucracy. The task is not easy. All that can be done now is to suggest a few lines of thought, some hypotheses that may serve to help some of the proper questions about the nature of representative democracy. They will be listed with little discussion.

1. The administrator, with supposed expertise, is firmly in formal control of both the details of government and often major policy proposals. When speaking of the "administrator," it is well to remember that administration is both public and private and that we are talking about the technostructures within and without the formal civil service. The myth to the contrary notwithstanding, the "popular rule" model of government does not reflect reality. Certainly the populace does not rule in any direct sense. Furthermore, it is clear that there is no true representative democracy in the sense of those who actually make important decisions representing anyone other than themselves, the group of which they are members, or surrogates, or (in the case of public officers) the "clients" whose interests they protect. Put another way, the bureaucrats of the corporate state are the servants of the holders of real power in America.

History, perhaps because it is clouded with idealism and with the value preferences of the historians, does not reveal a valid answer to the question of whether government by elite has always characterized the United States. Whatever has been the situation in the past, the reins of government in the corporate state are now, and increasingly will be, in the hands of the putative expert. Government by expert is far more prevalent today than it was in the past, even though it might always have been evident in some degree, with those experts tending to identify with the holders of real power. That, as suggested above, makes nonsense out of the idea of popular rule. The simplistic view of public affairs epitomized in that model has been described by Professor William C. Mitchell as follows:

> The objective of the popular rule model is to ensure that each and every citizen will participate with equal power in the deliberations of government, and that each will derive more or less equal values and share more or less equally in the maintenance of the system. The ideal image is one consisting of a society composed of individuals, rather than of groups and classes, and one that is motivated by public rather than self-interest. Not only is such a society expected to have little conflict, but what little it does have is expected to be readily handled or resolved through rational argumentation among well-intentioned citizens and with decisions by majority rule. It is assumed rather than stated that the types of political problems which will arise are of a kind that lend themselves to relatively quick and easy solutions. In other words, it is viewed as a simple society with a government performing little more than the most elementary functions that self-reliant citizens cannot do for themselves. [64]

The very statement of such a model is its own refutation. It is a statement of an ideal rather than a description of reality, an ideal predicated on a simple agricultural, small-shop type of economy. It is the "town meeting" model of democracy and one that is obviously unsuited for a continental, urbanized, industrialized nation with worldwide interests and responsibilities.

What, then, is a more accurate model? How is public policy made? The short answer to that question is that policy results from the interactions of the private bureaucracies of pluralistic groups and the public bureaucracies of government. To put it somewhat more precisely, an accurate model of decision making must focus on the members of an elite structure as the person or persons who make or greatly influence the flow of policy decisions.

Modern elite theory derives from Vilfredo Pareto and Gaetano Mosca. Their conceptual schema includes the following ideas: "In every society there is, and must be, a minority which rules over the rest of society; this minority—the 'political class' or 'governing elite' composed of those who occupy posts of political command and, more vaguely, those who can directly influence political decisions— undergoes changes in its membership over a period of time, ordinarily by the recruitment of new individual members from the lower strata of society, sometimes by the incorporation of new social groups, and occasionally by the complete replacement of the established elite by a 'counter-elite,' as occurs in revolutions."[65] Contemporary scholars tend to concentrate upon the political elite— those who hold formal authority within the body politic. But those power wielders, according to Harold D. Lasswell, also include "the leadership and social formations from which leaders typically come, and to which accountability is maintained, during a given period."[66] In the corporate state, the formal power holders are the technocrats, those with expertise in given complex areas—in other words, the engineers that Thorstein Veblen visualized or the managers that James Burnham saw.[67] There is a difference, however; Veblen and Burnham perceived rule by an industrial elite. What they failed to take into account was the question of accountability: to what, to whom, are the engineers, the managers, the technocrats accountable? And for what?

We merely pose those questions here. When they are answered, as they must be, then some idea of the structure of real power can be determined. Suffice it now merely to state that the rule by elites has resulted in the politicization of law and the legal process. And further: the tug within government is between rule by the technocrat and rule by politics and law; the former is in the ascendancy.

The strength of elite structures does not mean that what Professor C. Wright Mills described as the power elite has control of the decisional processes of government.[68] Mills, writing in 1956, saw power in America in the hands of a combination of corporate officials, military officers, and high government figures. His model may well be no more valid than is the notion of popular rule. It is suggested here that there are a number of elites, not excluding those that Mills saw.

Neither executive nor legislative officials can control the bureaucracy effectively. They are the organs of representative "democracy," but that representation tends to be functional—of interest groups rather than of "the people."[69] The "nonrepresentative" institution, the judiciary, is even less effective. Judicial review of administration is sporadic. There is little reason to believe that it seriously limits what policymakers want to do at the highest level; and even at the lower rungs of the bureaucracy, it is a seldom used device of dubious merit. Perhaps it is because it has been so inconsequential that searches are made for other institutional means, such as the ombudsman, to put checks on the exercise of administrative power.[70]

Even more significant, however, is the impotence of the individual citizen, whose single vote is a meaningless gesture, who gets significance only as a member of a group. When one looks at the citizenry of the modern nation-state, one can see some truth in Ellul's wry observation that "democracy is no longer actually a means of controlling state power, but of organizing the masses."[71] If there is any lesson to be drawn from the quadrennial political conventions, it is that they are a device whereby the machinery of the state is used to organize the citizenry. Only ostensible attention is paid to the notion of popular sovereignty. The party administrations make the decisions, which are then ratified by the conventions.

The net conclusion is clear: the bureaucracy, topped by elites, is in formal control. That conclusion is valid for the public bureaucracy and is even more so for the private bureaucracies of the supercorporations. By definition, those administrators are beyond popular control. If control exists at all, it is by members of the public administration. But that cannot reflect reality, for often, perhaps usually, the officials of both work quite closely together. Theirs is a symbiotic relationship, not one of governor and governed. The technocrats in these organizations are at times at loggerheads with the politicians, but more often they enter into working liaisons with them.

2. The consequence is not the monolithic state but a state made up of a set of diversified decision-making centers interacting with each other. These centers are those clothed with formal authority (the true "public" administration) and those with effective control

(private centers of administrative power). There is little overall centralized direction from the "man on top" but rather a complex series of brokerage agreements among the leaders of the various power centers. [72]

3. The resulting "organism"—which has drives and purposes of its own, separate from any of the individual parts—acts in consonance with certain sociological laws of organization. Outwardly it operates in conformance with constitutions and statutes and the established rules of administrative law; but that is the facade, beneath which lurks the dark reality. The laws of continuity and of stability are followed, even with changes of personnel (or of administration, as with the election of a new President). [73] Furthermore, the organism acts in accordance with the laws of specialization and rationalization. Efficiency is its ultimate goal. In that quest, each segment of the bureaucracy is interested in its own sector; it does not take the whole into consideration. (A consequence, to be sure, is the lack of consistency or congruency in governmental policies.) [74]

Finally, there are two other "laws" of importance: anonymity and secrecy. [75] Decisions tend to be anonymous. The head of a bureau or other top official issues a general directive, which then must be interpreted to fit specific factual situations. In so doing, the decision is collective and is taken in the name of the bureau or agency or corporation or "the government." It is independent of the individuals who participated in part in its formulation.

Just as the decision is anonymous, even though it bears the nominal signature of some official, the criteria of judgment and the processes—the procedure for reaching decisions—remain secret. One must distinguish, however, between official rules of administrative procedure, which interested parties and their counsel can learn but which are too numerous and complex for anyone to know all of them, and the informal methods of procedure that remain hidden. How decisions are in fact made within government is a closely held secret, whether the government organ be legislative or executive or judicial or whether it be a private center of power (such as the supercorporation). The ultimate law of the bureaucracy is necessity. Decisions get made because of this—but one would be foolish to think that he can describe in exact detail the process that took place. [76]

One has only to compare such a decision as the Apollo program (putting an American on the moon by 1970) with that for building the B-1 aircraft. Here were high visibility decisions of great import, committing a large portion of the gross national product to their realization. Both were made in the bureaucracy, taking the term broadly and loosely, and ratified by Congress. Both were, in effect, anonymous and secret; few know who influenced whom, who had the ultimate power of decision, the criteria of choice, the methodology followed. Both exemplify in clearest terms the operation of the "military-space-industrial-scientific complex." [77] The role of traditional law—as a set of interdictory rules—was minimal. That, be it noted, is also true when the decisions become those of low visibility. At that level, even though the bureaucrat seems to be circumscribed by regulations and rules, discretion prevails. [78] Choices have to be made. Again, anonymity and secrecy characterize the situation. The result often is a Kafkaesque situation where no one decides and what is decided is merely announced.

5. The bureaucracy is amoral; it acts to maximize efficiency and is not concerned with abstract notions of good or bad. In so doing, it justifies its actions by pointing to "the book"—the regulations that purportedly leave no discretion but that can be and are bent at times in the interests of specific persons. [79]

6. The bureaucracy attempts to reduce the impression of arbitrariness and omnipotence through carefully designed public-relations programs. This can be most clearly seen in the campaigns of the supercorporations—through institutional advertising—to convince the public that the firm operates only to further the public good. But the avowedly "public" bureaucracy does it as well, as when, to take just one example, the National Aeronautics and Space Administration retained a public-relations firm to help convince the American people that the vast sums spent on space would have undoubted "spin-off" benefits through the development of new techniques and products. The ultimate in this can be seen in the manner in which modern Presidents employ the mass media as propaganda organs to orchestrate and manipulate public opinion on specific issues.

7. The inability of citizens to control the flow of decisions, the

very desuetude of the concept of representative government, reveals the lack of validity in the Supreme Court's enunciation of the marketplace theory of truth. Under this idea, truth is the resultant of the clash of ideas in the marketplace. [80] It presupposes a free flow of information about all aspects of decision making, a desire on the part of all to make the marketplace the locus of decision making, an aptitude and desire on the part of the citizenry to be informed and to participate, and free access to the media by anyone who wants his point of view expressed. None of these assumptions accords with reality. The actual processes of decision making are often kept secret; there is no desire to create a modern-day version of the New England town meeting (even though such a procedure may be technologically possible); likely most citizens have neither the capacity nor the wish to be fully informed on all of the intricacies going into any one decision; and the mass media simply do not give access to divergent points of view. The marketplace theory of truth is one of those quaint bits of mythology that continues to persist. If it ever had any validity, it was during yesteryear when the United States was a nation of small towns and small shops, agriculturally oriented. But it is probable that even then, even during the alleged golden age of the nineteenth century, the idea that truth—which is roughly translatable as decisions made by the populace—emanated from the marketplace is fictional. This is not an argument for the abolition of the First Amendment's freedoms of expression. Far from it. But the sociological and philosophical bases of that amendment, the assumptions underlying the Supreme Court's interpretation of it, simply do not accord with reality.

The clear conclusion from such an analysis is that representative government does not exist in the United States. This, we suggest, is a consequence of the coming of the corporate state; however, quite possibly a similar situation always existed. The democratic ideal may never have been approximated in the past. The American experiment, therefore, has been just that—an experiment—and little more. If so, the most portentous consequences become apparent. The liberal dream—the idea of progress and the perfectability of man—is ended. That, ironically, comes at precisely the time in history when scientists and technologists tell us that man can invent the future if so desired. Man's ability to control the physical world has never been greater, but his ability to control himself has never been more shaky. The end of the road is *1984*.

The summary treatment that has been given to the decline and fall of the ideal of representative government in the United States should not obscure its great significance. The theoretical nature of the American government has been thoroughly warped, probably irretrievably so. But another constitutional consequence of corporativism merits attention, albeit briefly. The next in this listing is the trend toward multinationalism in public policies.

THE MERGER OF "FOREIGN" AND "DOMESTIC"

If representative government is a myth, in the sense that the people generally are not represented, then it is equally fallacious to divide the problems of government between domestic and foreign. While it is true that the national government is organized along those lines, with the President being the only person in the entire structure with dual responsibilities, nonetheless the consequence of new communications and transportation technologies, coupled with the growth of multinational business, has all but erased the line between foreign and domestic policy. There is scarcely a government office that does not have some larger-than-national aspects; and there is scarcely any public policy problem that does not cut across the historical lines. The consequence is that the United States is deeply and irretrievably immersed in world affairs. That means that a Constitution largely drafted for domestic affairs has to do duty in an increasingly interdependent world.

This adumbrates one central hypothesis: the growth of giant business, particularly the multinational enterprise (MNE)—the one truly supranational organization thus far created—has had and will continue to have a major impact upon the political order. In brief, some of the political (that is, constitutional) consequences of economic power as it is exercised in the world arena will be examined. "This," says economist Sidney E. Rolfe, "is an undefined region whose exploration is bound to be a thankless task." [81] Thankless, perhaps, but necessary if an understanding of the political economy of the modern era is to be attained. But since this is terra incognita for the most part, the exposition will be more in the nature of posing questions than of asserting answers. It is too early to do more.

The supercorporations dominate and set the economic tone for many economies on both sides of the Iron Curtain. The "principle of convergence" noted by Professor John Kenneth Galbraith as characteristic of modern industrialized nations includes both the large privately owned enterprises of the West (consisting roughly of those countries which are members of the Organization of Economic Cooperation and Development) and the state-owned enterprises of the Soviet Union. [82] Nevertheless the giant firms constitute only one of at least two forms of business organization in a country such as the United States, the other being the world of small business. The latter is far greater numerically and of far less apparent social and political (including legal) power than the supercorporations, simply because the small companies tend not to join together in common fronts of power. Furthermore they often exist as satellites of the giant companies, either as suppliers to the latter or as franchise dealers.

We have concentrated thus far on domestic economies. It is fast becoming a cliché that the major economic development in the post-World War II world is the rise of the MNE. The majority are American in origin, but they come from other countries as well. J.-J. Servan-Schreiber's notion, which received wide currency a few years ago, about the "American challenge"—*le defi Americain*—is more *le defi economique* of companies from a number of nations presenting a major challenge to the political order of the nation-states. [83] For whatever reason, and doubtless the reasons are multiple, corporate giants have proliferated within domestic economies and in world trade. Corporate managers and owners in one country have devised techniques by which an enterprise can have centralized management and decentralized operations. Tight control is retained over major policies through managerial hierarchies that "see the world as their oyster" [84] and that consider the world to be an economic unit. Techniques of multiple incorporation, particularly that most useful of inventions—allowing one corporation to form another or even a series of others—enables the parent company and its managers to establish and maintain a bewildering variety of interlocking corporations. In net effect, this means, as Professors Nye and Keohane have recently said, that "transnational organizations whose principal goals are social and economic have increased in importance. By far the most important of these organizations is the multinational business enterprise." [85] Modern communications and transportation technologies permit imposing a central strategy on widely scattered subsidiaries.

To understand the significance of this to the constitutional order it is useful to remember the American experience. American business, small and local in 1800, became multistate in the late nineteenth and early twentieth centuries. Corporations spread throughout the country, aided by new developments in communications. The history of American constitutional law reflects, as Felix Frankfurter once said, the way in which finance capitalism developed. [86] In no small part, changes in the system of federalism and in the separation of national governmental powers can be traced to reactions to the growth of the giant corporations. Both are major constitutional changes, resulting in a concentration of power in the central government and, within that government, in the executive. In recent years corporate growth has accelerated. The result is the new industrial state, to use Galbraith's label, a peculiarly American form of corporativism that has so altered the mix between public and private as to create a new constitutional order.

The growth of multistate business enterprise was merely a prologue to the multinational or global firm. [87] Taking 1800 as a point of departure, the trend is clearly toward larger size in business units and toward expansion of the activities of those companies to planetary dimensions. "The emergence of the multinational private corporation as a powerful agent of world social and economic change has been a signal development of the postwar era." [88] Richard J. Barber put the movement in effective focus in 1970:

The opportunities presented by the booming world economy have been clearly recognized by American and foreign business interests. Partly through trade but primarily through multinational investment and operations, corporations are becoming genuine economic citizens of the world. This fact, with its obvious economic implications, presents even more critical politi-

cal problems for it draws into serious question both the suf-
ficiency and the relevance of existing legal arrangements to
control, and service, corporations which have severed their ties
with any single nation.

No longer is it accurate to think of most of our large corporations as "American." The oil companies, the big auto, drug,
and chemical producers, and the makers of computers and
electrical equipment, among many others, are so heavily committed to foreign markets that they have in fact lost their U. S.
identity and assumed a multinational character. Just as regulation of business corporations by the states became outmoded
sixty or so years ago as an integrated U. S. economy supplanted
the local and regional markets which had characterized the
nation in its first century, today the global scope of commercial activity by major U. S. and foreign companies is rendering
national regulation obsolete.

With firms like Standard Oil of New Jersey, Mobil Oil,
Woolworth, National Cash Register, Burroughs, Colgate-Pal-
molive, Standard Oil of California, and Singer deriving more
than half their income or earnings from "foreign" sales, and
with a long list of others, including such familiar giants as
Eastman Kodak, Pfizer, Caterpillar Tractor, International
Harvester, Corn Products, and Minnesota Mining (MMM)
making from 30 to 50 percent of their sales abroad, even those
once-American companies are beginning to acknowledge openly—indeed with occasional enthusiasm and a frequent boast—
their new *supranational status*. In explaining why it changed
its corporate name and trademark to Uniroyal, U. S. Rubber
proclaimed that "it is now meeting the research and manufacturing needs of the whole polyglot world."[89]

That statement points up three hypotheses we now advance. Business—the business of the "first economy" of the supercorporations—is indeed achieving a new supranational status. This can lead
to one of three ends when it is viewed in conjunction with the role of
the political order (the nation-states); those possible consequences
are essentially constitutional in nature. They include the following
hypotheses, which are tentatively advanced as being the most prob-

able. The suggestion is that one of them—or what may be more likely, a combination of the second and third—will eventuate.

Hypothesis 1. Multinational business provides a basis in the "living law" (to adapt Eugen Ehrlich's term)—for multinational constitutionalism. A necessary corollary is that the nation-state is becoming obsolescent (but not obsolete) as a form of social order and that the trend will be toward political integration on regional, and perhaps ideological, bases. In other words, supranationalism in giant business will eventually have the same ultimate effect in erasing national boundaries as did suprastate (multistate) business for American federalism.

Hypothesis 2. Multinational corporations will themselves become a principal unit of governance; they will, if that is valid, challenge the nation-states for dominance. To analogize: just as the territorial nation-state supplanted the church (in the Western world) as the dominant force and became the characteristic type of social order in the world community, so the supercorporation may eventually emerge victorious over the political entity.

Hypothesis 3. The MNEs and the nation-states both need each other; their leaders, perceiving this, will enter into closer and closer relationships—into a symbiotic situation of corporativism writ large.

These alternatives do not necessarily exhaust all possibilities of the emergent constitutional order. Even so, it is not unduly rash to predict that one of them will eventuate or that a combination of the latter two will emerge (some sort of a grouping of supra- or multinational corporate states). But it would be rash indeed to be confident in this regard. What shape the future will take is at best problematical. How constitutional forms and mechanisms evolve may be outside man's capacity to control. Science and technology, as yet unharnessed, may be more influential than other factors in shaping the future.

Even if the future remains unpredictable, on the basis of existing evidence the nation-states and the corporations will, outwardly at least, compete for dominance. To speak sententiously: that contest will result in a coalescence or fusion of the political power of the territorial states and the economic power of the giant companies into a global type of corporativism. Put another way, by the year 2025, a new form of social order will have emerged, one that renders obsolescent the traditional nation-state. In that process, the rise of multinationalism in business affairs will be a major contributing factor.

If present trends continue, the last part of the twentieth century will probably be called by future economic historians the age of transition from an international—nationally based—to a global economy. [90] The image that many, perhaps most, people still hold of economic affairs is that of Adam Smith and David Ricardo: the world consists of several dozen nation-states, among which products—manufactured or primary—move relatively freely but with the "factors of production" (labor, capital, management) moving only with great difficulty and perhaps not at all. The same sort of belief patterns hold for the political order: the nation-state is considered to be the most appropriate method of organizing economic activity; one of its main functions today is to regulate, manipulate, stimulate, and even own its industry. A final tenet in the conventional wisdom is that the chief purpose of the nation-state in "its" economic activities is to attain and maintain a favorable balance (a surplus) in international payments so as to enable it to acquire or to hold gold (or, more recently, "paper gold"—special drawing rights [SDRs] within the framework of the International Monetary Fund).

The trouble with that model is that it simply does not accord with reality. Production of goods is no longer a purely national matter. This is the age of international production, the instrument for which is the multinational corporation. That it is as yet an imperfect institution does not belie the fact that for at least a half-century, and with increasing speed in recent years, a trend toward the internationalization of production has been visible. Goods move between nations, to be sure, but trade as such has diminished in importance; the factors of production also move between nations. International investment is here, apparently to stay, despite rumblings of discontent in some sectors. A new breed of corporate executive is appearing— the multinational manager, he who really has no home because the whole world is his home. He is based, for short or long periods, in one place (say Geneva), and he still doubtless retains his political citizenship (say, that of the United States); but he is as truly an international citizen (Arnold Toynbee once opined that they would be international "civil servants") [91] as are, for example, the Eurocrats who man the offices of the European Economic Community in Brussels. Probably the multinational manager is more truly a "citizen" of the corporation he serves than of any nation-state.

If international production is indeed here to stay, says Rolfe, "it becomes a matter of central importance for every person concerned with the future of his nation's or the world's economy to understand what is involved." [92] A significant aspect of "what is involved" is the impact on the political order. As has been noted, multinational firms come from nations other than the United States. That was historically true, also, as with the East India Company, which conquered and ruled India in Britain's name for centuries. [93] One need look only to such giants as Italy's National Hydrocarbon Agency (ENI), Britain's Unilever, British Petroleum, and Philips of Eindhoven (The Netherlands) to realize that multinationalism is not a uniquely American phenomenon. For that matter, the United States itself is now the target of multinational investment by firms from other countries—British Petroleum and Olivetti, to name but two.

The political (constitutional) consequences of the internationalization of production can be summed up as the challenge that the corporate giant, which exercises economic sovereignty in the world community, poses to the nation-state, the repository of political sovereignty. The tensions, the inevitable clashes, and the compromises struck between the two types of sovereignty will create much, perhaps most, of the international law in the future. The "one world" of the supercorporations confronts the splintered world of the nation-states. There can be no question that much new law will evolve out of that massive confrontation.

This can be put in another way: there is a built-in dynamic in the corporate enterprise of industrialized nations to continue expanding exemplifying Gunnar Myrdal's sociological "principle of cumulative causation." [94] According to Myrdal, social affairs are never in equilibrium; a given institution is always in a spiral upward or downward, W. W. Rostow's theory of economic development, propounded in *The Stages of Economic Growth*, being more fancy than fact. [95] For corporations, on the other hand, success begets success. "The way to achieve and retain [business] greatness," Osborn Elliott has said in *Men at the Top*, "is always to be striving for something more." [96] That "something more" is now making the world a single economic unit for a number of transnational supercorporations. Once having made a breakthrough, certain firms become giants through a process of upward causation. National boundaries do not confine them, and the nation-states tend to be important only because they at times provide some protection to them and because of largely ineffectual attempts to regulate them. "Yet," Judd Polk commented recently, "we find ourselves trapped in such anomalies as balance-of-payments accounting that tends to force world operations into national perspectives. There is a lack of intergovernmental machinery to assure suitable money and credit conditions. The international legal structure is far from coherent—uncertainties and conflicts of laws are a constant embarrassment to international producers. Furthermore, conditions affecting the operation of international companies differ—to a large extent arbitrarily—from country to country."[97]

What, more specifically, are some of the political (that is, constitutional) consequences of multinational economic power? Three can be mentioned to illustrate what is occurring: (1) the erosion of the historical sovereignty of the nation-states in important areas of public policy; (2) the growing indication that a concept of corporate citizenship is evolving; and (3) a high degree of cooperation between enterprise and state, coupled with an apparent desire of corporate executives to retain the present forms of political order. Each will be briefly discussed.

Striking resemblances exist between growing tensions of the nation-states vis-à-vis the MNEs and the development of giant domestic corporations within the United States and the strains placed upon the historical structure of states within the federal union. In both, the economic entities in their totality are superimposed over and transcend decentralized political units. And in each case, traditional attributes of sovereignty (as exclusive power) have been and are diminishing. The analogy, to be sure, is not exact, for the states within the United States were never sovereign in the strict Bodinian sense, but it is sufficiently close to provide a clue to a constitutional change.

The peoples of the planet are now governed by at least two (perhaps more) overlapping, interacting institutions: (1) the *public* instrument of governance, the nation-state, plus the alliances, regional organizations, and worldwide groupings into which nations enter, and (2) the *private* instrument, the voluntary association, of which the supercorporations are the most important; these also enter into supracorporate groupings (cartels, shipping conferences, trade associations, etc.). Both governing institutions have strikingly similar characteristics and functions. Save for the employment of violence, over which the nation-state has, if not a monopoly over the legitimate use, at least effective control over most uses, the corporation is as much a government as is the nation. It allocates resources, affects the values of hundreds of millions of human beings, enters into alliances with other corporations and with public governments (as in concession contracts for development in extractive industries), has an intelligence function, sets prices, carves up markets, and in its internal operations is a political order. The development has reached the point where A. A. Berle could assert in 1954 that the international corporation does a better job governing its part of world affairs than does the nation-state. [98]

The basic difference between state and company is that the former is limited geographically, whereas the latter is not terrestrially bound. Both are hierarchically structured and bureaucratically managed, with the managers being technocrats (or members of a meritocracy). Common principles of organizational behavior govern the public and private bureaucracies. Both have an elite sitting atop each bureaucracy. (That dual elite system, in American domestic affairs at least, is interlocking; a flow of personnel routinely takes place between the two organizational structures, corporate officials being a main source of manpower for high-level governmental positions.) Two decades ago Sigmund Timberg described the situation thus:

> England, Holland, and the other great trading powers of the seventeenth and eithteenth centuries were delegating *political* power to their foreign merchants, when they permitted those merchants to engage—collectively and under the corporate aegis—in foreign trade. In Maitland's classic phrase, these were "the companies that became colonies, the companies that make war." The same proposition holds for the modern large corporation. The modern state undeniably delegates *political*

power to large private corporations, as it does to the large labor
unions with which the corporate behemoths deal. The authorization of collective activity has, at least since the early Christian and Jewish communities had their difficulties with the
Roman Emperors, always been a state prerogative. Furthermore, the activities authorized for a large corporation involve
such functions as price-fixing, the division of markets, the setting of wages, and the general development of local communities, functions which in a pre-Industrial Revolution era had
been the primary responsibility of the State. It has been said of
international cartels that some of the more powerful of them
"are little empires in themselves, and their decisions are often
more important than those of 'sovereign political' entities like
Holland, Denmark or Portugal." The same could be said even
more forcefully of the political strength of that more cohesive
unit, the international combine; the notion that international
combines and cartels are strong *political* entities is no longer a
monopoly of the intuitively minded economist or political scientist. Judges have described international cartels as instruments of "private regulation", and have called an American
subsidiary the "commercial legation" of its British parent.
Even the counsel involved in drafting international cartel
agreements speak of a trade area as so-called neutral territory,
or to put it another way as "spoils" belonging to the British and
ourselves as allies in the late war. Such a consistent use of political terms is more than a mere metaphor; it is a recognition
of an underlying reality. [99]

That is the political dimension. The economic sphere is equally
impressive. In terms of totality of assets, the largest corporations
overshadow all save about a dozen of the nation-states of the planet.
Such a concentration of economic wealth is unknown in history; it
makes the supercorporation an institution that is sui generis, one
that has the important political—read constitutional—consequence
of diluting the monopoly of the nation-state on governing power.
Ever increasingly, significant decisions affecting people everywhere
are made by corporate managers, not political officers. That means
a diminution in fact of sovereignty, however much the theory re-

mains the same. A recent observation of Stephen Hymer is apposite:

> How far will this tendency of corporations to create a world
> in their own image proceed? The situation is a dynamic one,
> moving dialectically. Right now, we seem to be in the midst of a
> major revolution in international relationships as modern sci-
> ence establishes the technological basis for a major advance in
> the conquest of material world and the beginnings of truly cos-
> mopolitan production. Multinational corporations are in the
> vanguard of this revolution, because of their great financial
> and administrative strength and their close contact with the
> new technology. Governments . . . are far behind, because of
> their narrower horizons and perspectives, as are labor organi-
> zations and most non-business institutions and associations.
> (As John Powers, President of Charles Pfizer Corporation, has
> put it, "Practice is ahead of theory and policy.") Therefore,
> . . . multinational corporations are likely to have a certain de-
> gree of success in organizing markets, decision making, and
> the spread of information in their own interest. However, their
> very success will create tensions and conflicts which will lead to
> further development. [100]

That "further development" of which Hymer speaks is, in my judgment, the third of the constitutional implications herein discussed—
multinational corporativism.

We have alluded previously to a notion of citizenship of the corporation—of allegiances being owed to a nonstatist collective body. So
considered, citizenship must, of course, be based upon a theory of
political organization on a functional or occupational-industrial
basis rather than upon a territorial or a geographic basis. The suggestion is that for the MNE's international executive staff, and indeed for members of the technostructure far down the corporate
hierarchy, citizenship is tending to become dual. Allegiances are
owed both to the nation-state and to the corporation, and it is by no
means certain which is the stronger tie.

Under the orthodox conception, the status of citizenship is conferred by the positive law; it is an attribute of the state. Normally only one nation-state is involved, but in some instances dual nationality (the international law analogue of the municipal concept of citizenship) is possible. Some nations permit a person to renounce his citizenship to acquire another; others, however, do not recognize voluntary divestiture. Furthermore, one nation-state—Israel—claims that Jews everywhere are also nationals of Israel because of religious ties and because Israel is said to be the "national home" of Jews, regardless of whether an individual wishes it. [101]

The frontier question is whether a person can be considered to be a citizen of both the territorial state and a nongeographic entity, such as the corporation. An affirmative answer to that question is possible if the corporation is viewed, as indeed it should be, as something more than an economic organization or a constitutional (legal) person, but also as a political order and a social system. Then it may validly be held, as Professor Andrew Hacker said several years ago, that the time has come "for us to recognize a new kind of citizenship: corporation citizenship." [102]

The crucial issue is this: with which group does the employee, mainly but not entirely white collar, identify? In the MNEs, managers tend to view themselves as being at least a-national. Overall company goals are rigorously, even ruthlessly, pursued. As David Finn put it, "Not only personal concerns but the special interests of individual departments or subsidiaries must be subordinated to the good of the company as a whole." [103] Citizenship, then, should be viewed functionally rather than as solely a characteristic that can be conferred only by the state. So considered, it then becomes necessary to ask: With whom does the individual identify? Which organizations command his loyalties and allegiances? What type of reciprocal obligations flow from the organization to the individual? Such questions can only be posed here, much empirical research being necessary to develop a factual base for valid answers. Suffice it at the present to quote Professor Hacker again:

. . . Managers and workers alike are uprooted, but it is the former—the middle class—who seek adjustment and new roots

because of the profound changes they have undergone in environment, expectations, and status. Eastman Kodak's medical
plans, IBM's country clubs, Richfield Oil's model homes, du
Pont's psychiatrists, Reynolds Tobacco's chaplains, and even
RCA's neckties with the corporate insignia—all are sympto-
matic of the effort to establish a feeling of community within
the corporation. The middle-class employee no longer has an
alternative community in which he can find a sense of belonging. The national government is too large and unwieldy to provide this satisfaction; and local governments are too ineffectual
to cater to such deep-seated needs. Government provides various welfare services at various levels, but they are far from
being programs that will meet the social and psychological
needs of the middle class.

    Thus there has emerged the equivalent of a new kind of
citizenship; corporate citizenship. It is not the same as our
traditional view of citizenship. . . . [104]

Hacker, of course, spoke there of the domestic corporation. But if
his views are valid, as I believe they are, then they are applicable with
even greater force to the MNEs. Those who toil and spin for the
MNEs are a part of a community, nongeographical but nevertheless identifiable, that has its rewards and punishments and, even
more importantly, gives satisfactions greater than the orthodox political order.

    It goes without saying that the state for centuries has claimed and
attempts to enforce a monopoly on loyalty. However, if one takes the
span of historical time, even this is a development of relatively recent origin, as Robert Nisbet has shown.[105] And to the extent that it
had viability in public international law, it has broken down in recent years. New groupings have emerged. The United Nations, for
example, has been recognized by the International Court of Justice
as an international public body.[106] The subjects of international law
are no longer limited to nation-states; as the former Secretary-
General of the United Nations put it, "Practice has abandoned the
doctrine that States are the exclusive subjects of international rights
and duties."[107] Other transnational organizations that are beginning to achieve some recognition, albeit limited, as international

public bodies include the Knights of Malta, the Ismaili sect, and the Roman Catholic church. [108] And surely corporations that enter into concession agreements for, say, the extraction of petroleum can, with little distortion, be accorded a status in the world community, a status that no doubt is a shore dimly seen but one that is becoming more evident.

Whether a given organization has achieved the status of an international public body requires the application of empirical tests rather than abstract legal formulas. As Professor H. Lauterpacht said, "In each particular case the question of whether a person or a body is a subject of international law must be answered in a pragmatic manner by reference to actual experience and to the reason of the law as distinguished from a preconceived notion as to who can be subjects of international law." [109] An analysis of the role that corporations play in world affairs and the manner in which people cling to them, while simultaneously adhering to their formal allegiances to nation-states, tends to indicate that a concept of dual citizenship is emerging. Definitive proof of such a proposition would require data not yet available, not only about what the MNEs do in fact insofar as planetary decision making is concerned but also about the psychology—the motivations, the preferences, the values—of individual members of the sociological communities called the corporations.

The trend seems to be toward a multiplicity of loyalties. If that is so, then the clear implication is that reciprocal rights and duties attach to groups other than the nation-states. In traditional legal parlance, those rights and duties, as well as the identifications with the nonnation groupings, bespeak nationality or citizenship. Functionally, this is a practical consideration, as Professor Helen Silving has said: "Nationality law is closely connected with the political structure of a country, more so than most branches of law. It determines who should be a 'citizen', and thus what shall be the composition of the 'nation.'" [110] Or as the Supreme Court of the United States said in 1913: "Citizenship is membership in a political society and implies a duty of allegiance on the part of the member and a duty of protection on the part of the society. These are reciprocal obligations, one being a compensation for the other." [111]

The suggestion made here is not that corporate citizenship is full blown; quite the contrary. It is as yet an unformed concept, an inchoate notion, a tendency or trend rather than a settled proposition. I do not suggest that duality of citizenship means that the state and enterprise are equal in fact, whatever that may mean. Speaking generally, the nation-state is still the most visible and dominant organ in world affairs, but that does not necessarily mean that the situation will continue or that the nation will eventually triumph in any struggle for power between it and the MNE. Nor does it mean that the nation-state will vanish. To the contrary, it will continue to exist, in form or facade, but with much of the substance drained out of it.

The twentieth century is the century of corporativism. Indigenous to Europe, it is now spreading elsewhere. Anchored in theological pronouncements, exemplified in the abortive fascism of Mussolini and Hitler and the watered-down fascism of Franco, corporativism—the fusion of economic and political power—bids fair to become the ultimate social order on the planet. Whether it is "Japan, Inc." or the more subtle politico-economic arrangements of modern industrial nations, the trend seems to be clear and unmistakable: the *internal* constitutional order is corporativist. Can the same be said for the "world community"? The answer suggested here is in the affirmative.

The domestic corporate state provides a basis for validating that conclusion. A beginning may be made with a statement made in 1931 by lawyer Adolf Berle and economist Gardiner Means:

> The rise of the modern corporation has brought a concentration of economic power which can cope on equal terms with the modern state—economic power versus political power, each strong in its own field. The state seeks in some aspects to regulate the corporation, while the corporation, steadily becoming more powerful, seeks independence and not infrequently endeavors to avail itself, through indirect influence, of government power. Not impossibly the economic organism, now typified by the corporation, may win equality with the state and perhaps even supersede it as the dominant institution of social organization. The law of corporations, accordingly, might well be considered as a potential constitutional law for the new economic state; while business practice assumes many of the aspects of administrative government. [112]

If from that statement is extracted the phrase "the corporation . . . [both] seeks independence and not infrequently endeavors to avail itself, through indirect influence, of governmental power," then the germ of the corporate state, American style, may be perceived. The development is a two-way street, for the state seeks to employ the corporation for its ends. The resulting relationship, when one strips the facade off it, is a symbiosis. Each entity, enterprise and state, needs the other and uses the other. Indeed, it would be difficult to visualize either existing without the other, if one views only the United States and Japan.

A new constitutional order is in process of becoming in the United States, and probably elsewhere, a group-person that at once transcends the arithmetical sum of its parts, which are the public group of government and the private groups of the corporations (plus other important social organizations). To summarize what has been said before, the essential characteristics of the new order are: a merger, actual or tacit, between political and economic power; a legal nexus between the two; the result of the creation of a corporate body that both encompasses the two and is greater than the arithmetical sum of the two; and a diminution of the social and legal role of the individual qua natural person. The basic idea is that important societal decisions tend more and more to be the resultant of the interactions of public and private bureaucracies. Quite often, but not always, these decisions—they are matters of important public policy—are put into official form through the formal authority of governmental officials. This is not always so, for perhaps equally often corporate managers can do so, but only with express or tacit delegation of authority from the state, the state having what Wolfgang Friedmann once termed a "reserve function." [113] The flow of decisions thus made, which often are administrative rather than legislative or judicial, constitutes the living law. They need not be formalized in administrative rule or legislative enactment; they are, to vary the terminology of John R. Commons, the "working rules" of American corporativism. [114]

What has been suggested is that a system of law exists within the United States, and elsewhere, which consists of the informal transactions between government and pluralistic social groups—in present inquiry, the corporations. At times it is formalized, but more often it exists as a set of working rules that are understood by the participants but that seldom get a formal imprimatur, or, for that matter, that are often kept secret from all except a select few. This system is not necessarily cohesive and consistent; it is a series of laws rather than a logical whole. It is the means by which the various sub-governments within Washington, D. C., and other national capitals operate.[115] This complex web of informal interactions constitutes what, with Ehrlich, can be called the living law of contemporary corporativism. If the notion is valid, then it effects the legal nexus between the corporation and the state. It is law in that it enables power to be exercised, and it is invisible law in that it is not codified or otherwise buried in the musty volumes of law libraries. Commons's "working rules" appear to approximate this view; for example, he speaks of the corporation charter as a

> group of promises and commands which the state makes in the form of working rules indicating how the officials of the state shall act in the future in matters affecting the association, the members of the association, and the persons not members. It is these promises and commands, or working rules, of officials which constitute the charter and determine the status of the association. . . . This collective, intangible living process of individuals, the functionaries of the state find already in a trembling existence and then proceed "artificially" to guide the individuals concerned and give it a safer existence. The guidance is made through promising to them a certain line of behavior on the part of public officials, which sets forth the limits on their private behavior and the assistance they may expect on the part of public officials.[116]

Within the American constitutional system, that "assistance" about which Commons spoke is subject to the highest degree of discretion on the part of public officials, the constitutional and statutory law of delegation of legislative power having invested the bureaucracy with uncontrolled governing power—uncontrolled in the sense of interdictory rules of law.

So much for summary on the concept of corporativism. Can the same notions be applied to the larger-than-national scheme? The (admittedly) tentative answer is in the affirmative, coupled with the caveat that much research must be conducted in order to produce verified data that would validate such an hypothesis. Enough evidence is now available, however, for the state-centered view of world politics and world law to be an outdated paradigm; so much is shown in the seminal volume, *Transnational Relations and World Politics*, edited by Professors Robert O. Keohane and Joseph S. Nye, Jr. [117] As Seyom Brown, Senior Fellow at the Brookings Institution, has said: "The cumulative picture that emerges is one of governments losing their controlling influence over important transnational flows of people, material, money, and ideas, while other organizations—corporations, professional and trade associations, quasi-governments—gain in ability to allocate resources, privileges, and penalties across national boundaries." [118] At least three implications can be drawn from this. (1) The state-centered paradigm of world politics, which focuses on the strategies, capabilities, and interactions of nation-states, is no longer valid; indeed, it never was entirely valid, but it is becoming less so. (2) The nation-states do not (and will not) necessarily prevail over private transnational interests should conflicts occur; the orthodox assumption is that the nation-state *will* win out; the point, however, is not the ultimate power of the state in such clashes but whether the cumulative power of the transnational private interests often intimidate, and thus dominate, the very governmental agencies that purportedly regulate them. (3) It is not necessarily valid to maintain that creation of a single global economy within which goods and services can be exchanged freely on the basis of comparative advantages would be the optimum way of allocating the world's resources; despite the belief that it is, it may well be that "the transnationally mobile are rewarded at the expense of the nationally mobile." [119] In short, a just world order gradually evolving out of expanding socioeconomic intercourse, made possible by new transportation and communications technologies, might well increase conflict rather than eliminate it. [120]

Be that as it may, the implication of this analysis is that the rise of the MNEs is a postcolonial form of private economic imperialism. As Peter B. Evans has said, "With the growing predominance of the multinational corporation, increasing numbers of a poor country's economic actors become responsible to superiors and stockholders who are citizens of other countries. If a similar chain of command existed in public organizations, the poor country would be deemed a colony."[121] Even affluent countries, such as Canada, are subject to this type of neocolonialism. [122] The further implication is that the MNE quite often, although not always, is the "chosen instrument" of the powerful nation-state (such as the United States). [123] But the analogue is also noteworthy: as Professor Dennis M. Ray has said, quite often corporations can shape the environment in which the problems of American foreign relations grow and can also define the "axiomatic." "Axiomatic decisions," says Ray, "are those which are virtually automatic; those actions by government which no longer require explicit means-ends calculations and, indeed, are rarely accompanied by debate." [124] For example, it is "axiomatic" that the United States government should intervene to protect American life and property abroad. But whose life and whose property? And why? To what ends? The exposè of ITT's covert activities in Chile, carried on with the help of the American government, reveals hard evidence of business-government collaboration in the world community. Another name for it would be corporativism, American style.

It is, in sum, more than an a priori hypothesis that the MNEs and the state are often partners in fact, if not in theory. They ride on a bicycle built for two, with the unanswered question being who is doing the steering. Compare in this regard the statement of Professor Robert Gilpin with that of former Deputy Assistant Secretary of Defense Arthur Barber: "The role of the nation-state in economic as well as in political life is increasing and . . . the multinational corporation is actually a stimulant to the further extension of state power in the economic realm"; [125] Barber maintains that the MNE is "bringing an end to middle-class society and the dominance of the nation-state." [126] Just as the East India Company was, while privately owned and operated for the profit of shareholders, in effect an instrument of the British government, so too are the Fords and IBMs and Mitsuis and Unilevers and other corporate giants of the modern age.

That view, however, is being contested by some corporate officials who are beginning to think in terms of "anational" corporations. "We appear," said Carl A. Gerstacker, chairman of the board of Dow Chemical Company in early 1972, "to be moving strongly in the direction of what will not be really multinational or international companies as we know them today, but what we might call 'anational' companies—companies without any nationality, belonging to all nationalities." [127] If that should take place—the main obstacle now is the American tax laws—then corporations would no longer be instruments of American policy; they would be free from the laws of any nation save those in which they did business. No longer, says Gerstacker, would his company have to comply with United States law concerning his operations outside the United States. To achieve anationalism it would be necessary to incorporate in some principality, such as Monaco, or perhaps on some island in the Caribbean. Admittedly, however, this is not a present fact. It would be difficult, perhaps impossible, to predict the success of the drive for denationalizing the corporation. No doubt it would be strenuously resisted by the political leaders and, quite possibly, by the trade unions. Nationality of corporations, however, is at best a nebulous legal concept and has become more so with ownership of shares being held by citizens of many nation-states.

There is, furthermore, a strong reason for the corporation to retain ties to a nation-state such as the United States. As a superpower that, for better or worse, is the dominant political entity in the world, the United States can provide protection to corporations that they cannot themselves develop. There is, in other words, a reciprocal need of the two—corporation and nation-state—for each other. Through various techniques, including the use of violence, the political order can protect the property and assets of the companies. The price for that is paid through taxation and such regulation as can be effected. In the resolution of the conflicts between the two forms of social order—political and economic—a system of symbiotic cooperation and close partnership is likely to be the result; at times that cooperation may appear antagonistic, but only sporadically. The basic pattern will be for the corporation and the state to be the two sides of one coin; neither could exist in the modern world without the other.

The consequences of the foregoing analysis for American constitutionalism are several—and profound. The include the following: (a) Federalism will become even more moribund, despite a latter-day movement toward "participatory democracy"; the most significant units of our federal system will be "functional"—the corporations (and other pluralistic groups). (b) More power will flow to the executive-administrative branch, with both Congress and the courts suffering a marked diminution of status; the modern state is the "administate," and all modern governments, including that of the United States, are dominated by the executive. (c) In public policy matters, the lines between public and private and between foreign and domestic will be ever increasingly blurred; at times they will even be erased. (d) The Constitution, through some means, either must be able to work extraterritorially or it will gradually sink into oblivion.

So much seems to be becoming clear for the American system of government. It is perhaps more apparent in the United States than elsewhere because a long-lasting American ideology denies any effective role to government in economic affairs and sharply separates public and private matters as well as foreign and domestic affairs. Other nations not so dominated by a long repudiated (albeit seldom followed, even in the United States) view of government and business and that do not have a written fundamental law that has endured will not find such proposition so startling, as do Americans. Constitutional forms and mechanisms are not immutable. The future will see major changes in the constitutions of the industrialized powers. The form and facade may stay, but the content will change. The tide ceaselessly beating against the traditional political order is the force of economics.

EPILOGUE:
A Syzygetic Order

This essay has set forth a description of the emergent constitutional order. No attempt was made to prescribe what should be. It is, furthermore, illustrative rather than exhaustive; no doubt a number of constitutional issues have been left without mention or with too little discussion. The time, as was said in the preface, is too short to set out a more comprehensive analysis. The hope is that the foregoing exposition will help to pose some of the questions that must be answered in any modern systematic scrutiny of the American Constitution.

Nor should it be thought that the development of the corporate state reflects the personal values of the author. Far from it. The contrary would be closer to the truth. But one must describe matters as he sees them, rather than as he wishes them to be; and it is in that spirit that the essay was written.

The corporate state, American style, exemplifies a politico-legal form of syzygy—the conjunction of two organisms without loss of identity. Though they combine into an anthropomorphic super-person at once larger than either one or the sum of both, nonetheless corporation and state do retain their separate identities. Michael Kammen has suggested that "the condition of syzygy" is "central to a proper perspective upon American civilization."[1] So it is. The corporate state as group-person is syzygetic: each element retains its form but there are close interlocks between them. The modern constitutional order is made up of two governing structures—public and private—that are ostensibly at odds but really are not. Indeed it is not too much to say that modern constitutionalism cannot be understood unless the dimension of private governments is taken into consideration. And that is so even though the corporation, speaking generally, has not yet been "constitutionalized" by the Supreme Court.

Notes

NOTES TO THE PREFACE

1. Nagel, The Structure of Science: Problems in the Logic of Scientific Explanation (1961).

NOTES TO CHAPTER 1

1. Commons, The Economics of Collective Action 302 (1950).
2. As quoted in Henkin, Foreign Affairs and the Constitution (1973).
3. Neumann, The Democratic and the Authoritarian State 199 (1957).
4. Galbraith, The New Industrial State (rev. ed. 1972).
5. Reich, The Greening of America (1970).
6. Nieburg, In the Name of Science (1966).
7. For example, Spring, Education and the Rise of the Corporate State (1972); Brenner, Borosage, & Weidner, Exploring Contradictions: Political Economy in the Corporate State (1974).
8. Wilson, Constitutional Government in the United States 157 (1908).
9. Glidden v. Zdanok, 370 U.S. 530 (1962).
10. 384 U.S. 486 (1966).
11. See, for example, Frankel, The Democratic Prospect 189 (1962), quoting Kolakowski, *Permanent and Transitory Aspects of Marxism*, in The Broken Mirror 158-59 (Mayewski ed. 1958). Lenin said in his Marx, Engels Marxism (4th English ed. 1951): "The incontestable truth is that a Marxist must take cognizance of actual events, of the precise facts of reality, and must not cling to a theory of yesterday, which, like all theories, at best only outlines the main and general, and only approximates to an inclusive grasp of the complexities of life."
12. Lapp, The New Priesthood: The Scientific Elite and the Uses of Power 29 (1965).
13. Platt, Perception and Change: Projections for Survival 160 (1970).
14. 347 U.S. 483 (1954).
15. Missouri v. Holland, 252 U.S. 416 (1920).
16. Home Building & Loan Ass'n v. Blaisdell, 290 U.S. 398 (1934).
17. As set forth in The Brothers Karamazov.
18. Kammen, People of Paradox 56 (1972).
19. See Black, A Constitutional Faith (1968).
20. 381 U.S. 479 (1965).
21. Marbury v. Madison, 1 Cranch 137 (1803).
22. See Arnold, Fair Fights and Foul (1965).

23. On the power of the Court, see Miller, The Supreme Court and American Capitalism ch. 6 (1968).

24. Quoted in The New Republic, May 8, 1965.

25. Price, The Scientific Estate 163 (1965).

26. For example, Hand, The Bill of Rights (1958).

27. Freund, *Rationality in Judicial Decisions* (mimeographed 1962).

28. Compare Kammen, note 18 supra, with Roche, *The Founding Fathers: A Reform Caucus in Action*, in The Constitution Reconsidered 381 (Read ed. 1968) (hereinafter cited as Read).

29. Wilson, note 8 supra.

30. Bryce, The American Commonwealth 273 (1913).

31. Commons, Legal Foundations of Capitalism 7 (1924).

32. The Employment Act can be found in 15 U.S.C. §§. 1021-24 (1964); it has never reached the Supreme Court. The Civil Rights Act of 1964 was validated in Heart of Atlanta Motel v. United States, 379 U.S. 241 (1964) and Katzenbach v. McClung, 379 U.S. 294 (1964). The Sherman Act was judicially modified to include "the rule of reason" in Standard Oil Co. of New Jersey v. United States, 221 U.S. 1 (1911).

33. Riencourt, The Coming Caesars 330 (1957).

34. Hamilton, *Introduction* to Read, note 28 supra.

35. Ehrlich's book was published in an English edition in 1936, translated by W. Moll. The quotation is in Hall, Readings in Jurisprudence 825 (1938).

36. See Nichols, The Invention of American Political Parties (1967).

37. See Miller, *The Constitutional Law of the "Security State,"* 10 Stanford Law Review 620 (1958).

38. Quoted in Twiss, Lawyers and the Constitution (1942).

39. A good economic history of the early American period is Bruchey, The Roots of American Economic Growth, 1607-1861 (1965).

40. Gossett, Corporate Citizenship 157 (1957).

41. Michels, Political Parties (Paul & Paul trans. 1962).

42. Dartmouth College v. Woodward, 4 Wehaton 518 (1819).

43. Hobbes, Leviathan 218 (1651).

44. Quoted in Eells & Walton, Conceptual Foundations of Business 132 (1961).

45. Axelrod, *Schema Theory: An Information Processing Model of Perception and Cognition*, 67 American Political Science Review 1248 (1973).

NOTES TO CHAPTER 2

1. Fusfeld, *The Rise of the Corporate State in America*, 6 Journal of Economic Issues 1 (March 1972).

2. See Lindblom, The Policy-Making Process (1968).

3. Whitehead, Process and Reality 17 (1929). See also Whitehead, Modes of Thought 12-13 (1938); Miller & Howell, *The Myth of Neutrality in Constitutional Adjudication*, 27 University of Chicago Law Review 661 (1960).

4. Morgenthau, *The Perils of Political Empiricism*, 34 Commentary 60 (1962).

5. Rawls, A Theory of Justice (1970). Pragmatism is discussed in White, Pragmatism and the American Mind (1973).

6. Quoted in Elbow, French Corporative Theory, 1789-1948: A Chapter in the History of Ideas 11 (1953).

7. Bowen, German Theories of the Corporative State 2 (1947).

8. Maine, Ancient Law (1861).

9. Rist & Pirou, as quoted in Bowen, note 7 supra.

10. Marris, The Economic Theory of "Managerial" Capitalism 2 (1964).

11. The corporation became a constitutional person by Supreme Court fiat in 1886. Santa Clara County v. Southern Pacific Railway Co., 118 U. S. 394 (1886).

12. Whyte, The Organization Man 5 (1956).

13. Green, the English Idealist philosopher, is discussed in Richter, The Politics of Conscience: T. H. Green and His Age (1964).

14. Merriam, Public and Private Government 16 (1944).

15. Beard, The Economic Basis of Politics 45 (1945).

16. See Dewey, Human Nature and Conduct: An Introduction to Social Psychology (1922) and Dewey, The Public and Its Problems (1932). The source of the quote in the text is Latham, The Group Basis of Politics 1 (1952).

17. Notably in NAACP v. Alabama, 357 U.S. 449 (1958). See Fellman, The Constitutional Right of Association (1963); Horn, Groups and the Constitution (1956).

18. Hacker, *Introduction* to The Corporation Take-Over 8 (Hacker ed. 1964).

19. The quotation is repeated from Chapter 1. There was a brief flurry of interest in Ehrlichian jurisprudence in the 1920s and 1930s, but the movement has dwindled since.

20. As quoted in the New York Times, March 8, 1962.

21. Korematsu v. United States, 323 U. S. 214 (1944).

22. Berle, *Coherency and the Social Sciences*, in People, Power, and Politics 10 (Gould & Steele eds. 1961). See also Eells, The Government of Corporations (1962).

NOTES TO CHAPTER 3

1. Adams, Relation of the State to Industrial Action, and Economics and Jurisprudence 145 (Dorfman ed. 1954).

2. The Corporation in Modern Society 1 (Mason ed. 1959); Galbraith, The New Industrial State (1967).

3. Hale v. Henkel, 201 U. S. 43 (1905).

4. In Trustees of Dartmouth College v. Woodward, 4 Wheaton 518 (1819).

5. Stone, Where the Law Ends: The Social Control of Corporate Behavior 3 (1975). The internal quotations are from: first, Mencken, A New Dictionary of Quotations on Historical Principles from Ancient and Modern Sources 223 (1942); and second, from Maitland *Introduction* to Gierke, Political Theories of the Middle Ages *xxi* (Maitland trans. 1900). See also Hamilton, The Politics of Industry (1957).

6. Coleman, Power and the Structure of Society 14 (1974).

7. But not, be it noted, a constitutional "citizen."

8. Quoted by Maitland, note 5 supra.

9. McCulloch v. Maryland, 17 U. S. 316 (1819).

10. As quoted in Coleman, note 6 supra, at 30-1.

11. Dodd, American Business Corporations Until 1860 at 7 (1954).

12. Cahn, *Book Review* (of Hale, Freedom Through Law [1952]), New York Times, Jan. 18, 1953.

13. Fletcher v. Peck, 10 U. S. 87 (1810); Trustees of Dartmouth College v. Woodward, 4 Wheaton 518 (1819).

14. See Magrath, Yazoo: Law and Politics in the New Republic (1966).

15. Corwin, *The Basic Doctrine of American Constitutional Law*, 12 Michigan Law Review (1914), reprinted in American Constitutional History: Essays by Edward S. Corwin 25 (Mason & Garvey eds. 1964).

16. The "ruling class" hypothesis is suggested in a later chapter.

17. Mendelson, Capitalism, Democracy, and the Supreme Court 24 (1960).

18. Jones, The Consumer Society: A History of American Capitalism (1965).

19. Slaughterhouse Cases, 83 U. S. 36 (1873); Munn v. Illinois, 94 U. S. 113 (1877).

20. For illustrative cases, see Lochner v. New York, 198 U. S. 45 (1905); Adair v. United States, 208 U. S. 161 (1908); Coppage v. Kansas, 236 U. S. 1 (1915); Adkins v. Children's Hospital, 261 U. S. 525 (1923).

21. Hamilton, of course, was merely stating a truism, albeit one that the Supreme Court has neglected at times over the years.

22. For a recent account, see Levy, Against the Law (1974).

23. Quoted in Fairman, Mr. Justice Miller and the Supreme Court 374 (1939).

24. Twiss, Lawyers and the Constitution 149 (1942).

25. Miranda v. Arizona, 384 U. S. 436 (1966).

26. Commons, Legal Foundations of Capitalism 7 (1924).

27. Muller v. Oregon, 208 U. S. 412 (1908).

NOTES TO CHAPTER 4

1. Marris, The Economic Theory of "Managerial" Capitalism 13 (1964).

2. Adolf Berle was the leading theorist on the implications of the rise of collective capitalism. See, for example, Berle, The 20th-Century Capitalist Revolution (1954); Berle, Power Without Property (1958).

3. There is no such thing as "the" corporation, for the corporate form typifies many different organizations. For a brief discussion, see Coleman, Power and the Structure of Society (1974).

4. Quoted in Dewing, The Financial Policy of Corporations 16-17 (5th ed. 1953).

5. Machlup, *Theories of the Firm: Marginalist, Behavioral, Managerial*, 57 American Economics Review 1 (1967).

6. Louis K. Liggett Co. v. Lee, 288 U. S. 517 (1933).

7. In Trustees of Dartmouth College v. Woodward, 4 Wheaton 518 (1819).

8. Berle & Means, The Modern Corporation and Private Property (1932).

9. Galbraith, The New Industrial State (1967).

10. See American Law Institute, Restatement of the Law of Property § 1.

11. Young, *Preface* to Burnham, The Managerial Revolution 11 (paperback ed. 1961).

12. Compare Ginzberg and Associates, The Pluralistic Economy (1965) with Harrington, Toward a Democratic Left (1968), and Holton, *Business and Government*, Daedalus 41-59 (Winter 1969).

13. Federalist No. 10.

14. See the works cited in note 12 supra.

15. See note 11 supra.

16. Drucker, The End of Economic Man (1940); Drucker, The Future of Industrial Man (1942).

17. Price, The Scientific Estate 186 (1965).

18. The Corporation in Modern Society 1 (Mason ed. 1960).

19. Carr, What Is History? (1961).

20. Letwin, A Documentary History of American Economic Policy Since 1789 (1961).

21. Boulding, The Organizational Revolution (1953).

22. Landes, The Unbound Prometheus: Technological Change and Industrial Development in Western Europe from 1750 to the Present 21 (1969).

23. See Berle, The American Economic Republic (1962); Lilienthal, Big Business: A New Era (1953); Jessup, *A Political Role for the Corporation*, Fortune, Aug. 1952.

24. Frankfurter, *Justice Holmes Defines the Constitution*, in Law and Politics 61 (MacLeish & Prichard eds. 1939).

25. Max Weber's hypothesis about the rise of capitalism may be found in Weber, The Protestant Ethic and the Spirit of Capitalism (translation 1930). See also Tawney, Religion and the Rise of Capitalism (1926).

26. Letwin, note 20 supra, at 13.

27. H. R. Hood & Sons v. DuMond, 336 U. S. 525 (1949).

28. Northern Securities Co. v. United States, 193 U. S. 197 (1904).

29. Standard Oil Co. v. United States, 221 U. S. 1 (1911).

30. Adams & Gray, Monopoly in America (1955). See Baran & Sweezy, Monopoly Capital (1966).

31. Arnold, The Folklore of Capitalism (1937).

32. Quoted in Jaffe, Judicial Control of Administrative Action 11 (1966).

33. Emerson, *Politics*, in The Complete Essays and Other Writings of Ralph Waldo Emerson 422 (Modern Library ed. 1940).

34. See note 30 supra.

35. Kaplan, Big Business in a Competitive System (1954).

36. Berle, The 20th Century Capitalist Revolution 51 (1954).

37. Adams & Gray, supra note 30, at 2.

38. Heilbroner, The Limits of American Capitalism (1966).

39. Withers, Freedom Through Power 8 (1965).

40. Weinstein, The Corporate Ideal in the Liberal State (1968); Domhoff, Who Rules America? (1967); Mills, The Power Elite (1956); Harrington, Toward a Democratic Left (1968); Domhoff, The Higher Circles (1972).

41. According to Myrdal, social conditions are never in equilibrium but are always on an upward and downward spiral vis-à-vis each other. His views can be found in Myrdal, An American Dilemma (1944) and Economic Theory and Underdeveloped Regions (1957).

42. See, for example, Magdoff, The Age of Imperialism (1969); Corporations and the Cold War (Horowitz ed. 1969); Baran & Sweezy, supra note 30.

43. Kelso & Adler, The Capitalist Manifesto (1958).
44. Veblen, The Theory of Business Enterprise 24-25 (1904).
45. See Berle, Power Without Property (1958).
46. Earley, American Economic Review, Papers and Proceedings 330 (1956).
47. Elliott, Men at the Top 40 (1959).
48. Schumpeter's views are set forth in his Capitalism, Socialism and Democracy (3d ed. 1950).
49. Galbraith, American Capitalism: The Concept of Countervailing Power (1952).
50. See Simon, Administrative Behavior (rev. ed. 1957); and comments on Simon's views set out in Earley, supra note 46.
51. See Domhoff, The Higher Circles (1972).
52. Rose, The Power Structure: Political Process in American Society 101 (1967).
53. Nagel, The Structure of Science: Problems in the Logic of Scientific Explanation (1961).
54. Potter, People of Plenty: Economic Abundance and the American Character (1954). See also Penrose, The Theory of the Growth of the Firm (1959).
55. Perlmutter, *Three Conceptions of a World Enterprise*, Revue Economique et Sociale (May 1965); Perlmutter, *Multinational Corporations*, Columbia Journal of World Business (Jan.-Feb. 1969). See Barnet & Muller, Global Reach: The Power of the Multinational Corporations (1974).
56. See, for example, Schmookler, *Technological Progress and the Modern American Corporation*, in The Corporation in Modern Society 141 (Mason ed. 1960).
57. See Webb, The Great Frontier (1952). See also North, The Economic Growth of the United States, 1790-1860 (1961).
58. Landes's book was published in 1969.
59. See the discussion in Landes, note 58 supra.
60. Ibid. at 19.
61. Turner, The Frontier in American History (1920).
62. Sumner, *Earth-Hunger or the Philosophy of Land Grabbing*, in Earth-Hunger and Other Essays 31 (Keller ed. 1913).
63. Webb, note 57 supra, at 101.
64. Published in 1969.
65. Jones, The Consumer Society: A History of American Capitalism 1 (1965).
66. Timberg, *The Corporation as a Technique of International Administration*, 19 University of Chicago Law Review 739 (1952).
67. Duerr, *Alternative Methods of Operation Within the EEC: Factors to Weigh in Doing Business in Europe*, in Doing Business in the Common Market 3 (Miller ed. 1963).
68. Kerr & Associates, Industrialism and Industrial Man (1964).
69. Berle, note 36 supra; Drucker, The Age of Discontinuity (1969).
70. Barber, as quoted in Galloway, *Worldwide Corporations and International Integration: The Case of INTELSAT*, 24 International Organization 506 (1970).
71. Perlmutter, *Super-Giant Firms in the Future*, Wharton Quarterly (Winter 1968).

NOTES TO CHAPTER 5

1. Rostow, Planning for Freedom: The Public Law of American Capitalism 10, 12 (1959).

2. Anderson, *Federalism—Then and Now*, 16 State Government 107 (May 1943), quoted in Corwin, *The Passing of Dual Federalism*, 36 Virginia Law Review 1 (1950).

3. Horsky, The Washington Lawyer 68 (1952).

4. The Supreme Court historically was mainly interested in what Professor Felix Frankfurter once called "the evolution of finance capital"—that is, the problems of the growth of American capitalism. Frankfurter, *Justice Holmes Defines the Constitution*, in Law and Politics 61 (MacLeish & Prichard eds. 1939). An interesting passage on the relationship between personal freedoms and "popular dictatorship" is in Auguste Comte, System of Positive Polity 307 (first English language ed. 1875): "The principal features of . . . government should be perfect freedom of speech and discussion, and at the same time political preponderance of the central authority with proper guarantees for its purity." That quotation bears the subhead, "Popular dictatorship with freedom of speech." The relationship, if any, between greater judicial attention to First Amendment freedoms and the rise of executive hegemony in American government has not, to my knowledge, been explored.

5. Duguit, Law in the Modern State 26 (1919).

6. Alexis de Tocqueville said that political questions tended to be judicialized and to be decided eventually by the Supreme Court. Tocqueville, Democracy in America (Bradley ed. 1945). The notion is criticized in Miller, *Book Review*, 71 Columbia Law Review 502 (1971).

7. The idea is adumbrated in Miller, *Toward a Concept of Constitutional Duty*, 1968 Supreme Court Review 199.

8. Means, *Collective Capitalism and Economic Theory*, in The Corporation Take-Over 67 (Hacker ed. 1964).

9. As the late Professor Robert G. McCloskey said in 1957: "The meaning of the Constitution is profoundly influenced by the actual course of legislative and executive action; . . . constitutional interpretation is *not* a judicial monopoly." Essays in Constitutional Law 183 (McCloskey ed. 1957).

10. The Employment Act is in 15 U. S. C. §§ 1021-24.

11. See Weinstein, The Corporate Ideal in the Liberal State (1968).

12. The cases are in Cases and Materials on Constitutional Law 5 & 6 (Gunther ed., 8th ed. 1970).

13. 300 U. S. 379 (1937).

14. Corwin, Liberty Against Government 161 (1948).

15. Sabine, A History of Political Theory 674 (1937).

16. 3 Green, Works: Miscellanies and Memoirs 371 (3d ed. 1891). See Richter, The Politics of Conscience: T. H. Green and His Age (1964); Bay, The Structure of Freedom (1958); Bosanquet, The Philosophical Theory of the State (1899); Chin, The Political Theory of Thomas Hill Green (1920).

17. Helvering v. Davis, 301 U. S. 619 (1937); Steward Machine Co. v. Davis, 301 U. S. 548 (1937).

18. Henry, *The Railroad Land Grant Legend in American History Texts*, in Pivotal Interpretations of American History (Degler ed. 1966).

19. The cases are discussed in Miller, note 7 supra.

20. Pekelis, *The Case for a Jurisprudence of Welfare*, in Law and Social Action 1 (Konvitz ed. 1950).

21. George, Progress and Poverty ch. 8 (1879).

22. For discussion of an aspect of this question, see Miller & Barron, *The Supreme Court, the Adversary System, and the Flow of Information to the Justices: A Preliminary Inquiry*, 61 Virginia Law Review 1187 (1975).

23. For example, the Social Security program upheld in the cases cited in note 17 supra.

24. Santa Clara County v. Southern Pacific Railway Co., 118 U. S. 394 (1886). The idea of corporate personality was challenged in 1938 by Justice Hugo L. Black and in 1949 by Justice William O. Douglas. See Connecticut Life Insurance Co. v. Johnson, 303 U. S. 77 (1938); Wheeling Steel Corp. v. Glander, 337 U. S. 552 (1949).

25. Tyler, The Political Imperative: The Corporate Character of Unions 92 (1968).

26. Krabbe, The Modern Idea of the State *xliv* (Sabine & Shepard trans. 1922).

27. Tyler, note 25 supra, at 78.

28. Berle, The American Economic Republic 165 (1965).

29. NAACP v. Alabama, 357 U. S. 449 (1958).

30 361 U. S. 516 (1960).

31. Communist Party v. Subversive Activities Control Board, 367 U. S. 1 (1961).

32. Discussed in Fellman, The Constitutional Right of Association 70-77 (1963).

33. Ibid. at 104.

34. McConnell, The Decline of Agrarian Democracy (1953).

35. Ibid. at 173.

36. See Gilb, Hidden Hierarchies (1966).

37. See, for example, Gellhorn, Individual Freedom and Government Restraints (1957); Wirtz, *Government by Private Groups*, 13 Louisiana Law Review 440 (1953).

38. Chorafas, The Knowledge Revolution (1968).

39. Drucker, The Age of Discontinuity (1969).

40. See Bell, The Post-Industrial Society (1974).

41. Chorafas, note 38 supra.

42. See Baritz, The Servants of Power: A History of the Use of Social Science in American Industry (1960).

43. Lundberg, The Rich and the Super-Rich (1968).

44. Baritz, note 42 supra. Cf. Elsner, The Technocrats: Prophets of Automation (1967).

45. Meynaud, Technocracy (1968).

46. See Domhoff, The Higher Circles (1972); Lundberg, note 43 supra.

47. Meynaud, note 45 supra. Ferkiss, Technological Man: The Myth and the Reality (1969).

48. Ferkiss, note 47 supra.

49. Wood, as quoted in Mesthene, *Introduction* to Mesthene, Technology and Social Change 6 (1967).

50. Ibid.
51. Baritz, note 42 supra.
52. Ridgeway, The Closed Corporation: American Universities in Crisis (1968).
53. Kerr, The Uses of the University (1963).
54. Ridgeway, note 52 supra.
55. Brzezinski, *America in the Technetronic Age*, Encounter 16 (Jan. 1968). See also Brzezinski, Between Two Ages (1972).

NOTES TO CHAPTER 6

1. McConnell, Private Power and American Democracy 339, 361 (1966).
2. Ellul, The Political Illusion 178 (1967).
3. Quoted in Nevins, John D. Rockefeller 622 (1940).
4. Quoted in Fallaci, If the Sun Dies (1966). See Miller, *Science vs. Law: Some Legal Problems Raised by "Big Science,"* 17 Buffalo Law Review 591 (1968).
5. Ward, *The Ideal of Individualism and the Reality of Organization*, in The Business Establishment 37 (Cheit ed. 1964).
6. Withers, Freedom Through Power 8 (1965).
7. Nieburg, In the Name of Science 190 (1966).
8. Baker's statement appears in the Christian Science Monitor, July 2, 1959.
9. Ikard's is in *Where Business and Government Meet*, 7 Petroleum Today no. 4, p. 24 (Fall 1966).
10. Wilson, The New Freedom 29 (1913).
11. Reagan, The Managed Economy (1963).
12. Galbraith, The New Industrial State 71 (1967).
13. Soule, Planning U. S. A. (1967).
14. Chamberlain, Private and Public Planning (1965).
15. Soule, note 13 supra.
16. See Reich, *The New Property*, 73 Yale Law Journal 733 (1964).
17. Not only corporations but the unions, among other groups. "In reality, the growing integration of unions into the state mechanism makes them increasingly an element of state power, and their tendency is to reinforce that power; at that moment a union becomes a mechanism of organizing the laboring masses for the benefit of the state. It is not by itself a 'counter-power'; it could be that only if it maintained its anarcho-syndicalist character." Ellul, note 2 supra, at 174.
18. Kidron, Western Capitalism Since the War (1968).
19. For discussion, see Barnet & Muller, Global Reach: The Power of the Multinational Corporations (1974).
20. See Miller, *Foreign Trade and the "Security State": A Study in Conflicting National Policies*, 7 Journal of Public Law 37 (1957).
21. See Lampman, The Share of Top Wealth-Holders in National Wealth, 1922-1956 (1962); Lundberg, The Rich and the Super-Rich (1968).
22. See *The Economics of Federal Subsidy Programs*, A Staff Study Prepared for the Joint Economic Committee of Congress (1972).
23. See, for example, Ridgeway, The Closed Corporation (1968).
24. Myrdal's principle is set out in, for example, Myrdal, Economic Theory and Un-

derdeveloped Regions ch. 2 (1957).

25. Kaysen, *The Corporation: How Much Power? What Scope?* in The Corporation in Modern Society 85 (Mason ed. 1960).

26. Lasswell & Kaplan, Power and Society 75 (1950).

27. See Walton & Cleveland, Corporations on Trial: The Electric Cases (1964).

28. The theory of administered prices owes much to economist Gardiner Means. See, for example, Means, The Corporate Revolution in America (1962).

29. See Pillai, The Air Net: The Case Against the World Aviation Cartel (1969).

30. The concept of "veto groups" (but not this particular action) is discussed in Riesman, The Lonely Crowd (1951).

31. In a conversation with the author. Used by permission.

32. Cleveland, *The Blurred Line Between "Public" and "Private,"* in Ethics and Bigness (Lasswell & Cleveland eds. 1962). For another statement, see Cleveland, The Future Executive (1972).

33. See Latham, *The Body Politic of the Corporation*, in The Corporation in Modern Society 218 (Mason ed. 1960). Says Latham: "A mature political conception of the corporation must view it as a rationalized system for the accumulation, control, and administration of power." Ibid., p. 220.

34. Michels, Political Parties (Paul & Paul trans. 1962).

35. See Kessler & Sharp, Contracts: Cases and Materials 1-13 (1953).

36. Ellul, Propaganda (1965).

37. First enunciated by Justice Oliver Wendell Holmes in Abrams v. United States, 250 U.S. 616 (1919). See Barron, Freedom of the Press for Whom? (1972).

38. Mill, On Liberty 97 (1947 ed.).

39. See, in addition to Weinstein, Kolko, Railroad and Regulation 1877-1916 (1965).

40. Adams, Relation of the State to Industrial Action, and Economics and Jurisprudence 145 (Dorfman ed. 1954).

41. The point has been taken from an earlier essay: Miller, *The Corporation as a Private Government in the World Community*, 46 Virginia Law Review 1539 (1960).

42. See, for example, Redford, *Business as Government*, in Public Administration and Democracy 63 (Martin ed. 1965).

43. Timberg, *The Corporation as a Technique of International Administration*, 19 University of Chicago Law Review 739 (1952).

44. Bryce, The American Commonwealth (1914 ed.), quoted in Miller, *Transitional Transnational Law*, 65 Columbia Law Review 836 (1965).

45. Timberg, note 43 supra, at 744.

46. Friedmann & van Themaat, *International Cartels and Combines*, in Antitrust Laws 508 (Friedmann ed. 1956).

47. 326 U.S. 501 (1946).

48. 391 U.S. 308 (1968).

49. See Reich, *The New Property*, 73 Yale Law Journal 733 (1964).

50. Bernstein, *The Regulatory Process: A Framework for Analysis*, 26 Law & Contemporary Problems 329 (1961).

51. Eugen Ehrlich had a considerable vogue in the 1930s and 1940s but has since, save for occasional mention, disappeared. Why this is so is itself an interesting specu-

lation but beyond the scope of this volume. It is sufficient to point out that present-day legal scholarship has largely reverted to the arid conceptualism of analytical positivism. See Shklar, Legalism (1964), for discussion.

52. Ibid.

53. Pound, *Introduction*, to Ehrlich, Fundamental Principles of the Sociology of Law (Moll trans 1936).

54. See Ehrlich, note 53 supra, at ch. 21.

55. See Commons, Legal Foundations of Capitalism (1924).

56. Schick, *The Cybernetic Revolution*, Trans-action, Feb. 1970.

NOTES TO CHAPTER 7

1. Barber, The American Corporation (1970).

2. See also Mintz & Cohen, America, Inc. (1971).

3. See Nagel, The Structure of Science: Problems in the Logic of Scientific Explanation (1961), for a superb discussion of the difficulties inherent in explaining any phenomenon.

4. Dahl, *Business and Politics: A Critical Appraisal of Political Science*, in Dahl, Haire, & Lazarsfeld, Social Science Research on Business: Product and Potential 1 (1959).

5. Even the literature of the businessman—for example, Fortune, Business Week, and the Wall Street Journal—is replete with discussions of the shortcomings of business. Often these discussions are apologetic or are cast in terms of the social responsibility of business. There is, of course, a history of antibusiness (or antimonopoly) sentiment since colonial days.

6. Sorensen, *How the President Makes a Decision*, Saturday Review, July 27, 1963.

7. Estate of Rogers v. Commissioner, 320 U.S. 410 (1943). See also Justice Frankfurter's statement in Priebe & Sons v. United States, 332 U.S. 407 (1947): "But answers are not obtained by putting the wrong question and thereby begging the real one."

8. Dill, *Administrative Decision-Making*, in Concepts and Issues in Administrative Behavior 29 (Maileck & Van Ness eds. 1962).

9. Sorensen, note 6 supra.

10. Lorenz, On Aggression (1966).

11. Koestler, The Ghost in the Machine (1967).

12. Ulmer, *Scientific Method and the Judicial Process*, 7 American Behavioral Scientist 21 (1963).

13. Boulding, *Social Justice in Social Dynamics*, in Social Justice 73 (Brandt ed. 1962).

14. See Lindblom, The Policy-Making Process (1968).

15. Weinberg, *Can Technology Replace Social Engineering?* University of Chicago Magazine, Oct. 1966.

16. Dewey, Logic: The Theory of Inquiry (1938).

17. Schon, Technology and Change 204 (1967).

18. Lowi, The End of Liberalism (1969).

19. Published in 1949. See also White, Pragmatism and the American Mind: Essays

and Reviews in Philosophy and Intellectual History (1973); Commager, The American Mind (1950).

20. Platt, Perception and Change: Projections for Survival (1970).

21. Note 18 supra.

22. Johnson's statements are quoted in Wormuth, The Vietnam War: The President versus the Constitution (1968).

23. See United States v. United States District Court, 407 U.S. 297 (1972).

24. Validated by the Supreme Court in, for example, the Prize Cases, 2 Black 635 (1863); these cases dealt with the presidentially ordered blockade of Confederate ports before a declaration of war. See also Korematsu v. United States, 323 U.S. 214 (1944), upholding exclusion of Japanese Americans from the West Coast during World War II.

25. See Friedrich, Constitutional Reason of State (1957).

26. Riencourt, The Coming Caesars (1957).

27. Ibid.

28. Quoted in ibid.

29. See Gierke, Natural Law and the Theory of the State, 1500-1800 (Barker trans. 1933).

30. Ibid.

31. Barker, *Introduction*, to Gierke, note 29 supra.

32. The term "society" is often used by the Supreme Court in such matters as free speech and other civil liberties matters. One of the many failures of legal (and political science) scholarship is the complete lack of any attempt to give substantive content to the term. It is fair to say that insofar as the law is concerned no one knows what "society" means, save on the level of the highest abstraction.

33. Of many examples in the literature, see Frantz, *The First Amendment in the Balance*, 71 Yale Law Journal 1424 (1962).

34. Latham, *The Body Politic of the Corporation*, in The Corporation in Modern Society 319 (Mason ed. 1959).

35. Barker, note 31 supra.

36. Ibid.

37. See the discussion in Elbow, French Corporative Theory, 1789-1948 (1953).

38. Professor Wolfgang Friedmann has suggested that Figgis wrote in an attempt to counteract the overweening power of the state. See Friedmann, *Corporate Power, Government by Private Groups, and the Law*, 57 Columbia Law Review 155 (1957). See also Friedmann, Law in a Changing Society (2nd ed. 1972).

39. Quoted in Barker, note 31 supra.

40. McConnell, Private Power and American Democracy (1966).

41. Lippmann, The Public Philosophy (1955).

42. Bailey, *The Public Interest: Some Operational Dilemmas*, in Nomos V: The Public Interest 96 (Friedrich ed. 1962).

43. See Friedrich, Man and His Government (1963).

44. Mason, *Introduction* in The Corporation in Modern Society (Mason ed. 1959).

45. These subsidies and other benefits for the supercorporations are "brokered" by the "Washington lawyer"—the major law firms of the country. Compare Horsky, The Washington Lawyer (1952), with Goulden, The Superlawyers (1971), and Green, The

Other Government: The Unseen Power of Washington Lawyers (1975).

46. Baratz, *Corporate Giants and the Power Structure*, 9 Western Political Quarterly 406 (1956).

47. Keynes, The General Theory of Employment, Interest, and Money 383 (1936).

48. Mason, *The Apologetics of Managerialism*, 31 Journal of Business 1 (1958).

49. Quoted in Martyn, *Multinational Corporations in a Nationalistic World*, Challenge: The Magazine of Economic Affairs (Nov.-Dec. 1965), p. 13.

50. Heilbroner, The Limits of American Capitalism (1966).

51. For example, Mintz & Cohen, America, Inc. (1971).

52. There is little evidence that such an effort is being made.

53. See Davis, Discretionary Justice: A Preliminary Inquiry (1969).

54. Lowi, note 18 supra. For a later statement, see Lowi, The Politics of Disorder (1971).

55. Friendly, The Federal Administrative Agencies: The Need for Better Definition of Standards (1962).

56. Michels, Political Parties (1911).

57. Lipset, *Introduction*, to ibid.

58. Lipset, Trow, & Coleman, Union Democracy ch. 18 (1956).

59. Rose, The Power Structure: Political Process in American Society (1967).

60. Domhoff, Who Rules America? (1967).

61. Dahl, *Business and Politics: A Critical Appraisal of Political Science*, in Dahl, Haire, & Lazarsfeld, Social Science Research on Business: Product and Potential (1959).

62. This is particularly to be noted among government lawyers. See Miller, *The Attorney General as the President's Lawyer*, in Huston, Miller, Krislov, & Dixon, Roles of the Attorney General of the United States (1968).

63. See Glasser, The New High Priesthood (1967).

64. Taylor, *Is the Corporation Above the Law?* Harvard Business Review (March-April 1965), p. 128.

65. Evan, *Organization Man and Due Process of Law*, 26 American Sociological Review 540 (1961).

66. The Automobile Dealers Day in Court Act is in 15 U.S.C. §§ 1221-25.

67. See, for example, Wellington, *The Constitution, the Labor Union, and "Governmental Action,"* 70 Yale Law Journal 345 (1961).

68. Civil Rights Cases, 109 U.S. 3 (1883).

69. Santa Clara County v. Southern Pacific Railway, 118 U.S. 394 (1886).

70. 321 U.S. 649 (1944).

71. Marsh v. Alabama, 326 U.S. 501 (1946); Amalgamated Food Employees Union v. Logan Valley Plaza, Inc., 391 U.S. 308 (1968).

72. Pollak v. Public Utilities Commission, 343 U.S. 451 (1952).

73. 95 Sup. Ct. 449 (1974).

74. For example, Lloyd v. Tanner, 407 U.S. 551 (1972).

NOTES TO CHAPTER 8

1. Bentley, The Process of Government 268 (1908).

2. The "counterculture" got its most effective statement in Roszak, The Making of a Counterculture (1969).

3. Michener, The Drifters (1971).

4. Fromm, Escape from Freedom (1941).

5. Tocqueville, Democracy in America (Bradley ed. 1945).

6. Riesman, The Lonely Crowd (1951).

7. See, for example, Lundberg, The Rich and the Super-Rich (1968).

8. The civil-rights movement of the 1960s is now ended, with the result that black Americans find themselves (with some exceptions) outside the mainstream of American life. Cf. Bennett, Confrontation: Black and White (1965): "The basic fact of the Negro situation is shattered community. Negro and white Americans do not belong to the same social body. They do not share that body of consensus or common feeling that usually binds people sharing a common land."

9. See, for example, Wiener, The Human Use of Human Beings (1955).

10. Cf. Domhoff, The Higher Circles (1972).

11. Fitzgerald, The Crack-Up (1938).

12. Mayer, They Thought They Were Free (1966).

13. Ellul, Propaganda (1965).

14. See Barron, Freedom of the Press for Whom? (1972).

15. Lloyd, The Idea of Law (1964).

16. See Dulles, Labor in America: A History (3rd ed. 1966).

17. See Van Alstyne, The Rising American Empire (1960).

18. See Barnet & Muller, Global Reach: The Power of the Multinational Corporations (1974).

19. Platt, Perception and Change: Projections for Survival (1970).

20. Ibid.

21. Myrdal, Rich Lands and Poor (1968).

22. See Radosh, Prophets on the Right (1975).

23. See Miller & Ferrara, *Public and Private Enterprise in the United States: Co-Existence in an Unsteady Equilibrium*, in Public and Private Enterprise in Mixed Economics (Friedmann ed. 1974).

24. Nicely summarized in McCloskey, The American Supreme Court (1960).

25. An early and excellent discussion of the change is Corwin, *The Passing of Dual Federalism*, 36 Virginia Law Review 1 (1950).

26. For summary, see Miller, The Supreme Court and American Capitalism (1968).

27. Laski, *The Obsolescence of Federalism*, 98 The New Republic 367 (1939).

28. See Tawney, Religion and the Rise of Capitalism (1926).

29. Commons, The Economics of Collective Action 302 (1950).

30. Berle, The 20th-Century Capitalist Revolution (1954).

31. Renner, The Institutions of Private Law (Kahn-Freund ed. 1949).

32. The landmark case is Munn v. Illinois, 94 U.S. 113 (1877).

33. Carlston, Law and Structures of Social Action (1956).

34. Berle, note 30 supra, at 60.

35. Jessup, *A Political Role for the Corporation*, Fortune, Aug. 1952.

36. Wilson, Constitutional Government in the United States 173 (1908).

37. Lasswell & Kaplan, Power and Society 195 (1952). An earlier statement is Barnes, Sociology and Political Theory (1924).

38. For example, Drucker, The New Society (1950); Latham, *Anthropomorphic Corporations, Elites, and Monopoly Power*, 47 American Economic Review Proceedings 303 (1957).

39. Berle, in 4 Encyclopedia of the Social Sciences 423 (1931).

40. Drucker, The Future of Industrial Man 93 (1942).

41. Berle, *Evolving Capitalism and Political Federalism*, in Federalism: Mature and Emergent 48 (MacMahon ed. 1955).

42. Price, Government and Science (1954).

43. Cleveland, *The Blurred Line Between "Public" and "Private,"* in Ethics and Bigness: Scientific, Academic, Religious, Political, and Military (Cleveland & Lasswell eds. 1962).

44. Ibid.

45. 94 Sup. Ct. 3090 (1974).

46. Hurst's statement is in Federalism: Mature and Emergent 87 (MacMahon ed. 1955). See also Bickel & Wellington, *Legislative Purpose and the Judicial Process*, 71 Harvard Law Review 1 (1957).

47. See Miller, note 26 supra, at ch. 6.

48. See, however, Miller & Scheflin, *The Power of the Supreme Court in the Age of the Positive State*, 1967 Duke Law Journal 273, 522.

49. This is the term sometimes applied to the so-called independent regulatory commissions, the first of which was the Interstate Commerce Commission. For discussion, see Bernstein, Regulating Business by Independent Commission (1955).

50. Corwin, The Presidency: Office and Powers (4th ed. 1957).

51. Youngstown Sheet & Tube Co. v. Sawyer, 343 U.S. (1952).

52. See Schlesinger, The Imperial Presidency (1974).

53. For discussion from the standpoint of a psychologist, see Janis, Victims of Groupthink: A Psychological Study of Foreign-policy Decisions and Fiascoes (1973).

54. See, for an earlier discussion of this proposition, Miller, *"The Constitutional Law of the "Security State,"* 10 Stanford Law Review 620 (1958).

55. Ellul, The Political Illusion (1967).

56. There is little reason to believe that either the routine or the extraordinary tasks of government will revert to Congress, which occurred after the trial of Andrew Johnson. See Miller, *Implications of Watergate: Some Proposals of Cutting the Presidency Down to Size*, 2 Hastings Constitutional Law Quarterly 33 (1975).

57. McConnell, Private Power and American Democracy (1966).

58. Ibid.

59. Discussed in Neumann, The Democratic and the Authoritarian State (1953).

60. In Federalist No. 10.

61. See Miller, *The Public Interest Undefined*, 10 Journal of Public Law 184 (1961).

62. Ellul, note 55 supra.

63. See Mitchell, The American Polity (1962).

64. Ibid.

65. Bottomore, Elites and Society 6 (1964).

66. As quoted in ibid.

67. Veblen, The Engineers and the Price System (1921); Burnham, The Managerial Revolution (1942).

68. Mills, The Power Elite (1956).

69. See Ellul, note 55 supra; Huntington, *Congressional Responses to the Twentieth Century*, in The Congress and America's Future 24 (Truman ed. 1965). There is no reason to believe that the post-Nixon Congress will do any better.

70. See Gellhorn, When Americans Complain (1966).

71. Ellul, note 55 supra.

72. See Neustadt, Presidential Power (1960).

73. It is a Washington truism that the bureaucracy changes little with a change in elected administration. This has led recent Presidents to create their own apparatus within the executive offices of the President in such matters as national security.

74. For one example, see Miller & Pierson, *Observations on the Consistency of Federal Procurement Policies with Other Governmental Policies*, 29 Law & Contemporary Problems 277 (1964).

75. See Friedrich, The Pathology of Politics (1972).

76. See Lindblom, The Policy-Making Process (1968).

77. See Melman, Pentagon Capitalism (1970).

78. See Davis, Discretionary Justice: A Preliminary Inquiry (1969).

79. See, for example, Bernstein, Regulating Business by Independent Commission (1955).

80. Best discussed in Barron, Freedom of the Press for Whom? (1972).

81. Rolfe, The International Corporation 119 (1969).

82. See Galbraith, The New Industrial State (rev. ed. 1972).

83. Compare Rolfe, note 81 supra, with Barnet & Muller, Global Reach: The Power of the Multinational Corporations (1974).

84. Phrase used by Anthony M. Salomon in *International Aspects of Business*, Part I, Hearings before the Subcommittee on Antitrust and Monopoly of the Senate Committee on the Judiciary 19 (1966).

85. Transnational Relations and World Politics (Keohane & Nye eds. 1972).

86. Frankfurter, The Commerce Clause Under Marshall, Taney and Waite (1937).

87. See Hymer, *The Multinational Corporation and the Law of Uneven Development*, in Economics and World Order: From the 1970s to the 1990s 113 (Bhagwati ed. 1972).

88. Ibid.

89. Barber, The American Corporation (1970).

90. I have developed this point in Miller, Technology, the Evolution of the Transnational Corporation, and the Nation-State: A Speculative Essay (Monograph No. 14, George Washington University Program of Policy Studies in Science and Technology, October 1972).

91. Toynbee, *How Did We Get This Way—And Where Are We Going?* in Management's Mission in a New Society 16 (Fenn ed. 1959).

92. Rolfe, note 81 supra.

93. See Gardner, The East India Company (1972).

94. See Myrdal, An American Dilemma (1944).

95. Published in 1960.

96. Elliott, Men at the Top (1959).

97. Polk, *The Rise of World Corporations*, Saturday Review, Nov. 22, 1969.

98. Berle, note 30 supra.

99. Timberg, *The Corporation as a Technique of International Administration*, 19 University of Chicago Law Review 739 (1952).

100. Hymer, note 87 supra.

101. See Mallison, *The Zionist-Israel Juridical Claims to Constitute "The Jewish People" Nationality Entity and to Confer Membership Upon It*, 32 George Washington Law Review 963 (1964).

102. Hacker, *Politics and the Corporation*, in The Corporation Take-Over 260 (Hacker ed. 1964).

103. Finn, The Corporate Oligarch 135 (1969).

104. Hacker, The End of the American Era 72 (1970).

105. Nisbet, Community and Power (1962).

106. United Nations Reparations Case, International Court of Justice Reports 174 (1949).

107. Memorandum of the Secretary General of the United Nations, in Survey of International Law in Relation to the Work of Codification of the International Law Commission, (Feb. 10, 1949).

108. See McDougal, *International Law, Power and Policy: A Contemporary Conception*, 82 Recueil des Cours 137 (1953); Farran, *The Sovereign Order of Malta in International Law*, 3 International and Comparative Law Quarterly 217 (1954).

109. Lauterpacht, International Law and Human Rights 12 (1950).

110. Silving, *Nationality in Comparative Law*, 5 American Journal of Comparative Law 410 (1956).

111. Luria v. United States, 231 U.S. 9 (1913).

112. Quoted from the Encyclopedia of the Social Sciences, in Commons, The Economics of Collective Action (1950).

113. Friedmann, *Corporate Power, Government by Private Groups, and the Law*, 57 Columbia Law Review 155 (1957).

114. See Commons, Legal Foundations of Capitalism (1924).

115. See Cater, Power in Washington (1964).

116. Commons, note 114 supra.

117. Keohane & Nye, note 85 supra.

118. Brown, *A Study of Conglomerate Powers That Transcend Nations*, Saturday Review, May 20, 1972.

119. Keohane & Nye, note 85 supra.

120. See Brown, supra note 118.

121. Evans, *National Autonomy and Economic Development: Critical Perspectives on Multinational Corporations in Poor Countries*, in Keohane & Nye, note 85 supra.

122. See, for example, Levitt, Silent Surrender (1970).

123. As in the airlines industry.

124. Ray, *Corporations and American Foreign Relations*, 403 Annals of the

American Academy of Political and Social Science 80 (1972).

125. Gilpin, *The Politics of Transnational Economic Relations*, 25 International Organization 419 (1971).

126. Barber is quoted in Galloway, *Worldwide Corporations and International Integration: The Case of INTELSAT*, 24 International Organization 506 (1970).

127. Quoted in the New York Times. Feb. 13, 1972.

NOTES TO EPILOGUE

1. Kammen, People of Paradox (1972).

Index

White, Byron, 6, 47
White, Lynn, 58
White, Morton, 153-4
Wilson, Woodrow, 1, 5, 99, 116-
   17, 205

Withers, William, 69, 115
Wood, Robert, 109

Young, Michael, 54

ABOUT THE AUTHOR

Arthur Selwyn Miller, a Professor of Law at the National Law Center, George Washington University, is also Consultant for the Senate Subcommittee on Separation of Powers. In 1973-74, he was Chief Consultant, Senate Select Committee on Presidential Campaign Activities. Topics for his earlier published books include the Supreme Court, racial discrimination and private education, and the roles of the Attorney General of the United States. In addition, Professor Miller's many articles in the field of law have appeared in leading legal periodicals.